Palgrave Studies in Arab Cinema

Series Editors
Samirah Alkassim, Film and Video Studies, George Mason University,
Fairfax, VA, USA
Nezar Andary, College of Humanities and Social Sciences, Zayed
University, Abu Dhabi, United Arab Emirates

This series presents new perspectives and intimate analyses of Arab cinema. Providing distinct and unique scholarship, books in the series focus on well-known and new auteurs, historical and contemporary movements, specific films, and significant moments in Arab and North African film history and cultures. The use of multi-disciplinary and documentary methods creates an intimate contact with the diverse cultures and cinematic modes and genres of the Arab world. Primary documents and new interviews with directors and film professionals form a significant part of this series, which views filmmakers as intellectuals in their respective historical, geographic, and cultural contexts. Combining rigorous analysis with material documents and visual evidence, the authors address pertinent issues linking film texts to film studies and other disciplines. In tandem, this series will connect specific books to online access to films and digital material, providing future researchers and students with a hub to explore filmmakers, genres, and subjects in Arab cinema in greater depth, and provoking readers to see new frames of transnational cultures and cinemas.

Series Editors:
Samirah Alkassim is an experimental documentary filmmaker and Assistant Professor of Film Theory at George Mason University. She is the co-editor of the Palgrave Studies in Arab Cinema and her publications include the co-authored book The Cinema of Muhammad Malas (Palgrave, 2018), contributions to Cinema of the Arab World: Contemporary Directions in Theory and Practice (Palgrave, 2020), the Historical Dictionary of Middle Eastern Cinema, 2nd Edition (Rowman and Littlefield, 2020), as well as chapters in Refocus: The Films of Jocelyne Saab (Edinburgh University Press, 2021), Gaza on Screen (forthcoming 2022), and text book Global Horror: Hybridity and Alterity in Transnational Horror Film (Cognella Academic Publishing, forthcoming 2022) which she co-edited with Ziad El-Bayoumi Foty. She is currently writing a book, A Journey of Screens in 21st Century Arab Film and Media (Bloomsbury, forthcoming 2023) and editing a documentary about Jordanian artist Hani Hourani. She holds an MFA in Cinema from San Francisco State University and a BA in English Literature from Oberlin College.

Nezar Andary is Assistant Professor of Film and Literature at Zayed University in the College of Humanities and Sustainability Sciences. He has published literary translations, poetry, and articles on Arab documentary, and researched the relationship of Arab cinema to the recent Arab uprisings. Among his many involvements in Abu Dhabi, he directed a multilingual play for the Abu Dhabi Book Fair and organized an Environmental Documentary Film Series. In addition, he served as Artistic Director for Anasy Documentary Awards in 2010 and Artistic Director for the documentary series Perspectives and Retrospectives in 2013. He holds a PhD from the University of California, Los Angeles and was a Fulbright recipient conducting research in Syria.

Florence Martin

Farida Benlyazid and Moroccan Cinema

Florence Martin
Center for the Study of Modern
Languages, Literatures and Cultures
Goucher College
Baltimore, MD, USA

ISSN 2731-4898   ISSN 2731-4901 (electronic)
Palgrave Studies in Arab Cinema
ISBN 978-3-031-40615-7   ISBN 978-3-031-40616-4 (eBook)
https://doi.org/10.1007/978-3-031-40616-4

This Palgrave Macmillan imprint is published by the registered company Springer Nature
Switzerland AG
The registered company address is: Gewerbestrasse 11, 6330 Cham, Switzerland

Acknowledgements

This book would never have been possible without the warm and generous support of a transnational family of friends who have shared their time, memories, documents, laughter, teas, and dinners with me. I would like to thank Farida Benlyazid for her patience, her humor, her innumerable stories, and her trust, as well as her family, in particular her daughters Ayda and Kenza Diouri and her son Abdelhaye Adbib who kindly agreed to be interviewed; Fayçal al Gandouzi, Fatema Loukili, Zoubida Menebhi, Munir Abbar, Zakia Tahiri, Jillali Ferhati, Younes Megri, Hassan Benjelloun, and Nour-Eddine Lakhmari for having so graciously agreed to meet with me and talk about Farida and her films during my research.

My sustaining clan of close buddies in this adventure include Élodie Martellière and her son Naïm who welcomed me on numerous occasions with open arms in their house in Rabat, and Ahmed Boughaba and Hamid Aïdouni who shared their friendship and their precious insights into the history of Moroccan cinema.

My gratitude goes to Mifa Martin and Isabelle Favre for their loyalty and unflappable support, to Penny Cordish for her help on the proofs, to Robin for his patience and humor and to Will Higbee who is at the origin of it all, as the principal investigator of the British research grant from the Arts and Humanities Research Council which allowed me to spend extended periods of time in Tangier between 2016 and 2019.

Introduction: How to Write on Farida Benlyazid?

Farida the Subject

This book is an attempt to correct a grave injustice by zooming in on a free, spiritual, inventive Moroccan woman filmmaker who is little known outside Morocco where she is a cultural icon and a revered *dame du cinéma*.

Farida Benlyazid, a pioneer director in Morocco, the first kiss producer in Morocco, the first woman to film a kiss (in *A Door to the Sky*, 1988), a woman who decided early on that movies would be her life, that she would earn her living as a film director in a developing country, a pious Muslim who prays five time times a day and who was married four times, who does not believe in orthodoxy or religious diktats and whose spirituality is generous and radiant. Fluent in Darija, Spanish, and French, Farida has penned articles in Spanish and in French. She has written scripts, short stories, even a play in French. A mother of three, she is a feminist, and a politically engaged citizen in her country and beyond. How can one write about such a multi-dimensional subject and do her justice?

The project was daunting: how was I to capture all her talents and life movements in a few pages? situate her in the history of Tangier and in the history of Morocco, which became independent when she was eight years old? come to understand and represent as faithfully as possible the spirituality that presides over her daily life and creative work (especially since I come from a secular culture)? Furthermore, her film career is shaped in large parts by her liberal, anti-globalist, and above all feminist politics that become braided with her spirituality after her return to Morocco from a decade spent in France. The project thus entailed relating the dynamic unique journey undertaken by Farida Benlyazid through its course.

I started in Tangier, with Farida.

It is on the return of one of our slow walks in Tangier that I first thought of sketching the protagonist walking along a path with a myriad twists and turns, encounters, film projects to be made, film projects that are abandoned, yet other film projects that take considerable time. This book about Farida Benlyazid and her films therefore follows the path of a *road movie,* of a journey with discoveries and returns. In that sense, Farida's journey is replete with detours and loops like those of Ulysses or Ibn Batouta, a native of Tangier. She could even be the latest incarnation of the Maghrebi women travelers of yore who leave to better return.

These pages are an invitation to follow the itinerary of her career along a path that starts in Tangier, goes to Paris where she studies film, returns to Tangier, from which Farida leaves again to shoot films all over Morocco—and even, once, in Mali. Tangier remains the constant magnetic pull, the nurturing home between all film projects.

This study also examines and contextualizes her work in at least four areas: (1) the socio-politico-historical development of Morocco and its deep mutations as an independent country from 1956 to the present; (2) the impacts of drastically evolving film-making technologies on the economy of third world production, and the ensuing forms of adaptation and creativity in her f ilms; (3) the Muslim cultural and spiritual landscape in which Benlyazid's cinema evolved; (4) the intersectionality of gender, ethnicity and class in her film output. I also complemented this familiar, multifaceted academic approach to my subject with interviews with the director herself (conducted over the course of several years in Tangier) and individuals who have worked with her over the span of her career (e.g., Jillali Ferhati, Mohammed Abderrahman Tazi, Fatema Loukili, Fayçal al Gandouzi, Munir Abbar, Younes Negri, Dominique Caubet), family members (e.g., Kenza and Ayda Diouri, Abdelhaye Adbib), and film critics (e.g., Ahmed Boughaba, Abdellilah Jaouhary).

THE MAKING OF THE BOOK

The structure of the book therefore espouses the shape of a spiral: after each film venture, the traveler returns to Tangier which acquires a new meaning, like a recurring jazz theme after a wild improvisation.

Chapter 1, "Tangier and Paris—Multiculturalism and Feminism" focuses on Farida's formative years in international Tangier and her studies in Paris. An initial establishing shot of Tangier is followed by a zoom on Farida and establishes the roots of her cinema in her biographical story. This section presents the various influences on Farida as a child and as a young woman that will inform her cinematic work. This is the section where Farida Benlyazid's voice appears most (signaled in italics here and in the rest of the book).

Chapter 2, "Tangier & (Re)turn to Fes: *A Door to the Sky* (1988)" illuminates several meanings of the term "return": it shows the return of Farida to her country, her culture, her father's city, the "return of her soul" to a spiritual form of Islam. The chapter looks closely at how Farida Benlyazid fashions her own brand of Moroccan feminism. Farida Benlyazid's first feature film is analyzed from an autobiographical angle and probes the difficulties specific to making a film in Morocco in the late 1980s, even if it is a transnational co-production. The polyvocality of the text appears through excerpts of Moroccan pioneer Ahmed Bouanani's diary and of critical reviews.

A short section, "Intermezzo: anti-globalist feminist resistance" shows Farida facing the discontent of the CCM (Moroccan Cinema Center) at home, and deepening her feminist reflection to encompass a political solidarity with sub-Saharan women, as she films Malian anti-globalist Aminata Traoré for a documentary commissioned by the UN.

Chapter 4, "Farida's great *halqa* through Morocco and beyond" focuses on Farida as a storyteller in the Moroccan *halqa* oral tradition, with her various tales organized in concentric circles as they reach a wider and wider audience. Starting with an analysis of her itinerant play, *Aide-Toi, le ciel t'aidera/Help Thyself, Heaven Will Help Thee*, as part of a campaign to ensure the survival and wellbeing of pregnant women, then her second feature, *Keid Ensa*, the adaptation of a fairy tale, it proceeds to her third feature, *Casablanca, Casablanca*, a film against corruption in Morocco. The entire chapter highlights her writing and narrative techniques as a feminist *hlayqiya* (Moroccan taleteller).

Chapter 5, "Tangier and the world –*Juanita Narboni* (2005)" is a study in contrasts between her feature film (her latest fiction so far) as an historical and fictitious return to the international Tangier of her youth and her political activism (manifested in her writings and other film projects) at the beginning of the twenty-first century, in the wake of both the digital disruption and 9/11. Here, the study of the film focuses on a mature approach to multiculturalism, in the context of a Spanish-Moroccan production.

Chapter 6 "The Saharah, the Atlas, and Tangier" describes and analyzes her documentaries on the tradition of various groups (Imazighen, women) made over the past fifteen years or so. It reveals a possible misunderstanding about her controversial docu-fiction *Fronteras* (2013) and explores the series of shorts commissioned by the Leïla Benjelloun Foundation, to be housed in the future museum dedicated to Amazigh cultures in Casablanca. Farida's political voice makes itself heard during the Arab spring and the long-delayed elaboration of the new *mudawana*. The chapter highlights her position as an honored *dame du cinema* in her country.

Finally, "Coda—Tangier" offers an update on her current activities, her participation in a development initiative in Morocco, and her film and writing projects. The Coda takes the form of a three-act narrative: her participation in the Royal Commission for Development, her collaboration in the creation of *Tamayouz*, her work on Fatema Mernissi, and the revival of *A Door to the Sky*.

Finally, this book is imagined in part as a collage of various voices to give as polyvocal, as variegated an image as possible of Farida Benlyazid's cinema, inextricably linked as it is to her life and spirituality. The form is therefore hybrid: other texts come to feed the main body of the monograph as the narrative of Farida's career and work unfolds. As a result, the text features Farida's transcribed words (in italics) (and occasionally my deferred response), taken from numerous interviews and conversations conducted with her since 2015 (especially in Chapter 1); the translated transcript of filmed interview *of* Farida presenting *A Door to the Sky* (in "Coda"); excerpts of her play (in Chapter 4).

The interdisciplinary approach to her films also privileges one particular aspect of filmmaking over others, depending on the film. For instance, the study of *A Door* looks closely at two crucial elements: the difficulties of shooting a film in Morocco and its controversial reception in 1988, while the analysis of *Keid Ensa* focuses on narrative techniques, and that of *Juanita Narboni* explores adaptation and co-production challenges.

CONTENTS

CHAPTER 1

Tangier and Paris: Multiculturalism and Feminism

Abstract Context: Tangier and Farida's family. Farida grew up in multi-cultural, multilingual Tangier, a city in which foreign films were shot and which boasted numerous movie theaters. After her short-lived marriage with political dissident Moumen Diouri, she studied literature and film in Paris, France, where she made her first documentary for French TV (*Women's Identities*, 1978), became the first Moroccan woman producer (*A breach in the Wall*, Jillali Ferhati, 1978), and wrote her first script (*Reed Dolls*, Jillali Ferhati, 1982). She was also raising two daughters. This chapter is based in part on extended interviews with the filmmaker.

Keywords International · Islam · Feminism · Multicultural · Multilingual · Tangier · Postcolonial · Producer · Hindi film · Script · Producer · Lesieur films · Tradition · Modernity · Makhzen · Acousmêtre · Moumen Smihi · Jillali Ferhati · Moumen Diouri · Ahmed Maânouni · Noureddine Sail · Nelly Roussel · Marguerite Durand · Ula Stöckl · Łódź · Paris · Vincennes University · Cannes

Tinja, La perla del Norte, Tanger internationale, Tanjah… Farida Benlyazid's native city has been called many names throughout its history, depending on the language spoken by the long history of its visitors or invaders.

F. Martin, *Farida Benlyazid and Moroccan Cinema*, Palgrave Studies in Arab Cinema, https://doi.org/10.1007/978-3-031-40616-4_1

Most relevant to the beginning of this story, the city during the international mandate (1912–1956), in other words, just before Moroccan independence, is teeming with people from all walks of life and renowned for its artists and colorful visitors from the world over. It is in this cosmopolitan harbor, situated at the extreme Western point of the Arab world and at the extreme North of the African continent, facing the Spanish Southern coast, that Farida Benlyazid grows up. This unique environment will have multiple effects on her imagination, her sense of self, her outlook on the world. She likes to repeat "*I am international*", by which she means that both her mind and spirit know no borders. She identifies as Moroccan and as a daughter of "international Tangier."

Tangier's international status was idiosyncratic in the larger history of Morocco's double colonization by France and Spain. The two nations had divided the Moroccan spoils into two zones in 1912: France "protected" the larger, central zone, while Spain "protected" most of the Mediterranean coast all the way to the Western Sahara region. In order to resolve a dispute between European powers on the African continent, Tangier was given an international status in 1923 so that neither the French nor the Spanish could rule it unilaterally: the de-militarized zone was to be governed by France, Great-Britain, and Spain jointly. This particular arrangement ensured that European powers enjoyed free circulation in the Strait of Gibraltar and prevented all military deployment in neutral Tangier. In 1925, a longer list of signatories (Belgium, France, the Netherlands, Portugal, the United Kingdom, the United States, USSR, and, a bit later, Italy) confirmed the international status of the city where they sent their representatives. A local Moroccan representative, the Mendoub, presided over a legislative assembly (whose twenty-seven member included a total of... nine Moroccans!) while the executive power was in the hands of a French governor assisted by two attachés: one British, the other Spanish (except after France's defeat in 1940, when Franco's troops occupied the city and Spain governed Tangier for five years). *La Perla del Norte* returned to its international status after World War II, officially until independence in 1956 when it joined the Moroccan kingdom.[1] If its geopolitical history largely explains its cosmopolitan, multilingual culture, it does not account for its attitude toward religions. Tangier is idiosyncratic in Morocco because it does not have a *Mellah* (a Jewish city): Tangerines of all faiths were thus unsegregated neighbors in the old Arab city, the *Kasbah*, where little Farida's family lived.

By 1948, the year of the future filmmaker's birth, Tangier had already become a cinema city: the Lumière brothers first came to Morocco in 1897 and allegedly shot *The Moroccan Goat Herder* there (but is it one of Tangier's many urban legends?); shortly thereafter, Moulay Abdul Aziz IV (r. 1894–1908), fascinated by photography and cinema, invited Gabriel Veyre, one of their *opérateurs* (cameramen-projectionists), to his court. Veyre is said to have been the first to film Tangier in color (Schneider 2008: 81). Foreign directors, attracted by the cityscape and its mythological aura also came to shoot a number of films over the years, throughout the twentieth and the twenty-first centuries. "Since the nineteenth century the city has occupied an important place in the imagination of the West and East as an extremely complex, chaotic, dangerous and at the same time alluring and open city," writes Patricia Pisters as she traces the shifting images and values of Tangier in films made by Westerners before and after independence, as well as the various geopolitical scopes of the nostalgia they expressed (Pisters 2014: 175–189). Tangier thus became the set for European and American action and spy films, shot wholly or partially in the city, such as *S.O.S, Mediterranean* (Léo Joannon, France, 1938), *Mission in Tangier* (André Hunebelle, France, 1949), *007 Espionage in Tangier* (Gregg Tallas, Spain & Italy, 1964), or *The Living Daylights* (John Glen, UK, 1987). More recently, the James Bond series returned with *Spectre* (Sam Mendes, UK & USA, 2015), while the *Bourne Ultimatum* (Paul Greengrass, Germany & USA, 2007), had Matt Damon riding on a motorbike at implausible speed through the Kasbah. Since the end of the Cold War and its juicy spy narratives, foreign directors have come to Tangier to film other stories: encounters between tourists and locals (e.g., *Tangerine*, by Irene Von Alberti, Germany, 2008; *In/Out*, a short by Olivier Guerpillon, Sweden, 2015); drug trafficking (e.g., *El Niño*, Daniel Monzón, Spain, 2014), and films noirs (e.g., *The Two Lives of Daniel Shore*, Michael Dreher, Germany, 2009; *Goodbye Morocco*, Nadir Moknèche, France, 2013); a postcolonial return to the city (e.g., *Tenja*, Hassan Legzouli, France & Morocco, 2005; *Far*, 2001 and *Changing Times*, 2004, André Téchiné, France); the story of a French woman relocating for work in a factory of today's free zone (*Catch the Wind*, Gaël Morel, France, 2017); or the desperate attempts to rally Europe by the *brûleurs*[2] (*Return to Hansala*, Chus Gutiérrez, Spain, 2008; *Hope*, Boris Lojkine, France, 2014; *Roads*, by Sebastian Schipper, Germany, 2019). Finally, Jim Jarmusch's *Only Lovers Left Alive* (UK, Germany, Greece, France, 2013) presents a fantastic vampire rom-com set between Tangier and Detroit that inscribes the Pearl of the North on the straits of late capitalism and global culture. In short, Tangier has been a film set ever since the dawn of cinema.

When Farida was a little girl, Tangier also boasted a rich movie-going culture, as attested by the number and diversity of its theaters catering to diverse audiences. Back then, viewers spoke various languages, including Darija, Tamazight, French, Spanish, *Tangerian* (an English variant), Haketia (the Tangerine Jewish creole of old Spanish, Darija, and Hebrew), as well as Italian. The multicultural fabric of the city fostered a pluralistic milieu receptive to cinema and movie-going from very early on: films were shown as early as the 1910s in the Teatro de la Zarzuela or the Alcazar, and not just to the expatriate population. At the time, Tangier had an impressive number of movie theaters for a city of 150,000 inhabitants. Noureddine Saïl, a native of Tangier who went to the same school as Farida and who would later become the head of the CCM (Moroccan Cinema Center), described his childhood as a continuous initiation into various film traditions at the local picture houses, each of them with its own specialty: American Westerns dubbed in Spanish at the Capitole; romance and comedies at the Alcazar—including Antonio del Amo's film for children, *El Pequeño Ruiseñor* in 1957 (the Franquist messages of which went over the kids' heads); Egyptian cinema at the Cinema Vox; he saw his first film by Luis Buñuel at the Mauritania. Outside traditional commercial theaters, films were also screened in cheaper venues for targeted audiences. Children who were too young to go to the movies, for instance, could catch a Laurel & Hardy film for 10 centimes in M. Larbi's garage, in the working-class district of Emsallah (Berrada 2011: 176). Ahmed Boughaba remembers that, as a child, during the 1960s, free screenings were also held in poor neighborhoods: people would bring their own chairs or straw mats and assemble on the terrace of a house, where films were projected onto a white wall. At first, these films were part of the information campaigns of the state (on topics such as hygiene, vaccinations, birth control, as well as Moroccan heritage). Then, food industrial brands started to underwrite the screenings of what became known as the "Lesieur films" (named after the French brand of vegetal oil): Nescafé or Lesieur, for instance, would provide an Egyptian film, a European comedy, a Charlie Chaplin flick and insert their own ads at the reel change.

Growing up, Farida went to the movies a lot, with her mother, the formidable Fatima, who *was the freest woman I have ever known*, Farida says. Her life thus starts in a cinematic city, in the presence of cinema. And Farida learns to watch films very early on.

The composition of the Benlyazid family offers a fascinating look into the initial cultural make-up of the Tangerine filmmaker. Farida's father, Mohamed, came from a noble (Cherifian) dynasty that used to reside in Tlemcen (Algeria) until the French invasion: the Lyazid el Hassani (i.e., the Lyazid who descended from Hassan, one of Fatima and Ali's sons, in other words, from the prophet's grandson). *I am of Idrissid ancestry. Upon the death of Moulay Idriss II, his sons quarreled and a number of them left. The ancestor of our lineage went all the way to today's Algerian border—at the time, there was no border—in the region of Beni Znassen. His clan settled there before moving on to Tlemcen where they settled until the French landed in Algeria. But when the French arrived [in 1830], they moved to Morocco, to Fes. Some of them stopped elsewhere on the way. What is surprising is that our first Idrissid ancestor in Beni Znassen married an Amazigh woman named Azza, and that our name was actually her name for a long time. My father used to say: "Benlyazid is not our real name. That's the name we took in Fes, but our forefather who settled in Fes was named Lyazid Hassani, i. e. a descendant of Hassan." In the seventh century, our name was Ben Azza el Hassani: we bore the name of our Amazigh foremother. The first name was therefore the name of the mother! Then our name changed to Benlyazid Azza el Hassani. And that was way too many names!*[3] Hence, Farida's Arab ancestor, by enshrining the recognition of his indigenous spouse's name in the family patronym, altered the latter into a matronym, while retaining the noble Arab title. The family was noble. *At my father's, it was customary to address us as Moulay* [Prince] *Ibrahim, Moulay Mehdi, Lalla* [Princess] *Farida, imagine!*

Her aristocratic father, a pious Fassi,[4] had become a flourishing merchant, and led a comfortable life, in spite of difficult beginnings. When he was nine years old, his father, Abbas, had left the city for political and religious reasons. Abbas had been a member of the Derkawiya Zawiya (a Sufi brethren) led by a sheikh to whom he was very attached. After his death, the sheikh was succeeded by his son, *a young man who knew nothing ...* This took place at the start of the French protectorate. The French occupiers, eager to win the support of the population, had lavished presents upon the new sheikh, who had readily accepted them, to Abbas's utter disappointment. *My grandfather was so outraged that he decided to leave Fes immediately. He would have his family join him later.* In his search of a zawiya that would resist the French invaders, he left behind a wife, a son, and two daughters. His wife was now the head of the family and worked as a seamstress in order to feed her children. *He found a zawiya in Tadla which was colonized only in 1934. But he died two years after he left. So, actually, he got his wish: he never saw any French people again...* Yet neither Mohamed nor his mother had felt the slightest bit of resentment toward Abbas: *He was a man of God...* His decision was therefore accepted and respected.

Mohamed became a merchant and extended his trade route to Nador and Melilla, in the North. When he was twenty-one, the handsome young man was approached by Haj Ahmed Amor, a prosperous businessman who produced and sold uniforms to the Spanish army. El Haj offered him the hand of one of his four daughters. Among them, Fatima had by far the most spectacular independent streak, which she displayed at her wedding, at the age of fourteen: she was the first Moroccan young woman in Melilla to wear a white European dress for the ceremony. *Everybody was saying Mohamed had married a European woman! She would only do what she wanted. An idea came to her, and she would execute it immediately! Freer and more modern than anyone I have ever met!*

While Mohamed, raised in the sacred city of Fes, would pray and fast on Ramadan, Fatima did not. *He had never seen anyone remotely close to this creature who charmed him with her excesses, her beauty and gusto for life, here and now... She would have loved to have him drink, sing and dance with her. She would have liked him to take her to bars, restaurants, dancing halls... in short, to all the places of perdition the Christian colonizers wanted us to frequent so we could adopt a mode of life that was contrary to the true way of life Islam recommended. The Christian wanted life here and now, and God gave it to them.*[5]

Mohamed's love for Fatima never ceased over the course of their thirty-year marriage. While both spouses had different takes on life, they shared faith, an immense generosity, and eight children, who all went to school. *At home, we spoke Spanish. My mother was from the Spanish side* [Melilla] *and had attended school. Our parents wanted us girls to also go to school.*

Hence, from her very early childhood on, Farida experienced both what she would later call "tradition" (Moroccan, Muslim, with a long precolonial history) and "modernity" (under the Spanish and French influence on Tangier and the North of Morocco). Mohamed and Fatima decided it best to enroll their daughters in European schools. *I don't know what circumstances brought my mother to meet Mademoiselle Havre, the director of the French School in Tangier, and Fatima had invited her to my baptism. She had bent over my cradle and had asked my mother to enroll me, once I was old enough, in her school. And that's what happened. I went to primary school at the Lycée Saint-Aulaire—at the time every establishment representing French education was called 'lycée'; my sister went to Casa Riera, operated by nuns, in order to learn Spanish, embroidering and sewing, but she was excused from catechism, at my father's express request.* (Benlyazid 2014: 22–23).

Leila, younger than Farida, was sent to the Spanish school. Farida was the only daughter to receive a French education. On her first day of school, she spoke not a word of French, and nobody spoke to her in Arabic or Spanish. She remembers being amused by this game that everybody seemed to be playing, the code of which she had not mastered yet. After Saint-Aulaire, she attended the Lycée Regnault. Farida thus became trilingual.

Farida was eight years old when two dramatic events shook her world. On March 7, 1956, Mohamed V proclaimed the independence of Morocco from France. Joy erupted throughout the kingdom. Fatima came that day to take the little Tangerine girl out and they celebrated together in a fisherman's café, near the harbor all day and all night.

On November 18, the Sultan announced in another speech: "Morocco is coming out of the small jihad to tackle the big jihad:" the jihad of development. All citizens were asked to roll up their sleeves and enter the postcolonial era. The enormous work to be done in developing infrastructures, economy, access to education needed to be planned out and information about its advances needed to be shared. The Moroccan Cinematography Center (CCM), first created during the French Protectorate in 1941 (during the infamous Vichy régime that collaborated with Nazi Germany), under the (shady) auspices of the Moroccan Ministry of Information of the Protectorate, started to invite Moroccan directors to produce newsreels and films for the newly independent government. These films served multiple purposes: education as well as sharing political nationalist messages and consolidating the power of the *makhzen*.[6]

That same year, Fatima left the family home: *I was seven years old when my parents separated and I went to live with my mother at my maternal grand-parents, on rue San Francisco. We were leaving the big house at the entrance of the Kasbah, where my father, my five brothers and my little sister continued to live, together with my paternal grandmother who had come to care for them. I do not remember feeling any regrets, I think I was excited about residing in a more modern neighborhood, where my grandfather had acquired a beautiful building in which he had kept an entire floor for himself. I thought it fit my status as a pupil at the Lycée français. (...) This unforgettable period came to an end after the three months' interval the law required before my mother could marry the man for whom she had left my father.*

Farida's enchanted, flavorful memories of that time capture international Tangier: *Tangier was at the apex of its splendor at the dawn of independence. As the Arab proverb says, "If you hear the drum beat faster, know that it will soon be quiet." People were having fun everywhere on the streets, and we were part of it all. We would mix in the crowd on our way to Zoco Chico where the currency brokers gave the tempo, behind their red desks. Men in ties and hats and women in fur stoles or exquisite mantillas as if every day of the week was Sunday would cross paths with a few Nordic-looking couples, taller than them by a good head. All the eccentric people of the planet were represented, all sorts of languages were spoken, although predominantly Spanish. Hidalgos and ladies of the night became respectable at the terrace of the Café Central where we had our table.*[7]

Fatima wanted to keep Farida with her, but her father did not want to separate the children. *So my mother came to fetch me at school from time to time. She lived in Assilah, forty kilometers away from Tangier. My teachers knew: they would let me go.* Fatima had a flexible relationship with the rather rigid French rules of attendance: taking her daugher away from the Lycée for a few hours was also part of Farida's education. *We would go have lunch somewhere. She often took me to the movies. At first, she took me to see films for children. I remember* Cinderella... *But one day, she took me to see* Quo Vadis. *We arrived at the cinema late, in the middle of a scene where lions were devouring Christians. I thought: 'what on earth has she taken me to see this time?!' There were films that were totally inappropriate for my age!...She absolutely loved films, all the Hollywood films. I remember we saw films that I could not always understand very well. We went to see* Gone with the Wind *and I was perplexed: he was handsome, she was beautiful. Why did they split?! I remember the red curtain Scarlet O'hara took down to make a dress. That image made quite an impression on me...*

Fatima took Farida to see *Samson and Dalila* and the little girl saw the wiles of women on screen there for the first time: why had Dalila cut Samson's hair? How could she be so cruel with him? Farida has talked a lot about her early entrance into the world of screens. *In Tangier, when*

I was a child, we saw films from the entire world... American, Spanish, Italian, French, Egyptian and Hindi films.[8]

At the family house, two women tried to fill the void left by Fatima: the grandmother (Mohamed's mother) came from Fes and was soon joined by a stepmother, Aïcha. *My grandmother had an arrangement with her: grandma would take care of us and Aïcha would take care of her husband. This arrangement lasted. My stepmother was very kind, and things were going well, but since she did not understand Spanish, she asked us children to switch languages. So, we all started to speak Arabic at home.*

When we were too noisy, my impish grandmother would say: "Shush... Don't make too much noise or the bride will leave!...".

Aïcha knew the tales of the Moroccan folklore and loved to tell stories. She taught the girls the songs that the women would sing in *Darija*, out of male earshot; she told little Farida the spellbinding tale of *Keid Ensa. Really? A woman could do all that?! She could leave her father's house, make love with the man she loved, become pregnant, return, go out again? It was wonderful!....*

Farida's childhood was, by her own account, a happy one. Not only did she share a particular fondness for film with her mother, she also had a passion for books. She read in between classes at the Lycée Regnault, at home, everywhere. *Nobody was controlling what I was reading, and I took advantage of books to escape without leaving the house. Simone de Beauvoir became my model when I was fourteen. I led a parallel life in my head, while conforming to the life of a 'dutiful daughter'.*[9] Farida's parallel life also occasionally included movies. She remembers skipping class to see *Sundays and Cybèle* (Serge Bourguignon, 1962) and loving it. Her father had never been against cinema, although he thought there was nothing genuine about it. *He would laugh and tell us: "they are really leading you on! They take your money and tell you fanciful tales." He thought we were being manipulated. Actually, when you look at American film these days, you can see he was right! America has implanted its cinema everywhere!*

Her stepmother, Aïcha, had a brother, who was ten years younger than her: Moumen, a fiery, handsome, famous opponent to the makhzen. Their father, a political activist, had been incarcerated several times, initially at the sinister prison of Aïn Ali Moumen where he was tortured. A *shahid* (martyr) of the Moroccan struggle for independence, he died in 1953 from the after-effects of the torture he had endured (he never saw his dream of independence realized). Moumen—Abdelmoumen Diouri— thus bears the name of his father's jail.

Moumen was also a political activist, and fought against the regime of the new King, Hassan II, who ascended to the throne after the death of his father, Mohamed V, in 1961. Moumen, who had joined the party of opposition to the makhzen, was arrested for being one of the "conspirators of 1963," a group of opponents to the regime who were part of the UNFP (Union Nationale des Forces Populaires/National Union of the People's Forces) created by Mehdi Ben Barka and Abderrahmin Boubid in 1959, and who were accused of fomenting a coup against the King. In order to set an example, on July 16, 1963, the makhzen ordered the police to raid the office of the UNFP and arrest 100 militants. Ben Barka escaped abroad in the nick of time. A month later, the Ministry of Justice announced that the raid had prevented a coup against the King led by *fqih* Basri and former freedom fighters. A four-month long trial ensued and on March 14, 1964, Mohamed Basri, Omar Benjelloun, Moumen Diouri and eight others were sentenced to death (Cheikh el Arab and Ben Barka, in abstentia). However, the convicts received a royal pardon on August 20, 1964, and their sentence was then commuted to prison for life.

At the time, Farida was fifteen and Moumen twenty-five. She told her father she wanted to marry him. Mohamed showed no enthusiasm: "Why marry so young? Complete your studies first!" and "He will always be in jail. How is he going to take care of you?" *But I saw marriage as liberation, because every time I wanted to do anything, every time I wanted to travel, to go out, I was told: 'once you're married!' So, I thought: 'Fine! I'll get married! That's a pre-requisite!'"* Farida got engaged and took the bus once a week to go and visit Moumen in jail in Kenitra. *It was not very long: four hours by bus... and, while I was there, I would also see el fqih Basri, and Omar Benjelloun.*

In March 1965, after the brutally repressed rebellion of students and others (in Casablanca, in particular, where General Oufkir led the assault on the demonstrators), the King proposed a national union government which the parties of the opposition refused to join.[10] To show good will, Hassan II granted amnesty to political prisoners: Moumen was released from prison that year. Farida married him soon thereafter. She was seventeen. They settled down in Casablanca.

Farida's decision to lead the life she wanted and not necessarily along her father's or society's wishes was the first step of many during her life and illustrated a precocious sense of independence and confidence.

She gave birth to two daughters: Ayda was born in 1966, followed by Kenza, less than two years later. At the beginning of her married life, Farida worked as an accountant for OCE (Trade and Export Office). Three years later, since his business was doing well, Moumen suggested that she stay home and take care of the girls, and she accepted. However, she soon realized being a housewife did not fulfill her. She wanted to be a mother to her children *and* something else. Furthermore, her brave political activist hero had by now become... a husband. *In the beginning, we would laugh a lot. We were also marginal in some ways, on the fringes. We would see people from the high society of Casablanca, yet we felt different from them, apart. And then, I guess he just got swept up in it.*[11]

> This is when my father withdrew from politics, and opened a home appliance store, but he was not left alone. Every week, he was taken to the police station. They harassed him because he had touched upon something he was not supposed to. My parents' life became more and more unbearable. I know that we moved ten times or so in that period.[12]

Farida wanted to go to the movies, and Moumen tried to prevent her from doing so. She reminded him that she had always gone to the movies, even as a married woman. His response stunned her: "yes, but you were pregnant at the time. Now it's different!" Hence, it was acceptable for a woman with a bump to go to a movie theater, but not for a pretty, young woman showing no sign of pregnancy. Farida barely recognized her possessive husband who wanted to keep everybody at home, especially his wife who was *too attractive* to go out. Farida decided to return to her studies—she had interrupted them in order to get married—and finish high school. Things worsened at home, and Farida left Moumen. *It did not go well. First of all, it was an extremely painful divorce; a divorce that made me aware of what the mudawana really meant: women had no rights. When I told my father, he answered: "They have none, I agree with you. Someday, women will no longer want to get married. They've never had the rights to which they are entitled, you are right. They've never enjoyed the rights enshrined in Islam. But please don't become the leader of women's struggle!.»*[13]

In 1970, Farida left for Paris to study literature. Moumen and the girls joined her a few months later, in 1971. They tried to live together again as a family, but did not succeed. Their second separation was clouded by Moumen's intense and painful resentment following the torment of love gone awry. He had become a political refugee in France, after a second death sentence (in abstentia) and would stay in France for most of his life (he returned to Morocco only in 2006, and died in Rabat in 2012). In exile, and deeply hurt, he wanted to punish Farida and went as far as entrusting his two daughters to a nanny, in a secret location near Dijon. It took Farida an entire year of utter misery to find them and obtain custody. Finally reunited, Ayda, Kenza, and Farida, lived together on rue Berthollet in the Latin Quarter, in Paris.

By then, Farida needed to support her daughters and herself. She worked at a bank, first as a receptionist, then at the cashier's window, before she was put in charge of currency exchange. She describes what she did then with a smile: *I learned how to make estimates, and that is quite useful in filmmaking. Everything is useful to learn before making a film!* For years, Farida's multiple roles as mother, student, and bank employee left her exhausted. On one occasion, her father came for a visit in Paris and commented: *Is that the freedom you all wanted? You are working twice as much!*[14]

CINEMA AND TRAINING IN PARIS

Farida's student years in Paris coincide with a time of great upheaval and creativity at the university, and of militant cinema and manifestos in the Third World. She knew she wanted to study film. Everyone in her family thought this was a crazy idea, except for her aunt Fadéla—*the first to unveil was the only one telling me: "you are right. That's a good idea." I was impressed that one woman in my family would support me.* There was no film school yet in Morocco, and the government sent its promising students on scholarship to various schools in the North. They went to Paris (e.g., Ahmed Maânouni, Moumen Smihi, Jillali Ferhati), Moscow (e.g., Farida Bourquia), Łódz´ (e.g., Abdekader Lagtaâ, Mostafa, Abdelkrim Derkaoui), where they found a cosmopolitan student environment. Away from home, they got to know their peers from Algeria, Tunisia, Brazil, Argentina, Mexico, West Africa, East, and Europe. The future directors of postcolonial cinema all discussed similar issues in the smoke-filled cafés of Moscow, Łódz´, Paris, or Brussels: the politics and aesthetics of Third Cinema, and of Cinema Novo. Moroccan cinema would emerge from this fertile, transnational ground.

Farida joined the world of film apprentices, but not immediately, for the twists and turns of her itinerary started before she even left Morocco.

In 1970, I wanted to go to IDHEC [Institut des Hautes Études Ciné-matographiques, today's FEMIS] *but that year, IDHEC was in upheaval. I was offered a scholarship to go and study in Czechoslovakia, but I wanted to study in Paris... So, I went to Paris, and once there, friends of mine, including Noureddine Ayouch, advised me to go to Vincennes University where there was a minor in film studies within the literary major.*[15]

Meanwhile, under pressure from the May 1968 student and worker uprising in France, the state university system had started to decentralize. It hastily created a new university in Vincennes (outside Paris) that opened in January 1969: it was both an experiment and a showcase to demonstrate that the government was responding to the demands of students and professors. Vincennes welcomed traditional French students as well as students from abroad, factory workers and farm workers of all ages in night classes. It offered classes in disciplines hitherto absent from the university curriculum such as theater, music, visual arts, film studies. Lectures were abolished, and the Board of the University included equal numbers of faculty members and students. During its eleven-year existence (its buildings would be destroyed in 1980), it was at the cutting edge of intellectual radicalism: Vincennes is where Hélène Cixous founded the Center for Women and Gender Studies in 1974; where Gilles Deleuze, Michel Foucault, Jean-François Lyotard, Michel Serres, Giorgio Agamben, and many others gave talks and seminars. The canon was being revised and expanded: literary studies now included women's works as well as so-called "minor genres" such as science-fiction. It is in this heady, radical place, with daily calls for general assemblies of students and workers that Farida started her undergraduate studies.

She was stunned. She took part in discussions, attended her classes, studied, and read voraciously. An inquisitive, avid learner, she obtained her BA in literature with a minor in film studies in 1974. Her view on film at the time was much less radical than that of the passionate students around her who debated *cinéma-vérité* and Third Cinema. Solanas and Getino, in their famous Third Cinema manifesto, proposed:

> Pamphlet films, didactic films, report films, essay films, witness-bearing films – any militant form of expression is valid, and it would be absurd to lay down a set of aesthetic work norms. *Be receptive to all that the people have to offer, and offer them the best;* or, as Che put it, *respect the people by giving them quality.*[16]

Farida was not convinced that didactic cinema was the answer. "*We have to make films for the workers,*" people said. "*We can't make bourgeois films.*" But I thought: "*wait a minute! Workers have a right to see beautiful films! They are not going to like experimental research films!*" Ironically enough, she was perhaps more revolutionary than those around her, since she was following Che's directive to provide "quality" in the films she imagined for the workers.

In her literary studies, she enjoyed two courses in particular: one on women's literature and the other on science-fiction. She found science-fiction refreshing in its deployment of new imaginaries in which authors included incisive political comments on the human condition there and then. Here was a—literally—fantastic way to tackle current issues without seeming to! She was enchanted.

The second course began her initiation into the history of feminism in France and had rippling effects on her thinking about the role of women in society. Most days, she was to be found at the Bibliothèque Marguerite Durand, a feminist library where she discovered the history, narratives, theories of French feminists from revolutionary Olympe de Gouges to late nineteenth-century Marguerite Durand and Nelly Roussel. The latter, a socialist from the Belle Époque, was both a feminist activist who defended contraception as a right and an activist playwright who had written and directed plays to educate men, women, and children at the University for the People.

Farida probed the French texts and measured their political weight while pondering the condition of women in Morocco. She also commended Roussel's practice of giving a voice to the disenfranchised (women, children, workers) in her plays, applauded feminists for addressing the "people" in their fight for social justice rather than an intellectual bourgeois elite in their writings, conferences, or plays.

After her *licence* (BA), she enrolled at the *École Supérieure d'Études Cinématographiques de Paris* where she took classes until 1976. She left the bank and found odd jobs with more flexible hours in order to accommodate the various internships required in the audiovisual sector in Paris (either on film shoots or for the French TV). These exposed her to transnational feminist cinema in the making: for instance, she interned for Ula Stöckl, one of the leading figures of the New German Cinema from Ulm, on the shoot of the TV film *Eine Frau mit Verantwortung* (A Woman with Responsibilities, 1978). In 1977, she became a copy editor for the Parisian publishing house Sindbad. And she invited fellow

Tangerine Jillali Ferhati to join her as copy editor. Jillali (also an alumnus from the Lycée Regnault) had come to Paris to study cinema as well. They worked together for a year during which he had her read his script for a film he desperately wanted to shoot: *A Breach in the Wall*.

JARHA FI-L HÂ'IT/A BREACH IN THE WALL (1978)

Jillali and Farida were both young and passionate about film and decided to make the film, even though they had no money. Farida became the producer—and thus the first Moroccan woman producer. *In order to produce it, I sold my jewelry and the jewels of my sister, Leila Benlyazid, who gave me enormous support throughout my career.*[17] Investing in a film was more appealing than keeping the jewels their father had given them for rainy days. Jillali Ferhati remembers the film fondly: "We worked together and made a beautiful little film… You know, we had absolutely no dough to make it. It was produced by Kamar Films, a production company co-created by Farida… And yet, our film made it to the *Semaine de la Critique!*"[18] Indeed, the very first film she produced led Farida directly to the 31st edition of the Cannes International Film Festival in 1978, where it was screened in the critics' side-bar competition. The film had received a shooting permit but no funding from the CCM. In the 1970s, the mission of the CCM was mostly to produce Moroccan news-reels and short documentaries on Morocco of a didactic nature. With no help from the Moroccan state for feature films, directors became their own producers (for example, Souheil Ben Barka's *Thousand and One Hands*, 1971–1972, and *Blood Wedding*, 1977; or Moumen Smihi's *Chergui*, 1975).

SYNOPSIS—The narrative is situated in the contemporary period: Ringo, a deaf and mute public writer, gets out of jail after having served his sentence for the murder of a young female server. He roams the streets of Tangier as he re-acquaints himself with the city, with his past, and with freedom. He remembers the three friends he used to have and who were as marginal as he was: Khalid, the civil servant, and his beloved Khadija, who both played at being movie stars; and Chetba, the sickly tour guide whose mother did not want to see married. Tangier bears traces of colonialism, and the narrative mixes dreams and realism.

Farida and Jillali returned to Tangier to shoot the film. *We went back to film. Then we returned to Paris. And later, we thought that, in the end, we should really be back in Morocco. This is where we wanted to work.* The film appeared quintessentially Moroccan, from the very first lines of its credits that listed all the names of the future leaders of Moroccan filmmaking! Among its actors: Bachir Skiredj and Larbi Yacoubi; at the camera, Ahmed Maânouni, who had just finished his beautiful documentary *Alyam Alyam* (1978), and was working on his second one, *Trances* (1981); Izza Genini, who would later work on her own documentaries on Moroccan music, worked as an agent for the film and opened her address-book to make sure the film got screened. The director, Jillali Ferhati was also the actor playing the role of the protagonist, Ringo. Farida was both the producer and the first assistant.

Her first experience as a producer was far from easy, especially given her limited budget. She remembered one major player in the team suddenly demanding a raise and threatening to quit. *What could I do? We had no money!* She was so taken aback that she exclaimed: *Fine, then! We'll make the film without him!* Fortunately, Abdellah Bayahia, an experienced, older technician from the CCM, calmed her down: "No! You need the entire team for the film to work. Without him, the film won't exist. Do not worry! He'll be back!"[19] She learned an important lesson that would stay with her throughout her career: how to remain calm, keep her head above water, and be patient.

In Cannes, she further learned on the job: at the time, each film had press attachés who ensured that critics in the press and various special-ized journals were invited to the screenings of the films they represented. Needless to say, Jillali and Farida had no money for press attachés. They befriended a few who helped them for free. After the enormous prestige of having had their film selected in Cannes for the *Semaine de la Critique,* the film was released in Morocco, where, of course, Jillali and Farida were both eager to have the film screened and seen by the audience whom the film addressed: the Moroccan. The story of its arduous visibility in the kingdom reflects the situation of national film distribution at the time: … *no Moroccan distributor wanted it. I besought the manager of the Mauri-tania cinema in Tangier to screen it. I promised him, I swore to him that there would be viewers. With a group of girlfriends, we went everywhere in the kasbah and around the city to put up posters of the film in various cafés. We even found a van with a loudspeaker to drive through the streets downtown and in the suburbs to publicize the film screening. In the end, we managed to fill the theater and the film stayed on the marquis for one week. The manager confided that he had made more profit with it than with* Jaws, *the film that had beat all records that year!*[20]

At the time, Moroccan distributors favored foreign films, with no apparent desire to support their nascent national cinema. Instead, they would select Indian, Egyptian American, Spanish, and French films that came at a lesser price: the foreign films would arrive in Tangier or Casablanca long after their initial release abroad. As a result, these films had largely recouped their costs and already secured a profit, and their distribution rights in Morocco were thus bartered away sometimes as long as two years later, a real bargain for distributors and theater managers in the kingdom. Moroccans were thus saturated with images from all over the world (mostly from Egypt and France by the 1970s–1980s). So much so that film viewers were deeply surprised and felt odd when they first saw Moroccan characters and heard them speak in Darija.[21]

While the reception of *A Breach in the Wall* was unanimously positive in Cannes, it was mixed in Morocco: Jillali Ferhati was either celebrated as an upcoming Moroccan auteur or accused of having made too intellectual a film, inaccessible to a largely illiterate audience. Hence, the film enjoyed both enviable international critical accolades (it was also selected at the Mannheim Film Festival in Germany and at the Adelaide Film Festival in Australia), and poor national visibility (with a low score at the box office). And yet, the film clearly illustrates the élan and creativity of a young national cinema, and underscores the birth of a regional one: Tangerine Jillali Ferhati, Farida Benlyazid, and Moumen Smihi would become known as the *cinéastes du Nord,* the directors of the North. For the time being, in her first active role in a Moroccan production, Farida had succeeded in ushering the birth of a film on a shoe-string budget, no institutional aid, no publicity, and reluctant distributors. This state of affairs would slightly improve via institutional help over the years, but meager budgets and poor distribution would remain a constant in the cinema of the kingdom.

IDENTITÉS DE FEMMES/WOMEN'S IDENTITIES (1978)

Finally, Farida directed her first short film (16 min): a documentary made for Mouloud Mimoun's program *Mosaïques,* on French TV channel FR 3. First broadcast on January 22, 1978, it would rerun on January 1, 1987, in a "best of" montage to celebrate the 10-year anniversary of the program. The program focused on the diverse cultures of immigrants. Directed by Farida Benlyazid, in collaboration with journalist Jane Lagier, the documentary was structured along the interviews of four Maghrebi immigrant women, with a view to bridge two cultures: Maghrebi and French women's cultures. Kebira, the first interviewee, welcomes the team in her home, for instance, but on the condition that her face not be filmed. "It was important to us to respect her wishes and to show pictures while we listen to her voice," Jane Lagier's voice explains.

Farida's first challenge: how to visually represent an invisible woman. Kebira's acousmatic voice[22] justifies its status via a gendered detour: "It is still the case in the Muslim tradition that a woman must not appear in public, especially on television. We are in France, and we want to keep our country's traditions." The speaker's visual absence thus transforms her into an *acousmêtre*, a status usually reserved to masters and Gods according to Michel Chion: "God, in the three religions of the Book, Judaic, Christian and Muslim, is an *acousmêtre*." And, in cinema, "the voice of the acousmatic Master who hides behind a door, a curtain, or off-screen occurs in several major films."[23] Farida thus achieves a total revolution on screen: the interdiction to be seen—and for the non-diegetic viewer to see—allows for a subversion of the traditional power relationships. As Kebira's voice evokes the power of the Gods or the Master hidden from view, she usurps the power usually attached to patriarchy. Farida then proceeds to a slow pan of the walls of the apartment where Kebira lives to reveal elements of her life: leather poufs, a coffee table with a decorative tagine dish, the painting of a Marabout's sanctuary in the desert. The director bridges the distance to the "speaking God or Master" by giving an immigrant woman who is relegated to a political silent off-screen space in France a voice and a lived-in space. In order to give some corporeality to the invisible speaker, the camera zooms on the hands of women kneading the dough to make bread, and then on a collective couscous dish, while Kebira continues: "We are in France, and we have wanted to keep the traditions of our country alive so that, when our children go back to our country, they are no strangers to its habits, so that they can eat from the same dish. It is a sign of sharing." The director uses tactile images of her interior and of daily chores to enable the viewer to feel the relationship Kebira keeps with her original culture.

The second woman to speak is Fathia who brings to the screen her lucid and modern theory on the condition of Arab and French women: "French women are no different. They are exploited the same way, but they have the means to evolve, the means to express themselves–although they are crushed just like Arab women." Fathia's calm denunciation of the patriarchal yoke that weighs on both French and Maghrebi women casts a clear light on the experiential difference in both groups: it is at the inter-section of gender and (educated) class that the freedom of expression of women resides, whatever their culture of origin might be. French women have a little advantage here, given the difference in the percentage of girls who attend school in France and in Morocco at the time. Fathia is educated, speaks eloquently about her future outside French and/or Maghrebi cultural norms. Another young girl, Fatima, who wants to be an actress, is the most hybrid postcolonial subject among the interviewees who savvily negotiates the terms of her acculturation: "More than an evolution, it is above all an adaptation to a new culture. But what seems to me of utmost importance, is the right to make my own choices as a woman."

In their short documentary on immigrant Maghrebi women in and around Paris, Farida Benlyazid and Jane Lagier laid out several feminist postcolonial political principles for a francophone diverse audience. In order to avoid a reified commonly shared bicultural identity, the director showed four characters, four individual women with diverse origins in the Maghreb, singular modes of expression, and their own perceptions of themselves in a French environment—hence the plural title. On the one hand, Kebira's absent face signals a solemn interpretation of Muslim modesty. On the other hand, Fatima, a university student, reflects her own ambivalence after her trip to Algeria with an NGO (in order to understand her parents' culture). Once there, she felt like an "immigrant". She confesses to experiencing an acute sense of feeling caught, indeed suspended, between two worlds. The documentary explores the interstices or contradictory liminal spaces (so aptly described by Bhabha) of postcolonial subjects (and their descendants) transplanted out of their native land into Europe.[24] The camera then lingers on the objects evocative of a nostalgia for the Maghreb, next to the machines of modernity, before it films the exterior: a building on a grey, winter day. From beginning to end, the women all talk, eager to share their views. The camera gives hypervisibility to the varied degrees of attachment to the culture of origin by doing a close-up on the mother's couscous at noon and the young student's lonely cigarette at midnight.

ARAIS MIN KASSAB/REED DOLLS (1982)

After her first experience in the practice of cinema as producer, first assistant, and as director, Farida asked Jillali to read a short story she had turned into a script. This was her first script of many. Writing would become a large part of her life and career. She would write scripts for other filmmakers (notably Mohamed Abderrahmane Tazi), articles for various publications (not only on cinema, but on Morocco, on faith, on feminism, and more), a play, essays, short stories. She describes the process of writing as the intensely rewarding shaping of a vision of the world that is always in progress, always in the process of (re)creation. When you write, *you re-tell reality as you see it. In some ways, you are always writing. Very often, you write things that will never be written,* she explains. With the discoveries she makes while writing, comes the pleasure of writing in solitude, of holding the pen over the white page or starting to type on a keyboard, in a bubble of silence, away from the rumblings of the world. She speaks of writing as a *fulfilling experience.* Like most Maghrebi women educated in French, she writes in French and defends her linguistic "choice" in 1996: *I studied in France, therefore I write in French. I write for some people who read French. It would take me thirty years of study to be able to write in Arabic. And even if I could, I would face the same issue: it would be for a few literati who can read Arabic. Yet, I wanted to share stories with everybody. And I realized that film was the most appropriate tool for that. I can use* darija *and can thus reach every Moroccan.*[25]

Her explanation echoes the postcolonial position of her Algerian friend Assia Djebar: "So I write, and in French, the language of the former colonizer, which, however, has irreversibly become the language of my thinking; whereas I continue to love, suffer, and pray (when I happen to pray) in Arabic, my maternal language," the author declared in her acceptance speech for the Peace Prize, at the German Book Trade in 2000.[26] Here, using French is not a betrayal, she explained, but making use of a "near remoteness" that provides her with a lucid gaze on her own culture and country. Both women find in this "near remoteness" of the French language the terms to share their offbeat vision—at once clear-sighted and compassionate—of the Maghreb and its women. And for both women, writing is a vital necessity.

Upon reading it, Jillali was immediately enchanted by *Reed Dolls.* He offered to direct the film which came out in 1982. At the time, cinema in independent Morocco had a very short history and was entirely masculine, as attested by a quick look at the dossier on cinema published in the second issue of *Souffles* (1966) in which the discussion on national cinema was entirely conducted by men. In 1982, the camera still remained a male instrument of power in Morocco, before two women, Farida Bourquia and Farida Benlyazid seized it.[27]

Reed Dolls is the fruit of a true collaboration: co-produced by Jillali Ferhati's production company Héraclès and ZDF (*Zweites Deutsches Fernsehen,* the second TV channel in West Germany), it also received a comfortable 280.000 MAD in post-production aid from the CCM—the Support Fund (*Fonds de Soutien à la production cinématographique*) was created in 1980. The financial production montage is therefore transnational: Moroccan and German. Yet, even with the money they received to make the movie, their budget remained tight. Farida remembers finding an astute way to save money on costumes. *We had very little money. So, while we could buy clothes, distress them, and crumple them, why not rent them, already distressed and crumpled, from people in the kasbah? It would give them a little money which they really needed. Fatema Rifiya, who lived nearby, gave me a hand: she was our assistant for costumes... She was a woman of the people, free, intelligent, and with a great sense of humor. She was poor, she knew everybody in the kasbah, and she was invited everywhere. She was very proud. She would come to your house, holding her head high, and never asking for anything: you gave to her. So, she went to all the houses in the neighborhood and brought back heaps of clothes!*[28] This type of artisanal bricolage would become characteristic of Farida's way of stretching string-shoe budgets to enable her to make or finish a film throughout her career as a producer/director.

Jillali Ferhati's note of intent is clear on the teamwork that made the film possible:

Reed Dolls is not exclusively a film on women, it also comes to the defense of all beings who experience humiliation. I chose to direct this film, the scenario of which was written by Farida Benlyazid, because of the beauty, the power and the coherence of the topic. Nothing is artificial nor invented, it is a news story that makes your blood boil. I have never been as concerned – and there was so much more I would have liked to say – by the suffering of a being crushed by the century-old institutions that are customs and traditions, and that reinforce man's power and self-righteousness. But I consider my images not to be the end of Farida's and my words, because we are still pondering the issue, and many others are doing so with us.[29]

The film reaped awards in Morocco and abroad and was received with great enthusiasm by Moroccan critics. "In the institutional history of Moroccan cinema, Jillali Ferhati's *Reed Dolls* is the first film to have received the top award of the first edition of the National Film Festival in Rabat in 1982." notes Mohammed Bakrim.[30] And yet the competition at the initial National Film Festival was fierce, with highly creative films such as Bouanani's *Assarab/Mirage* (1979) and Mostafa Derkaoui's *Ayyaam Shahrazad al-hilwa/The Beautiful Days of Sheherazad* (1982). Moulay Driss-Jaïdi applauds the film's critique of the "gears of the social machine" relentlessly preying on the protagonist.[31] Ahmed Fertat salutes the cinematography by Abdelkrim Derkaoui (another pioneer in Moroccan film, back from Łódz' since 1972).[32] And Souad Filial, after quoting Noureddine Sail's positive take on the film underscores the strength of the script in her review:

"The authentic treatment of the status of woman linked to the precariousness of her living conditions is particularly poignant." While the film works on an affective mode, the affect is lucid and "does not devolve into demagogy like Egyptian films."

> Farida Benlyazid and Jillali Ferhati have transposed all the subtlety and elegance of the script in order to deliver a powerful message; indeed, Aïcha's progress takes place in an environment of warm human relationships: her mother-in-law's tenderness and unshakeable support, the respect of human dignity in the class rapport between the household mistress and the servant, the compassion of a fellow seamstress.[33]

The film is selected at the *Quinzaine des Réalisateurs,* another side-bar competition at the Cannes Film Festival in 1982. The French critics often review the film from an exoticizing angle, yet the film critic of *Le Monde* notes "Staying away from film as spectacle, the authors have recreated something akin to an ethnographic fiction full of sense and fury."[34] And Charles Tesson writes in July 1982 edition of the *Cahiers du Cinéma*:

> A rare pleasure. Here is a film about which you know nothing ahead of time and from which you come out moved beyond measure: because it is a superb melodrama, one of the darkest ones, and the gaze that guides it – with its passionate observation over the entire duration of the film of a character, a ritual, or a relevant gesture – succeeds in sketching an entire documentary perspective within the nagging, almost abstract framework of the film. *Reed Dolls* is an 'ethnographic melo'. (40)

SYNOPSIS—The narrative follows a young girl, Aïcha (<the living one>), who overcomes the many obstacles thrown in her way by traditional patriarchy throughout her life. She is first whisked away from her village as a little girl in order to be married to her cousin Mohamed who resides in Tangier. Growing up in the Kasbah under the guidance of her aunt and mother-in-law, she learns to become a woman and then the mother of three children. She suddenly becomes a widow with no resources, resists the advances of her brother-in-law, and finds employment outside the family home, which provides her with (meager) wages and a breath of freedom. Soon, she has an affair, becomes pregnant, and is sued by her brother-in-law. At the trial led by men, the custody of her children is wrenched away from her. Aïcha is illiterate and does not understand the verdict when it is announced in literary Arabic.

During the entire film, Aïcha measures the narrow space—both physical and mental—occupied by women in the patriarchal society in which she survives. In the international Tangier of 1953–1954 (the time of the narrative), she comes home one day and says: "The Spanish women go out with their husbands: I envy them," to which her aunt replies: "May God scatter them as they have scattered us. In the old days, women did not appear in front of men." Yet, as their friendship grows, the aunt becomes more and more conscious of the unfairness with which men treat her niece. She gradually changes her views and ends up defying the patriarchal laws by which she used to abide. It is the aunt, the matriarch, who suggests an abortion (which won't happen); and who admonishes her other, fearful, docile daughter-in-law: "Stop trembling! It is because of women like you that women are trampled down."

This script already contains the seeds of Farida's future films. It pleads for female solidarity as the only solution to free women from patriarchal shackles. Even if the film was directed by her partner, "the most feminist Moroccan film" as the critics said, bears the words and style of the Tangerine woman. Her grandmother is even quoted in the film, as Benlyazid would write much later: *My grandmother, who had had the opportunity to know women like Juanita, would say: "Make no mistake, some of my neighbors were Spanish women, and they are just like us!" This is a sentence I put in* Reed Dolls, *the first scenario I ever wrote.*[35] In fact, the quote is not the only element of the film that honors her grandmother. *Reed dolls refer to the hand-made dolls my grandmother taught us to make.* They represent *the strength of women who, like reeds, bend in stormy winds but never break...* The film espouses a vision of women in Morocco that is both anchored in a local experience and culture and irrigated by the international, multicultural, and multilingual context of Tangier as well as by the readings Farida absorbed at the Bibliothèque Durand. The script offers a view of Farida's ethics that exemplifies her political view on equity and social justice: it asserts the tranquil power of women while calling for mutual aid and compassion with all the oppressed. In that sense, Farida's feminism is, at this stage of her career, still close to the French feminism of the early 20th century: it rejects the status of woman as victim and extends the affirmation of solidarity across generations.

She had crossed the Mediterranean back to her country to collaborate on two films and she had decided to become a director in Morocco. She would still travel back and forth between Tangier and Paris to see her daughters, for a few years. Her return to Morocco would not happen in one clean break. But she bought her little *"snail's house"* house in the Kasbah, a few blocks away from the big family house. After ten exhausting years, Farida Benlyazid was now ready to move on to direct her own feature film.

NOTES

1. Tangier actually kept its former legislative and fiscal advantages until 1960.
2. The *brûleurs* (*harragas,* burners) are the clandestine migrants from Morocco and Sub-Saharan Africa who risk their lives in frail boats to rally the coast of Spain, the southern tip of Europe, and burn their papers prior to leaving, so that they cannot be deported back to their country if they are apprehended at any point in their journey or once they have arrived.
3. Interview with the author, March 24, 2018.
4. A Fassi is an inhabitant of Fes.
5. Benlyazid, Farida. "La Modernité," in *Fatimita*. Tangier: Editions Khbar Bladna, 2015: 8–9.
6. In Morocco, the term *makhzen* (<the warehouse> where the civil servants used to receive their wages) refers to the governing institution of the King and his entourage (e.g., his advisers, the leaders of his army, the economic, political, and intellectual elite that support the monarchy).

   "Makhzen" is a term that both Moroccans and Morocco observers use to refer to the network of power holders tied to the king and his associates through allegiance, patronage, and clientelism. It is not an official entity; nor is there a single agreed-upon list of its components. In some respects, the term could be analogous to "the deep state" as the term is applied to some segments of the governing authorities in other countries. The Makhzen refers to those who function as shadow decision makers in Morocco, with a preponderant role played by the security and intelligence services. In Morocco, the term "Makhzen" is also commonly understood to refer to security services and their members at large. (https://www.hrw.org/report/2022/07/28/theyll-get-you-no-matter-what/moroccos-playbook-crush-dissent#_ftn14).

7. Berrada, Hamid. Interview of Farida Benlyazid, *Mais encore? Avec Farida Benlyazid* (What else? With Farida Benlyazid), 2M, January 30, 2014.

8. Aidouni, Hamid. "L'œuvre au féminin, éloge du cinéma" (Female work, film praise), in *L'œuvre cinématographique de Farida Benlyazid* (Farida Benlyazid's cinematographical work). Rabat: Ministère de la Communication, 2010: 27.

9. Benlyazid, Farida. "Le cinéma au féminin" (Female cinema), *Quaderns de la Mediterrània*, No. 7, 2006: 221.

10. This strategy—coopting the opposition within the government—is the makhzen's solution to safeguard its survival: the regime adroitly appoints leaders of the opposition to occupy posts in precise spots on the political chessboard, in order to avoid the crises that threaten the very foundation of the monarchy.

11. Interview with the author, March 24, 2018.

12. Diouri, Kenza, interviewed by the author. Casablanca, March 20, 2018.

13. Berrada, Hamid. op. cit.

14. Benlyazid, Farida. "Le cinéma au féminin", op. cit.: 222.

15. Berrada, Hamid. op. cit.

16. Solanas, Fernando and Getino, Octavio. "Towards a third cinema: notes and experiences for the development of a cinema of liberation in the third world," *Black Camera: An International Film Journal*, Vol. 13, No. 1, Fall 2021: 391 [originally published in *Cinéaste*, Vol. 4, No. 3, 1970: 1–10].

17. Nesma, Didi. "Quand Farida s'entête, le succès se pointe" (When Farida's stubborn, success ensues/an interview of Farida Benlyazid). *Citadines*, No. 40, April 1999: 37.

18. Ferhati, Jillali, interviewed by the author. Tangier, November 30, 2017.

19. Benlyazid, Farida, interviewed by the author. Tangier, May 10, 2016.

20. Benlyazid, Farida. "Réception des cinémas du Maghreb au Maghreb" (The reception of Maghrebi film in the Maghreb), in Patricia Caillé, Florence Martin & Kamel Benouanès, eds. *Les Cinémas du Maghreb et leurs publics. Africultures* Nos. 89–90, 2012: 41.

21. *We were too late: the market was taken by the American, the Egyptian, the Indian who had implanted their networks early on. I remember that in the beginning, the viewers could not help but laugh when they saw characters speaking their language in sets that were familiar to them.* Benlyazid, Farida. "Le cinéma au féminin," op. cit.: 222.

22. A notion developed by French critic Michel Chion, an acousmatic voice is the voice we hear in a film without being able to see its origin.

23. Chion, Michel. *La Voix au cinéma* (Voice in film). Paris: Éditions de l'Étoile. Cahiers du Cinéma, 1993: 37 & 31.

24. Bhabha, Homi. *The location of culture*. London & New York: Routledge, 1994.

25. Salmas, Marianne. *Farida B., cinéaste marocaine*. France: Gaspacho Vidéo, 1996.

26. https://www.cairn.info/revue-etudes-2001-9-page-235.htm#:~:text=J'%C3%A9cris%20donc%2C%20et%20en,en%20arabe%2C%20ma%20langue%20maternelle [link active on April 5, 2021].

27. While Tangerine Farida was studying in Paris, and then lived in between Paris and Tangier for a couple of years, Casablancan Farida studied drama at the Lunatcharsky State for Theater Arts (GITIS) in Moscow where she graduated with an MA in play directing in 1973 before she returned to Morocco, taught drama, and worked for the Moroccan Radio and Television (RTM). She made her first fiction film in 1982: *Al Jamra/The Ember*, followed, in 1988 by Farida Benlyazid's *A Door to the Sky*. But this is getting ahead of ourselves.

28. Benlyazid, Farida, interviewed by the author. Tangier, November 23, 2017.

29. http://www.africine.org/film/poupees-de-roseau/1658 [link active on March 27, 2022].

30. http://albayane.press.ma/poupees-de-roseaux-de-jilali-ferhati-1982.html [link active on March 27, 2022].

31. Driss-Jaïdi, Moulay. "Figures de la féminité dans trois films de Jillali Ferhati: Aïcha, Mina, Saïda et les autres" (Female figures in three films by Jillali Ferhati: Aïcha, Mina, Saïda, and others). Groupe de Recherche. *Jillali Ferhati: Une Expérience unique*. Tangier: Association Marocaine des Critiques de Cinéma, 2011: 41–50.

32. Fertat, Ahmed. "La force expressive de l'image dans les films de Jillali Ferhati" (The expressive power of the image in Jillali Ferhati's films). Ibid.: 51–61.

33. Filal, Souad. "À propos de *Poupées de roseaux*" (About *Reed Dolls*). *Revue Lamalif*, No. 144, March–April 1983.

34. Lefebvre, Jean-Pierre & de Leon, Mike. "Les autres films à la Quinzaine des réalisateurs: *Poupées de roseaux*" (The other films at the Quinzaine des réalisateurs: *Reed Dolls*), May 21, 1982: 17.

35. Benlyazid, Farida. "Le cinéma au féminin," op. cit.: 223.

CHAPTER 2

Tangier & (Re)turn to Fes: *A Door to the Sky* (1988)

Abstract Context: Morocco in the 1980s. Farida Benlyazid experiences several "returns": a physical one to the postcolonial, political and economic space and culture of Morocco; a Muslim "return of the soul" which sets off her life-long spiritual quest, outside the constraints of religious parameters, and inspires her to compose the auto-fictional script of her first feature film, *A Door to the Sky* (1988). She directs her first film in Fes—excerpts of Ahmed Bouanani's diary on the film shoot detail the specific challenges of filmmaking in Morocco at the time. Upon its release, the film is met with controversy in the Muslim world and in the European feminist circles, for different reasons and lauded in the United States, before it becomes a classic in Moroccan cinema. She also writes the script of Mohammed Abderrah-mane Tazi's *Badis* (1989).

Keywords Feminism · Islam · Screenwriting · Reception · Fiction · Auto-fiction · Autobiographical "return of the soul," festivals · Qurʾān · Artisanal cinema · Ibn Arabi · Fatema Mernissi · Farqzaid · Homi Bhabha · Catherine Chalier · Ahmed Bouanani · Hassan Daldoul · Věra Chytilová · Ella Shohat · Miriam Cooke · Zakia Tahiri · Mohammed Abderrahmane Tazi · Noureddine Sail · Asma Lammrabet · Fes

F. Martin, *Farida Benlyazid and Moroccan Cinema*,
Palgrave Studies in Arab Cinema,
https://doi.org/10.1007/978-3-031-40616-4_2

Farida's return to Morocco, so longed for, is not necessarily easy on several levels: in her personal life, the girls are still away from her, in their fancy boarding-school near Paris, and Jillali and she are growing apart; professionally, coming back to Morocco as a woman filmmaker presents its own multiple challenges; on a mystical level, she experiences another form of return which sends her into a life-long spiritual quest; in her deep dive into Moroccan culture, she seems engaged more in an apprenticeship than in a literal "return". All these variegated shades of return will inform the creation of her first feature film: *A Door to the Sky*.

During her decade spent in Paris, Morocco had made tremendous progress in development, but its gains were not distributed equitably.[1] Illiteracy had started to recede (from 87% in 1960 to 60% in 1982) but unequally between men (51%) and women (78%).[2] The King, Hassan II, had been the victim of several coup attempts during the 70s (including the coup attempt in Skhirat in 1971 and the assault led by the army headed by General Oufkir in 1972), and had repressed them with utter cruelty. As a result, hundreds of suspects were incarcerated and tortured in prisons and newly erected penitentiaries, some of them in the desert (such as Tazmamart, the subject of Aziz BineBine's sobering autobiographical account, *Tazmamort: Eighteen Years in Morocco's Prison*).[3] Hassan II's authoritarian regime known as "The Years of Lead" is ruthless in its attacks on freedom of expression.[4] The King, faced with a multi-headed opposition from multiple layers of society (e.g., the army, the intellectuals, the imams, the students), uses repression and communication. A gifted strategist in the latter, he launches a campaign to solidify a (somewhat threatened) national unity around the monarchy: the famous Green March in 1975. He convinces 350,000 people from all regions and all classes of Morocco to march to and peacefully cross the Southern border of Morocco in order to free their Sahrawi brothers and sisters from the ongoing Spanish occupation. This allows him to annex a large part of Western Sahara, sign a treaty with Spain and Mauritania and start a territorial dispute with Algeria that is still going on today. In 1979, Mauritania exits the Southern part of Western Sahara, which the Moroccan army immediately occupies.

In 1980, while Farida is in Tangier, the makhzen starts building the famous "wall of sand," a defense system in Western Sahara against the possible attacks by the Polisario based in Algeria. That same year, in Fes, the Islamists are confronted by the police, and many of them are arrested.[5] The 1980s are a decade of extreme economic slump (due in part to the years of drought that led to it) and political and social upheaval. Urban revolts throughout the kingdom are subdued by the police and the army, the most spectacular and brutally crushed ones being the "bread revolts" in 1981 (in Casablanca where the authorities shoot into the crowd of demonstrators, killing hundreds) and 1984. Finally, Hassan II launches a "voluntary" subscription to finance the building of the largest mosque in the country in Casablanca, thereby killing two birds with one stone: filling up the state coffers and cementing national unity.

How will Farida be able to make film in this frail economy indebted to the IMF? Where will she find the funds to produce? How can she create what she wants? How and to whom can she tell her stories? How can she enter the masculine postcolonial mine-field of filmmaking in her country? Furthermore, given the restricted freedom of expression, how can artists and writers address their messages to their Moroccan audience? *I think this forces you to be more creative. Frankly, I am not interested in creating a political manifesto. I find it way more interesting to suggest things. It yields many more possibilities to be creative, it seems to me.*

The Return of the Soul

Farida is in Tangier, in her little house in the Kasbah, and re-acclimating to the realities of Morocco, when her "return of the soul"—a term I am borrowing from theologian Catherine Chalier—occurs. It is not a conversion in the sense that Farida does not convert from one religion to another, but rather an inner revolution in the first sense of the term: a startling turn of the soul on itself that leads it to contemplate a "truth" that had hitherto been hidden from view. The initial jolt gives birth to an acute and new or renewed awareness of the divine, of being, and of one's place in the cosmos. It is a return in the sense that it circles back to that truth, or more precisely, to the delightfully bewildering moment of awareness of a truth that the soul has always contained but from which it has been long distracted. This type of spiritual cartwheeling motion does not indicate a return to the past, a nostalgia for a lost Eden or the faith of childhood. Rather, it is the vertiginous discovery within one's soul of clear certainty. Viewed in cinematic terms: an initial high-angle shot of the deep dive into the inner world of the soul cuts to a dynamic counter, low-angle shot that opens up to a luminous meaning that the subject suddenly realizes has always existed, beyond the self (and the ego). The shock of this colossal discovery in the silence of one's soul also comes with the realization that the place the subject occupies in the universe is infinitesimally small. The phenomenon is so private, so guarded, that the entourage of the transformed subject can only piece together the emanations of a change in the subject. Farida's intense return of the soul corresponds to Chalier's description of the fulfillment it provides, so intense and overwhelming that it is difficult if not impossible to share:

> .. many of the converted remain discrete about it, not to protect some shameful secret, but rather to allow the sparkle of a truth to breathe and grow in them, a sparkle that they sense, with gratitude and surprise, is orienting their existence but resists all appropriation; a sparkle that they do not seek to retain or secure by an effort of the mind, lest they lose the orientation it has given them.[6]

Given the inability of the words of our rational human languages to adequately translate a return of the soul, Farida describes hers through images, allegorical fragments, poetry. Furthermore, she experienced no single dramatic conversion, but rather a series of "events" that serenely led her to an awareness of the divine. She relates two flashes—two enlightening flash-backs—that led to the intense renewal of her faith, which she calls *the illumination*. The first episode was the revelation of her own intense connection to the world, one morning, as the sun was rising over the sea by the beach where she was sitting. Her narration of it mirrors many other similar "returns of the soul" or "conversions." As she was contemplating the birth of a new day, facing the scintillating reflection of the sun on the sea, she sensed the movement of a presence near her. Looking away from the sea, she discovered a very small insect flapping its iridescent wings and felt a surge of energy rising up within her, an energy she had never felt before: *the energy was circulating from the little insect to me, from me to the rising sun, and I knew we were parts of the whole.* (As Farida evokes the wave that transported her that morning, her arms point to the insect, the sun, herself, and her eyes recall the ecstasy of the moment). Her place in the world is a humble one, devoid of human hubris: she is in the world as the insect is in the world, no more and no less. She is as small as the pretty insect in this beautiful expansive universe.

In the second episode, she happened upon a book on Tao, read it and recognized her experience in the words of Tao. She was enchanted. *But, seriously, I was not about to go all the way to Asia to fetch a religion!* She started to read Sufi scriptures and Arthur John Arberry. Her initial poetic illumination thus immediately leads her to a spiritual and intellectual quest. She read the Qur'ān, practiced *ijtihad* as requested, read the Muslim mystics, like Ibn Arabi. She also started to pray five times a day, a practice she describes as a discipline that has helped her a lot, and also reminds her of her exact place in the cosmos at the time of prayer. A pious Muslim, she has gone twice to Mecca—in 2000 and 2008. Narrating her second haj in a religious journal, she marvels at her participation in a world that connects the human to the divine, her being to the Whole: *One night, at two in the morning, we did a penultimate tawâf under the celestial vault. We did our last rotation around the Ka'ba, on a planet that rotated amid the stars themselves rotating on their orbits. Every time I would look up, I was overwhelmed with cosmic vertigo.*[7]

Her initial bewilderment and elation have never served her ego. Once on her quest for meaning, they turned an ever-larger openness to others, an encompassing form of love. Her response to a question on her practice of Islam is clear: *It is faith, and tolerance, and love. It is faith in love.*[8] Her constant practice of patience, tolerance, and love for others would become central to her life, her quest for wisdom, and her filmic creation.

Not everyone understands her. Jillali predicts that one day she will levitate so high that she will be found praying above a television antenna! Both have moved away from each other since their success in Cannes. In 1982, she meets Major Hamadi Adbib, a former commander of the Royal Guard who looks like Charles Bronson, and marries him. They have a son, Abdelhaye, born on October 1, 1983. Her relatives do not understand this union: under the orderly appearance of the uniform, the commander is unpredictable. He is married, has five children, and Farida is his second wife. His first wife has no profession and had waited for him while he was serving a sentence in prison. Farida offers the following:*'Give her the choice. If she wants to stay, I agree. If she wants to leave, then let her go.'* This does not prevent Farida from adding: *It doesn't mean at all that I think polygamy is a panacea! But in some cases, instead of saying to a woman 'leave!' as men often do when they want to marry a younger woman, we give her the choice!*

Her paradoxical decision to enter a polygamous union also indicates a phenomenal, masterful, individual gesture of defiance, as "unique" as the meaning of her name, performed on the basis of her own multicultural Tangerine humus, her decade in Paris, her intellectual and artistic journey, and her wilingness to experiment with her return. Moreover, she chooses to embark on a polygamous marriage in the respect of the "rules" of polygamy, yet with no constraints. The turn she takes here in her journey as a woman is antithetical to the writings of the French feminists she read in Paris (and would probably elicit shuddering horror, dazed shock, anger, among some Western or Arab feminists). Interestingly enough, she is not the only one to tread this unexpected path among postcolonial Muslim women returning to their countries from Europe.[9]

Farida's (recent) return to Morocco means diving into a cultural universe that is both hers and not completely hers. Moroccan culture, familiar and close to her (the tales, stories, practices, and songs she knew) has also remained at arms' length, given her childhood in well-educated, multilingual Tangier, and her ability to slip from the Tangerine culture into the French one with the nimbleness of an eel. Her in-depth apprenticeship of Moroccan cultures (in the plural for Morocco is no monolith) after her return leads to the following possible reading of her act: she is critical (*ijtihad*) and defines the terms of *her* union with Hamadi. Her consent to it signifies neither a plea for polygamy nor a rejection of the monogamous model.

Sabah Mahmood's notion of "individual autonomy" as a crucial element of agency in Islamic feminism provides another element of response.[10] Mahmood demonstrates that the practice of Muslim piety by women has always included a way to resist patriarchal subjugation, through the agency of one's freedom of decision and through the constant exercise of patience (*sabr*). But this path, which each woman is free to choose or not, is part of a long-term plan, and does not lead to the flash of a revolution. Western feminism and its urgency have a vertical axis aiming for an imminent equality of resources and rights here and now, while Islamic feminism has a horizontal one, as it appropriates the virtues advocated by Islam and proceeds through reformist stages at a necessarily much slower pace tending toward a future horizon.[11]

Farida does not abandon the ideas of equality and social justice for women. She lives according to her feminist principles in a society which does not have the same rules as Nelly Roussel's. Never posing as a role model, she claims the freedom of a singular choice while she remains in solidarity with other women—and with her co-wife in particular. Her deep sense of fairness also makes her recognize that she is engaged to two entities: the first one is cinema—to which she remains faithful throughout her life—and the second one her husband. *My condition was: I continue. My other spouse is filmmaking. I thought it was fair.*[12] She knows herself well: cinema is her primary passion, her constant companion.

Her marriage will not last, however, and she divorces Hamadi three years later. While this is going on, in 1982, she will find herself *inspired by the necessity to write the script that would become* A Door to the Sky. *The words would come to me, and I would wonder: 'Wait…where is this coming rom? Why am I thinking this?'* But first, she is asked to write a script by a fellow pioneer filmmaker: Mohammed Abderrahman Tazi.

WRITING THE SCRIPT OF *BADIS* (MOHAMMED ABDERRAHMAN TAZI, MOROCCO & SPAIN, 1989)

In 1986, Mohammed Abderrahman Tazi asks her to write the script of his film *Badis,* a co-production with Spanish TV which will come out in 1989. Tazi had the idea, discussed it with Noureddine Saïl who wrote a five-page-long development then handed it to Farida. One immediately recognizes the author of the script, especially in the way the scenario presents female characters in the Morocco of the 1970s. As Sandra Gayle Carter noted, the narrative focused on:

> the disharmonious interrelationships between men and women caused by lack: lack of understanding, lack of trust, lack of equality socially and legally, lack of control over the desired body, lack of alternatives, and most clearly, lack of communication. (…) Benlyazid was able to complexify and humanize the characteristics of the women in this script, but overall the story and film reflect indelibly that Sail conceived the story and Tazi directed the film.[13]

The director films in a little fishing village, Badis, with a long history— it was described by both Ibn Khaldûn (*Al Muqaddimah,* 1377) and Leo Africanus (*The Description and History of Africa,* 1550)—in the Northern part of Morocco:

> The action takes place in the thousand-year-old site of Badis, on the Mediterranean Coast of Morocco. Connected to the continent, the island called 'Peñon de Velez' was coveted in turn by the Phoenicians, the Romans, the Portuguese, before the Spanish occupied it in 1564… We are in 1974. The island is peopled with General Franco's prisoners and their jailers. Their food comes from Spain, but their water comes from the territory of Morocco. Fetching the water is the daily task of a serviceman who crosses the village of Badis every morning, at sunrise…[14]

SYNOPSIS—Badis is therefore still Hispano-Moroccan in 1974, with a Spanish jail at one end, and a Moroccan village with one fountain where women fetch water at the other end. It becomes the site of encounters, in particular between young Moira (Maribel Verdú) and the young soldier. Moira is the daughter of a Spanish mother who ran away and from whom she has no news, and Ba Abdallah, her Moroccan father (a former soldier enrolled in the Spanish army). Moira dances the Flamenco when she is by herself (to the chagrin of Ba Abdallah), and dreams of finding her mother. The handsome recruit who comes to the fountain says he will help her find her mother.

Meanwhile, the new schoolteacher (Jillali Ferhati) and his beautiful spouse Touria (Zakia Tahiri) arrive from Casablanca. Shortly thereafter, he asks Touria to tutor Moira at their home, supposedly to teach the pretty teenager to read the Qurʾān (an offer pious Ba Abdallah cannot refuse), but mostly to attract the girl under his roof. The new teacher also mobilizes the other men in the village to request that the serviceman be sent away.

Touria and Moira become friends: one learns how to read and the other how to dance the flamenco. Both women eventually decide to leave the village together. But they are caught by the village men. In a disturbing and rather incongruous final scene, the women join the men and start stoning both fugitives.

The structure of the script is contrapuntal: the incarceration of Franco's political enemies in the Spanish prison mirrors the lack of movement of the village women, pent-up in their homes, leaving them only to fetch heavy buckets of water at the fountain or bringing home massive burdens of wood to cook with. The only exception is the café owner who is free from her husband's surveillance (he is in Europe). While little schoolboys are visible on the streets of Badis, the little girls who all stay at home remain publicly invisible. Arabic and Spanish alternate in this village near Al Hoceima. Moira wants to leave in order to marry the young Spanish recruit now in Spain (and find her mother) while Touria wants to leave her strict, hypocritical husband. As Gayle Carter underscored, the little boys' voices diverge from the mob's voices: "The translated subtitles have the boys crying 'The teacher's wife has run away!' when in Moroccan dialect they are yelling 'The teacher's wife has saved herself!'" (351).

The stoning scene in the film did not exist in the script: Farida had ended the narrative with Touria and Moira running away from Badis, with no indication about whether they would be caught by the men in the village (who had become aware of their departure) or successfully escape. Unbeknownst to her, Tazi added it during the shoot, reaching for a symbolic nod to the ritual stoning of Satan at Mecca during the pilgrimage. If so, then Touria and Moira would be... Satanic creatures? Furthermore, by filming women throwing the first stones in order to stop Moira's seductive dance on the beach, Tazi transforms them into the harshest deliverers of an age-old patriarchal tradition and punishment. Moira must not be seen by the leering males of the village. And yet, Tazi had some difficulties recruiting extras when he shot the film, as he confided to Kevin Dwyer:

> When I told them the love story between the soldier and a village girl, that was a big shock! (...) 'you can film us and everything, but there is absolutely no question of filming even one woman from our village or one of our girls.' (...) the women who encounter Moira at the well or elsewhere were women from other villages who agreed to participate.[15]

In the end, then, it is women from other villages (and Naïma Souadi) who participate in this controversial last scene.

Farida was stunned and did not understand. *Women do not attack other women in the violent scenes I have witnessed or that were reported to me. Quite the opposite: women are distressed when they see men attack prostitutes, for instance.* Farida also objected to the fact that women were victimized in this scene. At the time, she declared: "*I am happy he is talking about women, but there is a much subtler, more nuanced truth. Women are much stronger than he shows them to be.*"[16] Moroccan feminist Fatema Mernissi was also appalled, according to Kevin Dwyer: "Fatima told me that *Badis* 'shouldn't have ended in that defeatist, pessimistic manner, because the film was made at a time when Moroccan women were starting to take their lives into their own hands.'"[17] Ironically enough, the stoning scene caused audiences to shun the film upon its release, at a time when the Islamic Revolution in Iran was leading men to stone women again.[18]

Farida now turns to the script of her own film, written under the spell of her spiritual awakening.

FES: *A DOOR TO THE SKY*

It is 1987: here she is, plunging back into the script she had written earlier with a fervor she had never experienced. During our conversations about the *Door*, she speaks of it with amazement, even thirty-plus years later. For her, A Door to The Sky *is something amazing, something that surprised me when I was writing it. I was writing and then I thought: what the hell am I saying? I was inspired in an absolutely amazing way. That is, things were coming out that I didn't usually think of. You see, I studied in Vincennes, I was on the left... and then!...* Or again: *It's a film that's beyond me!*

The process of writing is different this time. She feels carried along by an unforeseen text, unpredictable even, which wants to express itself through her. *These were breaths that came to me, and I kept wondering: what is this?* The process of writing, as if haunted by a forceful voice expressing itself through a writer may be the experience of many an author, but most crucially that of postcolonial novelists. Maryse Condé, for instance, when she wrote *I, Tituba, Black Witch of Salem,* described the process as listening to and becoming the scribe of the spirit of Tituba, her muse protagonist. Similarly, Farida the scriptwriter seems haunted by her protagonist and her story, as if she were entirely driven by the voice of Nadia, her fictional double. The trance of writing that takes possession of her leads her not only to write but also to direct. *Between the moment I read the Tao and the writing of the script for the film, a lot of time passed... After this pause, I knew that I had to make the film. Until then, I was a scriptwriter and I thought: 'Other people won't understand. Another director isn't going to know what this is about: it's too personal.' I came to the conclusion that I really had to be the one to direct it.* She embarks on the adventure with "faith": only this term seems befit to the immense hope and imperative feeling that propel her into action.

She first assembles a crew to make her film. *Finding those who agree to participate, who believe in such a project is really the hardest part. Through this experience, I was able to realize that the private sector is not at all interested in national production.*[19] This time, she is alone, and she finds herself far from her familiar marks in Tangier. *I thought to myself: I'm crazy, I'm talking about making a film and I'm all alone in Fes.* Because it is in the medina of the holy city of Fes that she will shoot. The location of the film has multiple resonances: it is a holy city (the film opens with a vertical traveling from top to bottom of the minaret, as if descending from the sky into the old city), the city of al-Qarawiyyin mosque, the first university, founded (in 857–859) by a woman, Fatima al-Fihri, with her share of the inheritance received after the death of her father, a merchant of Tunisian origin (from the holy city of Kairouan—hence the name of the mosque); the city of feminist Fatema Mernissi (who became friends with Farida after *A Door*); the city of her paternal family. Farida's trip to her father's city at this precise moment in her life, after her years spent in Paris, and in the aftermath of her enlightenment, also signals a conscious return to her Muslim, Moroccan spiritual roots.

She is adamant and insists on going to Fes. [The CCM] *wanted to make me shoot in Marrakech and I had said:'no, it is Fes!' They even offered the Club Med of Marrakech. But I said to Daldoul* [her producer]: *no! it is not Marrakech! I'm sorry, but we'll manage without the Club Med!* The old city of Fes is the urban nest where she looks for the house of her film. Farida visited *many houses until* she found her home: Dar Hadara. *You know, when I saw myself in this big house that I had found by myself, I thought: 'I am crazy to make a film! I have nothing...' But you know, you have to start somewhere. Then, things happen, things get done, with all sorts of difficulties, but they get done.* Farida rented it both for the shoot and to live in it with her team: she designed a women's dormitory and a men's dormitory. Bouanani was enthusiastic, Farida remembers. *The house reminded him of Satyajit Ray's film,* The Chess Players. *He would say,'I want to stay here and play chess!'*[20] (December 1st, 2017]. In the diary that Bouanani kept as he recorded this film shoot, he even personified it[21]:

We return to the House. I prefer to call it "Dar al Hadara".

It is a house with a soul. It looks at you, breathes with you, adopts you or rejects you. It rarely rejects, it is generous, good. It is an old nanny, a Deda. I will describe her throughout this journal: she is an important character. Her presence is felt twenty-four hours a day. (May 31, 1987)

The magnificent house, built in the old style with a traditional interior patio, tiled walls, and an open terrace allows the filmmaker to turn it into a pivotal space between interior and exterior. The architecture of the palatial villa allows the camera to film the high- and low-angle shots that Farida requested, and move from interior to exterior shots with a rare fluidity. Bouanani was moved by its magic: "All it takes is a moment of isolation, a moment when you wander into one of its many nooks and crannies to suddenly find yourself in a suspended space, like an invisible dawn mist" (June 2, 1987).

To help her produce the film, she called on one of Tunisia's most successful producers, Hassan Daldoul, creator of France-Médias in France. They had met in Cannes, where he had come to support the film *Beirut The Encounter* by Borhane Alaouié (Lebanon, 1981) which he had produced. *It is thanks to Hassan Daldoul, my producer, a Tunisian living in France, that I was able to have French and Tunisian co-productions. He is someone I admire because he has not chosen an easy path. But as he says himself, he works for the long term and believes that, one day, we will have our place in the concert of nations, so to speak. The list of films in which he participated became long. It was he who produced Borhan Aalaouié's* Beirut The Encounter. *It is this kind of profile that is missing in our film industry in Morocco.*[22]

The production obtained funds from various national institutions—Moroccan (the CCM in Rabat), Tunisian (the SATPEC, the Tunisian state laboratory), and French (the Ministry of Foreign Affairs and the Ministry of Culture)—as well as from a Moroccan production company Interfilms (in Casablanca, at the time) through which Farida is co-producer. The transnationalism of this Maghrebi production (very rare at the time) is not only what Mette Hjort would describe as "opportunistic," that is to say, essentially financial (crossing borders in search of funds available elsewhere) but also "creative."[23] Indeed, Farida assembled a top tiered creative and technical team, which included Moroccan actors, a Tunisian sound engineer (Faouzi Thabet), a Tunisian music composer, Anouar Brahem, a French director of photography, Georges Barsky (with a rich transnational filmography at the time), a renowned Tunisian editor, Moufida Tlatli. She also invited, alongside the film professionals, some of her relatives: her toddler son, Abdelhaye Adbib, played in the film; her sister Leila plays a small role—that of the lawyer—and supported Farida in many other capacities throughout the making of the film. Naïma Souadi, Ahmed Bouanani's wife, also played a small role, as did the great theater and film actor Bachir Skirej (*A Breach in the Wall* and *Badis*) and Ahmed Bouanani (the dying father). Naïma was also the first assistant director, Ahmed Bouanani the artistic director, and their daughter Batoul the costume designer. The interior decor of Dar Hadara was the combined work of Khalida Lahman who lent hangings and embroideries from her own collection and Latifa Amor (Farida's cousin and painter). Her faithful key grip was Ba Salah, from the CCM, who had worked with her since *A Breach in the Wall,* and who thus expressed his confidence in Farida's talents as director to Souheil Ben Barka (then head of CCM): "You see, she has no money, but she has a sweet tongue. You can work for her for nothing!".[24]

The actress who played the role of Nadia, Zakia Tahiri, whose father was Moroccan and whose mother was French, was a student in theater and cinema in Paris at the time. Zakia remembers Farida telling her, "You know, our meeting is no coincidence, because the heroine of the film, Nadia, is you!"[25] The narrative of *Une Porte* even echoed her own situation, that of "a rebellious girl who had gone to France... I was rebellious like her, and my father was seriously ill at the time. (...) And just like Nadia, I knew nothing about Islam...".

The non-professional actor who faces Zakia in *A Door* is Mourad Gamra. Farida met him at the Omar Khayam bookstore in Casablanca. *It was him! I was in a restaurant with him one day, and everything he said echoed the character in my script!* Not only would he play the role of Abdelkrim in the film, but he also married Farida. Their *journey* lasted seven years.

After three years spent setting up the production and an additional year preparing for the shoot in Fes,[26] she finally shot her film. Those who experienced the shoot all agree about the joyful atmosphere that reigned in Dar Hadara. Abdelhaye, who was four years old, entertained the crew. *In the morning, he would come to see me and he would say, "Today, am I working or not?" Because when he was working he stayed home and when he wasn't working he went to kindergarten. The production manager always said to me: "Oh, if all the actors could be like your son! When they line up to get paid, he too lines up: he receives a piece of chewing gum and leaves!"* Abdelhaye takes things very seriously. *One day, he had to play and I made a comment to him that he did not like. He got up, grabbed his sandals and walked out saying, "I'm not working anymore!" And the whole team applauded! One morning, he came in and said to me: "Hey, everyone is still sleeping! What is going on? Nobody is working!" I told him, "Well, go wake them up, if you want!"—"Great!" And you know who he started with? The producer! "Come on! Time to work, right?" Hassan was laughing his head off....*[27]

Bouanani's diary, which he scrupulously kept in the hope of constituting "a living image of the many obstacles faced by filmmakers of [his] generation," is a mine of invaluable information about the hazards of shooting *Une Porte,* and, beyond that, about the constant obstacles that stand in the way of filmmakers in Morocco at the time. The "adventures" began immediately, from the delayed arrival of Daldoul, who was supposed to bring the camera and sound equipment from Paris, thus postponing the beginning of the shoot: "the telephone is a beautiful instrument of torture" noted Bouanani, on June 2, before describing the anguish of waiting, then the disappointment experienced when the long awaited CCM technicians and equipment still had not made it by the start of the shoot.[28] A series of impediments followed, that reflected the reality of the "House" and the material obstacles Benlyazid encountered. On June 5, for example, there is a power failure in the area, and again a week later; similarly, the water is cut several times. On June 13, Bouanani shared his frustration: "We couldn't plan anything for that day: the Jilalas [The members of the oldest Sufi brotherhood in Morocco invited by Farida to play music for the Night of Destiny scene] are only available on Sunday evening. In other scenes, the actors or the props or the sets or the costumes are missing." On June 22, the technician Belkeziz had to travel to the airport in Rabat-Salé (a four-hour drive) to pick up the film. These pages illuminate in real time the challenges posed to the director for her first feature film: a thousand thorny problems of various origins and magnitudes dot her journey. When the crew shoots indoors everything is fine (when there is no power cut or a light bulb malfunction, that is), but shooting outdoors is a challenge: "As usual, it is very difficult to control the movement of passers-by in these narrow streets. We had to move the camera and the Nagra to let the vehicles pass: two donkeys heavily loaded with garbage." (June 4) Or again:

> As expected, it is not easy to shoot in the alleys of the medina. Extreme waste of time for transition shots. It is like clearing an anthill. This kind of shots must be taken fast, the camera well out of sight, otherwise... The result is not very convincing. Four passages of Nadia in jellaba going to the lawyer, were recorded. The last two were very difficult, in the middle of a market crowd. The presence of the police didn't change a thing. The camera always attracts crowds like honey attracts flies. On the other hand, no one pays any attention to the sound crew. The eye is more indiscreet than the ear. (June 6)

Over the pages, the recorded adventures highlight the flexibility of the film crew who adapted to the vagaries of the environment and the setbacks: "I must say that, on the whole, the Moroccan-Tunisian team is doing everything possible – without a grudge, without a complaint – so Farida can make her film." (June 15). And then, moments of grace arise at the turn of a scene. The French director of photography, Georges Barsky, is bewitched by the voice of little Malika. "I was so caught up in the Quránic recitation that I didn't pay attention to the pole!" says Barsky (June 18). There are also funny moments:

> Souad [Ferhati], in the role of the old Tsi-Tsi (it changes her from *Reed Dolls* !) intervenes in the last shot: she pities Khaddouj and asks her to go and drop off her things and then turns her back to the camera to fill the kettle. First shot: good. Everything goes well until the end when the sound engineer, Faouzi, interrupts the take. Tsi-Tsi bursts out laughing. We wonder what's going on. Explanation: as she wants to fill the kettle, Tsi-Tsi cannot remove the lid; her back to the camera, she runs the tap. She deceives the lens, but not the microphone. With this gag, the day ends. (June 16)

This is a testament to the excellence of the sound engineer, Faouzi Thabet, who is not fooled by the sound of running water... The team, transnational as we have seen, does not necessarily have a unified vision of Farida's project at the beginning of the shoot, as Bouanani notes. "Discussion after dinner. I realize that everyone sees the film they want. We each have our own film within us. It is impossible for all to adhere to one and the same vision" (June 4)—a new challenge for Farida. "She has to make the film that she carries inside her," he notes.

After the shoot, Farida goes to Tunis where Moufida Tlatli edits the film, and Anouar Brahem composes the music.

SYNOPSIS—The film opens with a flashback from the point of view of Nadia's dying father, who recalls returning from a business trip to his home in the medina of Fes, next to al-Qarawiyyn mosque. In the flowered patio of the house, his French wife (pregnant with Nadia at the time) is listening to Bach's *St. Matthew Passion* while her mother-in-law is trying to teach her the Muslim profession of faith. Thus, from the first seconds, the soundtrack mixes Christianity and Islam.

Nadia returns to Fes from Paris where she lives. Her mother, a French painter, died during her childhood. When she gets off the plane, she looks a bit punkish, she smokes, drinks, and categorically rejects the local rules of propriety that her sister Leïla tells her to follow.

Her father's death triggers a strong depression in Nadia that isolates her. She suddenly feels totally uprooted. However, the voice of Kirana chanting the litanies of the Qurʾān to honor the memory of the deceased awakens childhood memories (in flashbacks) that unlock a flooding of emotions previously out of her reach. Gentle, pious Kirana pulls Nadia out of her depression and grief and introduces her to a woman-centered interpretation of Islam. Nadia begins to read Sufi texts and during her initiation to Muslim mysticism, she discovers great female figures in Islamic history whom she had never heard of before. She also discovers the parts of the Moroccan-Muslim spiritual tradition that she had repressed until then and that are nevertheless part of her dual family culture. She begins to distance herself from the French part of her identity.

She decides to transform the family home into a *zawiya* (a spiritual center and refuge here) for women. She ends up opening this shelter to women who are beaten, lost, seeking shelter, spirituality or both. She also enters a legal dispute with her brother, Driss, as she challenges the law of inheritance that gives twice as much to a son as to a daughter. Nadia soon finds herself on the verge of bankruptcy. But the spirit of Ba Sissi, a painter and close friend of her mother who also died a long time ago, appears to her several times and reveals to her where to find a treasure buried in the garden. The zawiya can survive thanks to Nadia's *cherifa* powers (she discovers she is a healer and has access to Ba Sissi's world).

The residents of the shelter confront Nadia: they deplore the presence of Bahia, a new arrival fresh out of prison (whose rebellious look is reminiscent of Nadia's at the beginning of the film), whose behavior they decry; they also refuse to admit Abdelkrim, a sick young man whom Nadia is healing and with whom she is falling in love. Nadia can no longer endorse the strict and discriminatory rules of the zawiya: she leaves the house and Fes with Abdelkrim.

This is a film that many critics (myself included[29]) have already written about, without probing the autobiographical dimension of its spiritual story: that of the reversal of the soul of a woman who "returns" to Morocco.

Following the biographical breadcrumb trail of this film made at this point in Farida's life, several elements emerge that point to a personal film in its details, from the very opening of the credits. Two dedications high-light two gendered values of Fes: the first honors Farida's and Zakia's fathers (who are ailing during the shooting): "To our two fathers, Sidi Mohammed Benlyazid el Hassani and Sidi Larbi Tahiri, both of the generation of the beginning of the century." Farida spells out the complete identity of her father here, clearly inscribing him in his Cherifian dynasty (descendant of Hassan) and rooting the film in the space of the father—while the second dedication underlines the contribution of a woman to Islam in Fes ("Fatima, daughter of Mohammed al-Fihriya, founder of al-Qarawwyin Mosque in the ninth century, one of the first universities in the world"). Moreover, as we have seen, Farida assembles around her a community of actors and participants familiar to her: her partner, sister, and son appear in the film, as well as her friends (the Bouananis). Her American friend from Tangier, Stuart Church, painted the unfinished portraits of Nadia's mother. Surrounding herself with relatives and friends becomes a constant feature in Farida's work throughout her career and takes on various forms over the years. Here, her warm "family of the film" might cater to her emotional side, but also acquires a bright symbolic dimension. Nadia/Farida's return to the world of the Father, in Fes, is both literal and figurative (his Muslim culture, his Moroccanness, and his Cherifian dynasty, with its religious powers and privileges) and is central to the narrative.[30] Nadia will discover that she has the power of a cherifa, i.e., clairvoyance, magic, thaumaturgy. Farida the filmmaker dives into the Moroccan Sunni culture, with its saints, its *moussems* [Moroccan religious festivals], its practices of trances and beliefs in miracles which are antithetical to Sunni Islam orthodoxy. She thus constructs the character of "returned" Nadia—the one who returns from France to Morocco, and the one who experiences a "return of the soul"—in the specific cultural and spiritual context of Fes. In order to fully shape the narrative and its protagonist, she proceeds with the meticulousness and the delight of a naïve painter, such as Mohamed Ben Ali R'bati.

R'bati (born in Rabat as his name indicates), having found himself in the service of Sir John Lavery (portraitist of the British royal family) in Tangier at the turn of the twentieth century, started to teach himself how to paint, and ended up being offered a space at the Goupil Gallery in London to exhibit some of his works in 1916. He is said to be naïve, almost a miniaturist in his fine drawings of small figures, but not orientalist in the sense that he painted what he saw, not what he imagined.

Unlike Western painters, R'Bati was able to enter the world of women. He was known to cross-dress at times to entertain the women who then let him enter the kitchen, from where he could observe the world invisible to men other than the master of the house. His inner eye carried the vibrant memory of lively and colorful scenes that he would then render on the canvas: "more like a *taleb* [student of the Qur'ān] who magnifies his tablet before the *khatma* [recitation] than a painter (…) the artist gathers all his energy to give birth to true visions, such as he has internalized them and not such as he has only seen them."[31] No orientalist fantasy here: the representation of an everyday scene—located in a specific Moroccan space (the house, the mosque, the street), with individual characters and a profusion of details—is depicted by a Moroccan artist who gives life to a familiar universe with naive aesthetics and an empathetic gesture. It is in the liminal space between the intimate connection to a visual experience and aesthetic creation that the artist's vision emerges and exceeds both in a "sacred dimension of culture".[32] The latter may remain in the blind spot upon the viewer's first contemplation, given the abundance of details whose minuteness can distract from the whole. You need a second, more serene, contemplation to appreciate the staging of the culture and its aura in the carefully elaborated composition.

In her first film, Farida embraces some of R'bati's gestures: she creates a character who enters a world that is both familiar and unknown, just as R'bati once entered the women's space. She films the re-enactment of Moroccan traditions with a plus. *I like to interpret traditions and not serve them as they are because, as I say in* A Door, *traditions must not become straitjackets.*[33] Her (re)presentation of rituals (trance and others) in her fictional narrative is imbued with an additional aura. The filmmaker builds a fictional world with an abundance of details in her mise-en-scène, and puts her vision of the Moroccan spiritual culture of Fes into images with a simplicity that also rings true. This is why the accusation of catering to "folklore" or "orientalism" made by some critics in Morocco and elsewhere, seems unfounded.[34] Nadia's journey through certain Moroccan cultural and spiritual dimensions hitherto outside her reach allows the viewer (in Morocco and elsewhere) to identify with her through a set of emotions parallel to her own, especially when she witnesses strange phenomena. To wit, her mother appears to her fleetingly in a dream, and Nadia is upset. She gets up, disturbed by her dream/nightmare, and goes downstairs to the kitchen, where she ends up "seeing" or hallucinating Ba Sissi—neither the viewer nor the protagonist knows exactly at this strange moment in the film. When Ba Sissi's apparition speaks to her, she reacts spontaneously with fright and refuses to engage with the spirit of a dead man: "Let everyone stay in their own world!"—a reaction completely shared by the extra-diegetic spectator… But Ba Sissi calmly reasons with her: "Listen to me. I have come for the zawiya. Don't be afraid. I didn't come for you. I am a believer. This house is sacred. You must slaughter a calf and make a night of Aïssaoua: this house needs perfumes and trances." Then he begins to sing to the glory of Allah.

Only Kirana will know how to decode such a phenomenon and the household will follow Ba Sissi's directives during the Night of Destiny. Farida described its significance to Roland Carrée through a tale: *It is said that the door to heaven opens on this night and that any wish one makes to God is granted. But one must be very careful and be precise in its formulation. When I was a child, it was said that a little girl, on that famous night, asked God to give her long hair, but she changed one letter in the word "hair", which became "rage" ... This was just a tale, but it says a lot, I think, about the magic that is attributed to the Night of Destiny.*[35]

Finally, the film's construction—and resulting texture—is a form of craftsmanship that derives from the many material constraints that stimulate creativity according to the pioneers of Moroccan cinema, such as Bouanani:

> The craft is an art, the factory is an industry. We may have a chance to make art (film) with little means. In the factory, we will be mere employees. (...) As long as the cinema - ours - is an adventure, with all the risks, dangers, disasters, surprises that an adventure entails, we may have a chance to flirt with art. (Bouanani, May 30)

Farida shares Bouanani's vision of Moroccan cinema, driven by the director's impetus, whose limited means (the film cost a total of one and a half million Dirhams, i.e., less than $ 150,000...) require constant innovative tinkering in order to make everything work. This characteristic will be found in all of Farida's other productions, as we shall see.

My history with this film is not new: I have written twice about it and keep returning to it, as one returns to a piano score for new emotions, new meanings. The first time, I wanted to decipher the film in its Franco-Moroccan intertextual dimension in a collection on Arab cinema in the Maghreb and the Middle East.[36] Situated in the context of Maghrebi women's cinema, it was the third feature film—after *Al-Jamr/ The Ember*, a television production by the Moroccan Farida Bourquia (1982) and *The Trace* by the Tunisian Neja Ben Mabrouk (1988)[37]— the subject matter of *A Door* nevertheless exceeded my expectations at the time. The film (before and after this first publication of mine) has been the subject of a number of academic studies, although more often by English-speaking scholars than from French or Moroccan scholars. Analyses continue to be published, as the film continues to intrigue, to this day. It has been interpreted as projecting a form of Muslim feminism,[38] Moroccan feminism,[39] flirting with orientalism and *queer* politics,[40] intended primarily for a transnational feminist audience (not a Moroccan one). In Morocco, scholars and critics organized a seminar to study Farida Benlyazid's work and published its proceedings.[41] In it, Bouchta Farqzaid proposes a semantic breakdown of the filmic narrative according to various codes (hermeneutic, feminist, historical, aesthetic, symbolic) that ultimately "establishes a bridge between Western theory and a Moroccan imaginary" and highlights the paradoxes of the filmic narrative that both make it rich and provoke an ever-renewed questioning of its subject. In his nuanced reading, Farqzaid, while delineating the different acts of an occasionally irrational character's ark, establishes *A Door* as a possible threshold between a Moroccan imaginary and a woman's life shaped by Western modernity.[42]

Ella Shohat gave it a feminist aesthetic: "*A Door to the Sky* envisions an aesthetic that affirms Islamic culture while also inscribing it with a feminist consciousness."[43] *A Door* thus opened the possibility for hitherto unexplored compatibilities. I had noted the threshold shots that punctuated the film, as if, at any given moment, the camera was pointing the way from one space to another, showing a liminal space that adjoined one room and another; an open patio and an interior; a space of retreat and a space of openness to the chaos of others. I had therefore approached the film mainly from its political, feminist, and bicultural perspectives, analyzing how Farida had quietly dismantled two sets of mechanisms emanating from two different ready-made ways of thinking: a certain European—especially French—feminist current that left no room for the possible existence of either a Muslim tradition of strong women or feminist schemes outside of Eurocentric credos; and the patriarchal reading of Islam made by the men who have held power over its readings and practices for a very long time. In her film, Farida proposes to look at the less readily apparent facets of Islam: the *zawiyas* (<the corners> of the mosque, where one debated away from the imam, originally), had become, for example, places of reflection, independent communities that hosted Sufi assemblies away from the religious prohibitions of the *f'qhaa* [male theologians] that would impede their spiritual practices. The name of the male protagonist in the film is a reminder of Morocco's capacity to rise up, through its evocation of the eponymous hero of the Rif, Abdelkrim, who united his Amazigh people, with whom he resisted against the French, the Spanish, and the Moroccan sultan, and succeeded in creating the Republic of the Rif from 1921 to 1926.[44] In *A Door*, the primary goal of resistance, through the practice of critical thinking, is put in the practical service of women: the zawiya (itself opened thanks to Nadia's resistance to the law on inheritance) is their sanctuary.

The second time, my attention was drawn to the film's initiation narrative beyond that of Nadia's individual story, which was aimed at viewers in Morocco and Europe: a kind of triple initiation, therefore.[45] As I followed Nadia on her spiritual quest, I came to see how she took side-ways off the beaten path she had taken a few minutes earlier. Her detours formed neither assiduous convergence (with feminism or the orthodox practice of a masculine Islam) nor radical divergence (away from either pattern), but rather a seemingly whimsical and powerfully free form of "transvergence."[46] Nadia followed the trail that led her to one discovery and then veered away from it to another. She thus fashioned a unique path to her own freedom and her own Muslim spiritual practice.

It had not occurred to me then that Nadia was her creator's fictitious double in the spirituality and purity of intent with which both follow their shared ethical compass. It is as impossible for Nadia/Farida to reject a punk (probably lesbian) from the female cenacle of the zawiya as it seems aberrant to her to exclude Abdelkrim because he is male.

Now that I realize to what extent this film was nourished by Farida's return of the soul, I see the film under yet a new prism, as the expression of what remains almost impossible to describe in words. This is where filmmaking becomes a privileged means of expression, as it summons up most of the senses and calls upon references located off-screen that resonate in the memory of each viewer's experience. If words fail to translate the dazzle and intense joy experienced, then the shots and their movement, their breath, the music, the vibrations of the voices and the narratives that animate a film might succeed in faithfully translating what now inhabits Farida. This film reaches a hitherto never attained dimension. This is why its cinematographer Georges Barsky exclaimed at the end of the shoot: "*Now that you have touched the sky, Farida, what are you going to do?*".

The question of the reception of her first film, a film so singular in its conception and in what it tries to achieve, highlights different cultural and political concerns in Morocco, in the Arab world, in Europe, and in the United States. The film has many fans and many detractors. It sparks controversies, some predictable, others quite surprising, which shock the director when they erupt. In the Muslim world still reeling from the 1979 Iranian revolution, the film scandalizes for, largely, a question of optics: that of the protagonist's choice to wear a veil. The Islamic revolution that had propelled Ayatollah Khomeini to the head of Iran and transformed the Shah's kingdom into a theocracy, had snatched away one by one the rights and freedoms granted to Iranian women since 1935. The most visible expression of women's oppression in Iran in the 1980s was the compulsory wearing of the chador, policed by the Revolutionary Guards. "On a bus, every time a female body brushes against a male body, the tremor makes the edifice of our revolution wobble," the Ayatollah had declared, to combat the inevitable overwheming temptation (فتنة) that an identifiable female body could unleash...[47] Nadia's sartorial transformation (she wears a white veil) fuels fears that the Islamic revolution will spread outside Iran (Although the film at no point shows any sign of imposing anything onto a woman, and Nadia rebels against Sharia law and orthodox readings of Islam).

Press reviews of the time reflect contradictory points of view. In Morocco, the film was shown for the first time in 1988 during a festival entitled "Women filmed by women" at the 7ième Art in Rabat. It took more than three years for the film to be released on national screens at the end of 1991. Thus, notwithstanding the article in *al-Mandjra* which awarded it a non-gendered prize, the film first appeared in a female setting alongside other films made by women. The reviews are varied and favorable overall. They sometimes reflect a certain discomfort with a woman's treatment of Islam, a discomfort that is expressed in different ways from one article to another. If Fouad Souiba, the journalist and film critic who will later move to the other side of the camera, notes a weakness (a slow pace "with added sequences ... that unnecessarily weigh it down"), he also highlights the "theme dear to F. Belyazid: the cause of women, illustrated by a strong character, who follows her own law."[48] Mina Zine Eddine begins by praising the talent of the filmmaker in her "sensitive and intelligent rendering of the city of Fes through image and sound," before criticizing her for "the impression of incompleteness that sometimes arises from the dialogue, especially on the topic of secrets and symbols in Islam," then praising the acting of Ahmed Bouanani, Bachir Skirej, Chaaïbia Aadraoui, and Zakia Tahiri. The story of Nadia is perceived here in a strangely reductive way: "In order to fight against socio-religious burdens, Nadia, the heroine, after she has recovered the family home to turn it into a haven for women, takes refuge in a religious practice marked by a Sufism as pure as it is naïve."[49] Fatima Haddadi begins with a look at the audience in the screening venue—"Those who expected (and they were many, that evening, in the room of the 7ième Art) to see the image of a Moroccan woman moving about in a Western-ized environment on screen, were sorely disappointed." The critic then emphasizes "the path to follow" traced by the protagonist who chooses, between "two civilizations," a "return to the fold," located at the oppo-site of Western modernity. The review ends with praise for the filmmaker and her lead actress.[50] In short, once they had recovered from the surprise of the subject and its treatment, Moroccan critics welcomed the first film by a daughter of the Cherifian Kingdom in a rather positive way. When the film was released years later, the critic Mohamed Bakrim noted the quality of the film and of its narrative and evoked its "beautiful text" and its "quest for beauty that guides the camera" before paying tribute to "a filmmaker who does not hesitate to express her own ideas about cinema as well as about the world."[51]

The critical reception of the film in the rest of the Arab world opens a window on its resonance at a precise moment in the history of Arab consciousness and its view of the West. *A Door* is selected in many festivals in the Arab world including the Carthage Film Festival in Tunisia and the Alexandria Festival in Egypt. From one North African country to another, audiences change: while Egyptian audiences seem to reject the film for its religious content, this is not the case for viewers in Annaba, Algeria, where *A Door* was awarded the Annaba de Bronze the same year: it is viewed as "the intimate story of a long quest for the national self" which asks Arab intellectuals how to "inscribe our culture, our national self in the universal without discoloring or compartmentalizing them" and advo-cates tolerance.[52] In her interviews, Farida has to defend herself against all sorts of accusations. A journalist who interviewed Farida seemed to suspect her of targeting a French audience (given the participation and support of French organizations), to which she replied: "*It's a film for everyone. Everyone can find in it what suits them and enlightens them. For the Maghrebi public, it is the image of a return, successful or not, that's not for me to say. For foreigner viewers, it is an opportunity to see us as we are …*". The film is then accused of exoticism, which elicits this reaction from Farida: "*… I'm a bit tired of miserabilist films. Take for example the magnificent house in the film. There are two hundred like it in Fes, and*

they are falling into ruin. It is my intention to show things that are disap-
pearing or have disappeared, but that are part of our heritage, part of who
we are."[53]

In Tunis, finally, this film is applauded as a woman's film (it was screened in parallel with another pioneering film, Nejia Ben Mabrouk's *Trace,* a Tunisian-Belgian co-production). Dorra Bouzid celebrated this "beautiful aesthetic and moral film. A beautiful story with superb images" that has its own woman's spiritual truth.[54] As diverse as they are, the reviews from the Arab world have one thing in common: this is an important film and marks a turning point in the history of Arab cinema, because it is a woman's film, because it images an open and spiritual vision of Islam, because the culture that it celebrates is Arab and Muslim.

In Europe, the film is rewarded by the A.C.C.T. in Namur, Belgium, and is shown at the Angers Festival in France, Valencia in Spain, Rimini and Bologna in Italy. It travels across the Atlantic where it is screened at film festivals in Montreal, Los Angeles, and Seattle. Western critics often offer yet another double discourse: that of feminists in France or Europe, such as the Czech new wave filmmaker Věra Chytilová, and that of American feminist orientalists. *I met Věra Chytilová at a festival in Rimini in 1988. She saw the film and when she came out of the theater, she told me, "You're a liar!" She got really angry. "Nothing you say is true! It doesn't exist!" I told her: 'you know, I didn't invent this house: it was there, I didn't build it!' I faced brutal reactions... In their eyes, I was a fundamentalist, you see! The film was much better received in the United States than in Europe. In Europe, they have a problem with religions...* The American academic Miriam Cooke, in contrast, interprets the film as a rare example of Islamic feminism,[55] as does Ella Shohat, as we have seen. Nadia thus becomes the Janus-like symbol of a return to harsh Islam, the veil and the lack of freedom decried by French critics, and of a post-colonial spiritual liberation for American critics. Hassan Daldoul sees in the French critics the sign of a colossal misunderstanding:

I remember Farida Benlyazid's first film, *A Door to the Sky,* which tells the story of the return of a Moroccan girl living in Europe and her encounter in Fes with the tradition of Islam. Europe does not understand that she wants to give up the freedom of Europe. It is unthinkable, almost porno-graphic. In Europe, after the war, sex was liberated and was thought of as freedom - but that is not freedom. Freedom is something else.[56]

The fallout from the release of *A Door* takes many forms, some of which will remain with Farida for many years. In particular, her deep friendship with Fatema Mernissi which lasted until the death of the Moroccan intellectual in 2015.[57]

Farida was well aware that her film was going to throw a splashing stone in the feminist pond: *I thought to myself: "Oh dear, what are my feminist friends going to say?"* The latter had reactions just as varied as those of the critics. *There were two reactions: those who liked it and those who hated it.* Moufida Tlatli, the editor of the film, also nourished by feminism, had a reaction of surprise similar to that of Fatema Mernissi, according to Farida. *In the middle of editing, she said to me: "Wow, Farida, what are you doing to us? Heavens! Gone, Freud! Sartre! and all the others! They had taken over our minds!".*[58]

Farida recalls her delight at the reception of her film in the United States, when she evokes a screening in Seattle. *At the end of the film, I went into the theater to talk to people. One viewer came to me and talked to me about reincarnation. And then another approached me like a zombie and said in English: 'this is the most beautiful film I've ever seen in my life!' Then she left without saying anything else... Holy shit! If an American woman says it's the most beautiful movie she's ever seen in her life, that's really something!*[59] The place that remains free of controversy will be North America, far from the French or Arab tensions between secularism and religion, between veils and non-veils (a question that does not arise in Farida's cinema), far from the colonial and postcolonial history of Morocco. There, one will not see her film as a nationalist ode, a song against orthodox Islam, or a back-pedaling move in feminism.

Later, in interviews, Farida would sometimes be asked the question: why did ten years pass between *A Door to the Sky* and *Keid Ensa*, her second feature film? The first seven years in particular (1988–1995) seem to distant observers to be a low point, even though Farida does a lot. At the end of *A Door*, she confides the project of a film to come. "Next year, Farida Benlyazid will start a female epic of Moroccan history.[60] A little later, she mentions *Clair-Obscur*, a project that *is again inspired by double culture through a woman character but it is no longer in religion but rather in psychoanalysis and traditional therapy.* But these projects will not bear fruit. However, this seven-year period is punctuated on the one hand by upsetting events on both a personal and international level, and on the other hand, by creation and experimentation in various fields. It is a time of endurance during which Farida will write (articles, short stories, a screenplay) and direct three short films, each very different from the other, that were commissioned. This productive period is also an obstacle course.

Indeed, *A Door* continues to tour in the world and to create debate: it is screened on all continents at the turn of the 1990s. Farida's caravan thus grows with fellow travelers and takes new detours to reach a destination pushed back on the horizon by a succession of setbacks. Her first feature film had exposed diverse tensions not only in interpretations of Islam, Western, and/or Maghrebi feminism, but also in its national and transnational dimensions, given the political *Zeitgeist* in Morocco and beyond. Sometimes with unforeseen and often very unfortunate consequences. Curiously, after having made a film "that touches the sky," Farida will come up against a series of slamming doors, suddenly hermetically closed. She then follows a process of adaptation and intellectual and emotional maturation like the essay she composes published in 1992, "Patience is beautiful," a superb lesson of stoicism to survive what one cannot control. She is going through a difficult phase on a personal level—her father, the pious and patient Mohamed dies in 1991—as well as on a professional and political level. Cultivating an unwavering patience, Farida will write, create her own production company, find her way back to cinema through documentaries, and continue her path toward spiritual knowledge, thanks to encounters that dazzle her. This time, following her path leads us outside the borders of Morocco on an African map: to Mali.

Notes

1. Between 1970 and 1980, the population grew from 16 to 20 million and doubled the number of 14–24-year-old entering the workforce. At the same time, the kingdom saw a massive exodus from the rural areas to urban centers (the rural population decreased from 70.7% in 1960 to 63.9% in 1989), and a constant stream of emigration out of the country. See Sabagh, Georges. "The challenge of population growth in Morocco," *Middle East Research and Information Project*, No. 181, March/April 1993. https://merip.org/1993/03/the-challenge-of-population-growth-in-morocco/ [link active on April 9, 2022].

2. «Le taux d'analphabétisme au Maroc a baissé de deux tiers sur un demi-siècle.» https://www.h24info.ma/maroc/taux-danalphab etisme-maroc-a-baisse-de-deux-tiers-demi-siecle/#:~:text=Le%20t aux%20d'analphab%C3%A9tisme%20au,sur%20un%20demi%20si% C3%A8cle%20%2C%20H24info.

3. Bine, Aziz, tr. Lulu Norman. *Tazmamart: eighteen years in Morocco's secret prison.* U. of Chicago Press, 2021.

4. In 1973, it bans The National Union of Moroccan Students (UNEM) and restricts the Code of public liberties. In 1974, the makhzen attacks a religious and political movement of dissidence, fearing a possible ques- tioning of one of its pillars: the King as "Leader of the Faithful." Hence the arrest of Cheikh Abdessalam Yacine after his publication of an open letter to the King titled "Islam or the Deluge.".

5. «La religion continuera à avoir une place prépondérante dans la définition des enjeux politiques parce qu'elle constituera une ressource importante pour produire des discours de délégitimation des régimes politiques en place comme pour alimenter les utopies contestataires.» Tozy, Mohamed.
   «L'évolution du champ religieux marocain au défi de la mondialisation,» *Revue internationale de politique comparée*, Vol. 16, No. 1, 2009 (63–81): 80.

6. Chalier, Catherine. *Le Désir de conversion.* Paris: Seuil, 2011: 29. (my translation).

7. Benlyazid, Farida. "Le Grand Voyage," *Parfaire l'homme*, No. 2, Spring 2011: 83.

8. Benlyazid, Farida, in Hamid Berrada, *Mais encore? Avec Farida Benlyazid*, 2M, January 12, 2012.

9. I am thinking in particular of the Senegalese writer Ken Bugul who, on her return from Europe, married a marabout or Serigne, and went to live with him and his 27 other wives in Lower Casamance, an experience that inspired her novel *Riwan ou chemin de sable.* Paris: Présence Africaine, 1999.

10. The anthropologist shows to what extent the behavior of pious Muslim women (Egyptian, in her study) perceived from a Western feminist point of view outside the community in question can lead to important misunderstandings. For instance, the (notorious)

wearing of the veil, understood and constructed in first-world feminist discourse as undeniable evidence of "deplorable passivity and
docility from a progressive point of view, can be fully understood as
a form of agentivity" that unfolds "not only in acts that bring about
progressive change but also in those that aim at continuity, stasis,
stability." Mahmood, Sabah. "Feminist theory, embodiment, and
the docile agent: some reflections on the Egyptian Islamic revival,"
Cultural Anthropology, Vol. 16, No. 2, 2001 (202–236): 212.

11. In her description of Islamic feminism over time, Sabah Mahmood
joins Moroccan Asma Lamrabet, although the latter describes the
need for a thorough re-reading of the Qurʾān to clear the way
for a Muslim feminism that would clearly establish the difference
between the text of the Qurʾān itself and the exegeses of the (male)
theologians of the other, constructed into Islamic jurisprudence
over the centuries. See *Femmes—Islam—Occident: Chemins vers
l'universel*. Casablanca: La Croisée des Chemins, 2011; and *Islam
et Femmes: les questions qui fâchent*. Casablanca: En Toutes Lettres,
2017.

12. Hamid Berrada, op. cit.

13. Carter, Sandra Gayle, "Farida Benlyazid's Moroccan women,"
Quarterly Review of Film & Video, Vol. 17, No. 4 (343–369): 349.

14. Text of the opening credits (my translation).

15. Tazi, Mohammed Abderrahman, in Kevin Dwyer. *Beyond
Casablanca: M. A. Tazi and the Adventure of Moroccan Cinema*.
Bloomington & Indianapolis: Indiana University Press, 2004: 193.

16. Teo Simarski, Lynn. "Through north African eyes," *Saudi Amraco
World*, January–February 1992: 35. https://archive.aramcoworld.
com/issue/199201/through.north.african.eyes.htm [link active
on April 2, 2022].

17. Ibid.: 193.

18. Carrée, Roland. «Mohammed Abderrahman Tazi: Rester Debout,»
Répliques, No. 7, 2016: 77.

19. Bradley, Ghita. "Five years of purgatory for a door to heaven," *The
Liberal*, April 1988.

20. Interview with author. Tangier, December 1, 2017.

21. May his daughter, Touda Bouanani, be thanked here for having
given me access to his *Diary*.

22. Farida quoted in an interview with Mohamed Chaoui, *Première
Heure No. 101*, March 10, 1991.

23. Hjort, Mette. "On the plurality of cinematic transnationalism," in Nataša Ďurovičová & Kathleen Newman, eds. *World cinemas, transnational perspectives.* New York: Routledge, 2010: 12–33.
24. Words reported by Farida, interview with the author on November 20, 2017.
25. Tahiri, Zakia. Interview with the author, January 15, 2017.
26. Bradley, Ghita. op. cit.
27. Interview with Farida, December 1, 2017. Tangier.
28. "It must be midnight. Exhausting day because the anxiety does not leave us. Late in the evening, Daldoul arrived. But not the three technicians (2ᵉ assistant-op, electrician and stagehand) nor the CCM equipment. The stage and the TRAV were needed for tomorrow, as well as additional lighting. We will see what we can do for tomorrow. But we absolutely must have the camera running. TO WARD OFF FATE. IF THERE IS SUCH A THING AS FATE!" (my translation).
29. See "*Bab al-samah Maftouh/A door to the sky,* Farida Benlyazid, 1988," (Gönül Dönmez-Colin, ed., *The cinema of North Africa and the Middle-East.* London: Wallflower Press, 2007: 123–132); and Chapter 2 of *Screens and veils: Maghrebi women's cinema.* Bloomington & Indianapolis: Indiana University Press, 2011.
30. It is also a spiral meant to overcome the father, hence the need to symbolically put him to death in the first minutes of the film....
31. Chraïbi, Zineb Abderrazik. *Mohamed Ben Ali R'bati, Naissance de la peinture marocaine, 1861–1936.* Rabat: Éditions Marsam, 2007: 16. (my translation).
32. De Pontcharra, Nicole. Ibid.: 44.
33. Berrada, Hamid. *But still? With Farida Benlyazid,* 2M, January 12, 2012.
34. This type of criticism persists, for example, in the rather recent criticism of the academic Lhoussain Simour, who sees in what he calls the representation of a "folklorized Islam" (19) and in the "excessive aesthetics of space" (21) of the film side effects of orientalist exoticism intended for a Western rather than a Moroccan audience. Simour, Lhoussain. "(Re)Locating space in Hakim Belabbas's *khāyṭ al-rūḥ* and Farida Benlyazid's *bāb sma maftūḥ.*" *International Journal of Francophone Studies,* Vol. 20, Nos. 1–2, 2017: 9–23.

35. Square, Roland. "Farida Benlyazid: turning to the sky." *Replicas*, No. 12, 2019 (120–145): 126.
36. See Martin, 2007.
37. The two women's films will be released at the same time in Tunis, giving rise to an article on the films of the two Maghrebi pioneers in counterpoint to each other. "We are far from the obscure daily revolts of the obstinate young girl from Gafsa so remarkably revealed to the public in 'The Trace'. Sabra fights to live, to study and that she will find her salvation by leaving.

In contrast, Najia, Farida Belyazid's heroine, is very rich and already gone. She is even a punk and lives in Paris with 'a guy'. If she comes back, it is in spite of herself, for the funeral of her father. And here comes the most beautiful song of the Islamic world. The Qurʾān (Aziza Tazi's moving voice). She is stuck. She will never leave…" (Bouzid, Dorra. *L'Hebdo Touristique*, No. 77, November 7, 1988). (my translation).
38. See Ella Shohat (1997), Miriam Cooke (2001), Viola Shafik (1998 and 2007).
39. See Sandra Gayle Carter (2009), Touria Khannous, 2001, Carine Bourget (2008). Gauch, Suzanne. "Now you see it, now you don't: transnational feminist spectatorship and Farida Benlyazid's *A Door to the Sky*," *Camera Obscura*, Vol. 71, No. 24.2, 2009: 106–137.
40. See Gauch, Suzanne (2002, 2009, 2016).
41. Aïdouni, Hamid et al. *The cinematographic work of Farida Benlyazid*. Rabat: Ministry of Communication, Moroccan Association of Film Critics, 2010.
42. "Thus, the character accomplishes a spiraling journey. Paradoxically, it is spiritual love - that of God - that constitutes a point of transition to human passion, even an initiation into the world, after which the conciliation of opposites becomes a guarantor of balance, namely the angel and the beast.

Then the foreigner, through returning to her roots, finds her own balance and identity. She puts an end to the absurdity of her life, to the doubt that gnaws at her and the fear of being crazy. In short, *A Door to the sky* is a film about individual happiness or how to be happy as a woman. To our humble knowledge, this theme has not yet been taken up by Moroccan cinema." (23) (my translation).

43. "The film's aesthetic, however, favors the rhythms of contemplation and spirituality, in slow camera movements that caress the contoured Arabic architecture of courtyards and fountains and soothing inner spaces. Dedicated to a historical Muslim woman, Fatima Fihra, the tenth-century founder of one of the world's first universities, A Door to the Sky envisions an aesthetic that affirms Islamic culture while also inscribing it with a feminist consciousness." Shohat. "Framing post-third-worldist culture: gender and nation in Middle Eastern North African film and video," 1997: 21. http://152.1.96.5/jouvert/v1i1/shohat.htm.
44. His *guerrilla* strategies had inspired other fighters such as Ho Chi Minh and Che Guevara, among other leaders of non-aligned nations.
45. *Screens and veils: Maghrebi women's cinema.* Bloomington: Indiana University Press, 2011: Chapter 2 (63–84).
46. Similarly, the writing of the film follows some of the neo-realist codes of Arab cinematography of the 70s and 80s, suddenly interrupted by the irruption of a form of magic realism to which viewers at the time did not necessarily subscribe.
47. Quoted in Forti, Marina. "Iran: La lunga marcia delle donne," *Il Manifesto*, June 25, 2005. https://www.feltrinellieditore.it/news/2005/06/27/marina-forti-iran--la-lunga-marcia-delle-donne-5067/.
48. "Une Porte sur le ciel," *Cinémasrah*. February 24, 1988.
49. Zine Eddine, Mina. "Cinéma: Farida Belyazid ouvre 'sa porte sur le ciel,'" *Maroc Soir*, February 26, 1988.
50. Haddadi, Fatima. "*Une Porte sur le ciel,*" *Le Matin*, August 7, 1988.
51. Bakrim, Mohamed. "*Une Porte sur le ciel*: Filmer la tolérance," *Libération*, March 15, 1991.
52. Benmedjahed, Fayçal. "La quête de soi," *El Moudjahid*, June 16, 1988.
53. F, Kader. "Images of a return on oneself.".
54. Bouzid, Dorra. "Les portes du ciel," *L'Hebdo touristique*, No. 77, November 1988.
55. Cooke, Miriam. "*A door to the sky*, directed by Farida Ben Lyazid," *MESA Bulletin No. 6*, 1992: 269–270.

56. Barlet, Olivier. "La crise du cinéma tunisien: entretien d'Olivier Barlet avec Hassen Daldoul, producteur tunisien," *Africultures*, Septembre, 14, 2004.
57. So much so that Farida, anxious to honor her friend, and worried that her thoughts, her writings, and her activism would be forgotten, wrote a script at the request of Mohamed Abderrahman Tazi and started a documentary project in tribute to the sociologist. (see Coda).
58. Interview with the author, December 15, 2017.
59. Interview with the author, December 1, 2017.
60. Statement at the Women's Film Festival, Salé, 1988.

CHAPTER 3

Intermezzo: Anti-Globalist Feminist Resistance

Abstract Context: Micro politics largely explain an apparent "pause" in Benlyazid's film production. Meanwhile, she writes articles and short stories in French (e.g., "A Day in the Life of Hajja Leimeth," "Patience is beautiful") and a second script for Tazi's comedy, *In Search of my Wife's Husband* (1993), a formidable success at the Moroccan box office. She goes to Mali to direct a documentary on anti-globalist activist Aminata Traoré: *Aminata Traoré: A Woman of the Sahel* (1993). She is also tasked with two other short documentaries: *Contrabando* (1994) made for Moroccan TV and *Sur la terrasse/On the Terrace* (1995), requested by the CCM to commemorate the centennial of cinema.

Keywords Anti-globalism · Feminism · African feminism · Patience · Oral literature · Bamako · Chefchaouen · Aminata Traoré · Homi Bhabha · Mohammed Abderrahmane Tazi · Noureddine Sail · Felwine Saar · Fatema Mernissi

The beginning of the 1990s is rife with political turmoil for Morocco and Farida on the macro-level of the nation and its foreign policy, and on the micro-level of the CCM. This period just after *A Door* is sometimes misunderstood as a vacant one in the life and career of Farida,

© The Author(s), under exclusive license to Springer Nature Switzerland AG 2024
F. Martin, *Farida Benlyazid and Moroccan Cinema*, Palgrave Studies in Arab Cinema, https://doi.org/10.1007/978-3-031-40616-4_3

but the circumstances of that decade show her resistance on several fronts: once again, her personal life becomes enmeshed with politics, even internationally.

1990 is a curious year for Morocco: on January 1st Amnesty International's report (on 1989 in Morocco) lists a series of human rights violations ranging from arbitrary arrests to the systematic use of torture in prisons and police custody centers, as well as the "disappearance" of many Sahrawis.[1] On May 8, the makhzen creates the Advisory Committee on Human Rights (CDDH); in the fall Gilles Perrault publishes *Notre ami le Roi* (*Our Friend the King*) in France. In December, a massive general strike leads to brutally repressed riots in Fes, Tangier, and Kenitra.

Meanwhile, Moumen Diouri, the father of Farida's daughters is still a political refugee in France where he does business and also writes, his readership consisting mostly of dissidents of the makhzen in exile and intellectuals on the left in France and in the kingdom.[2] In April, he gives an interview to the Spanish newspaper *El Cambio* about his latest forthcoming book (*À qui appartient le Maroc?/Who Owns Morocco?*[3]), in which he incriminates the makhzen and accuses the French of complicity.[4] Neither the makhzen nor the French state is amused. Mitterrand, a former supporter of Diouri, is ambivalent: he wants to neither offend Hassan II nor find himself with another Ben Barka affair on his hands.[5] His solution is to expel Moumen to Gabon on June 20, 1991, on account of his "repeated failure to respect the duty of reserve" attached to his status as political refugee. Farida flies to Paris to be with her daughters. This episode, called "the Diouri affair" mobilizes many people in France who circulate petitions, demonstrate in Paris, publish articles in the press (in particular, *L'Humanité* and *Carré Rouge*). Moumen Diouri returns to Paris on July 16.[6] Farida returns to Morocco where she faces other vendettas.

Farida, who follows her principles and intervenes when she perceives an injustice, will find herself blocked in several of her projects, as the following episode demonstrates. It all starts with an invitation to present *A Door* at the Hundred Flowers Festival in Beijing. Farida is thrilled: a perfect opportunity to discover China. The CCM, through its director, Souheil Ben Barka, will cover the cost of her ticket. First, Farida attends the JCC (Journées Cinématographiques de Carthage) in Tunis where her colleague Nabyl Lahlou asks her to sign a petition against the CCM's production assistance commission because the latter has just denied him the last instalment of the assistance granted for his film *La Nuit du crime/ The Night of the Crime* (this provocative film on abuses of power will earn him ten years of forced silence.) She agrees with him and signs. Among all the signatory filmmakers from the Maghreb and Sub-Saharan Africa in particular, she was the only Moroccan to do so... Once back from Tunisia, her suitcase packed for China, she receives a call from Souheil Ben Barka: *Have you lost your mind? Why did you sign the petition? It's very serious! What about the Polisario?! And I answered: "You talk to me as if you were the minister of the Interior! I don't understand. I just signed a petition and this commission is not the CCM! It's a separate commission!" Then Souheil Ben Barka's secretary called me: he said you were no longer going to China.* Farida, hurt and angry at this abuse of power, ends up writing about it in the press. *When someone throws me a ball, I throw it back... Of course, I dared to write against him. Then, it was war....*[7] For years, Souheil Ben Barka systematically blocks Farida's projects or gives her *crumbs* insufficient to start a film.[8] Farida persists in acting according to her principles year after year without deviating from her personal ethics. In fact, she later reconciles with Souheil Ben Barka: *It so happens that Souheil Ben Barka is Moroccan-Malian. When I went to Mali to work on Aminata Traoré, I sent him a postcard with a palaver tree. In Africa, it designates a traditional place of gathering, in the shade of which people talk about life in the community, the problems of the village, politics (...) On the back of the card, I wrote' No hard feelings, I hope! Only much later did we really reconcile.*[9] Meanwhile, not only are Farida's projects compromised or destroyed for lack of funds, but the Chamber of Producers (all male at the time) sends the black sheep that she has become to the disciplinary board *in abstentia* with a letter in which she is accused of having "signed the petition of the enemy of Moroccan cinema!" *I replied that I disagreed: he is not the enemy of cinema, he is an artist. You can say what you want, but in this particular case, he is right.... I left the Chamber and told them: "your story is of no interest to me."*[10] Hence, because she stands up out of loyalty and for what she believes is right, Farida finds herself ostracized, condemned to make her own journey through the desert.

In 1991, she founds her own production company, Tingitiana Films (from the ancient name of Tangier: Tingis, or *Tanja* in Darija) with her sister Leïla. *We were very complementary. Leïla was three years younger than me. Even when we were children, she was afraid of nothing. We worked together almost until her death.... She was not an intellectual, but a very practical woman who was always involved in good deeds.*[11]

Farida also writes during this period: articles in French or Spanish for *El Mundo, El País*, in Spain, or *Qantara*, as well as short stories and articles published by *Autrement*, in France. Here again, she writes about people from her life, from Tangier. In a candid interview with Paul Bowles, she captures his humor and his jaded tone (*When I asked him for an interview, he answered me kindly, with a smile, that he hated interviews, which, he added, have the same effect on him as taxes!*). He tells her about the dream that led him to settle in Tangier in 1931, yet he also has no illusions: "...everything here interests me intensely. This is the place where I live. But I am still a stranger to the religion, to the language, to the culture."[12]

In the same issue of *Autrement*, *Signs of the Invisible: Morocco*, she publishes a short story, "A Day in the Life of Hajja Leimeth." In it, Farida portrays "a leading woman," inspired by her former mother-in-law (Hamadi's mother), during the winter, in her home in Ketama. She describes Hajja's morning rituals: getting up, performing her ablutions, her prayer, and her tender thoughts for her favorite cow that she hears stirring in the small stable below in the same house. Composed in a very visual style (the short story could easily become a script), the text slips into Hajja Leimeth's consciousness and recounts her worries about her sons, her daughters-in-law, evokes past episodes of her life, the changes that have come with the intensive cultivation of kif (cannabis) in the region. The author ends the short story on Hajja's patience.[13]

She picks up the theme in her next short story, «La patience estbelle»/ "Patience is beautiful," written for a special issue on patience edited by none other than Catherine Chalier in 1992.[14] This second text opens with a quotation from the Sura of Joseph praising "those who encourage each other to be patient" before launching into an auto-fiction around the protagonist, Lalla Fadoul, who is modeled after Farida's paternal grand-mother. Surrounded by the children she raises after their mother left the family home, pious Lalla Fadoul teaches them patience when they are toddlers and as they grow up. When her granddaughter Ghita wants to leave her husband, she advocates "patience" not as resignation but as a strategy that can be slowly deployed.

> God created men stronger and women more cunning. As for patience, it is required of both. He who does not want to use it will suffer the consequences. Everyone, man or woman, will be judged for their own actions. So your actions must be well thought out and not dictated by reaction with an idea of revenge. If he does anything, it is up to you to organize yourself so that his actions have the smallest impact on the family that you wanted to build under the direction of God. This is what Islam

is all about, it's not just about fasting and praying. There will come a time when he himself will repent. (205)

Lalla Fadoul is the heiress of a traditional ethic in sharp contrast with the egalitarian notions of gender of the "Nazarene" couples of her time which can only lead to pain. And she concludes on the therapeutic benefits of patience: "Patience is the only way to overcome suffering. It soothes the burn of it" (205).

In the text, the narrator describes two other female characters who also come straight out of Farida's childhood: Malika, the first daughter-in-law, who is described as too free; and Aïcha, the second one (named after Farida's mother-in-law) who, having been widowed by her first husband, "had lost all right to speak" and turned into "the 'low wall,' the one that one jumps over without a second thought" (203). Then the author returns to the trio composed of Lalla Fadoul, Aisha, and Ghita, and sketches three portraits of women across three different generations with three distinct levels of consciousness within the same family. They all dialogue, listen, and support one another. Her short story brings to mind the scenarios of *Reed Dolls*, *Badis*, and *A Door* and their vision of women that is nuanced, diverse, and tender at the same time, just like the patience praised by the grandmother of the short story.

It is this patience that Farida cultivates in order to face the annoyances of the CCM, to help her daughters in Paris, to return to Tangier with little Abdelhaye who, according to his older sisters, likes to play hooky. Farida has the patience of Job (to whom she alludes in her text) to endure rejections, blows of fate, moments of disarray without suffering or losing hope, but by working actively to "organize" herself, as Lalla Fadoul would say, around the negative event, in order to attenuate its effects and not curl up in morose passivity. Here the term is understood in its Muslim sense—صَبْر/*sabr*—i.e., patience kneaded with perseverance, endurance (the antipodes of anger), a resource that one draws from within oneself to face the blows of fate. This practice and discipline of patience lead Farida to keep on writing short stories as she figures out her next film. And she also writes a second scenario for Mohammed Abderrahman Tazi.

LOOKING FOR MY WIFE'S HUSBAND (1993)

This time, she writes the script of a comedy: Mohammed Abderrahman Tazi's *In search of the husband of my wife*, the most popular film in the history of Moroccan cinema. Tazi, frustrated by the lack of a Moroccan audience for *Badis*, wants to make a film about the traditional bourgeoisie of Fes where he grew up (his father and grandfather had several wives in a bourgeois harem in the city) and about the law governing the third repudiation of a wife.[15] After having first toyed with the idea of directing a short film on the subject in an omnibus to be made with other Maghrebi filmmakers, Tazi turned to Noureddine Sail and Farida Benlyazid who thought there was enough material for a feature film.[16] Farida writes the exuberant script of the comedy in the space of two months!

SYNOPSIS—In the old city of Fes, a jeweler, Haj Ben Moussa, has three wives: Lalla Hobby (the oldest), Lalla Rabi'a (the mother of many young children), and young Houda, whom the Haj desires most. One day he catches her flirting with a sheep deliverer, goes into a fit of fierce jealousy and repudiates Houda for the third time—the equivalent of a divorce under Islamic law. Houda returns to her parents' home while the Haj mourns her loss loudly to his first two wives who are quite disinclined to pity him. The Haj wants Houda back, but he must undergo the punishment reserved for men who lose their minds, as prescribed by the Sharia: Houda must first marry another man, consummate her marriage, and then divorce him before she can remarry the Haj. The latter thus starts looking for a husband for... his wife! He ends up selecting an emigrant who has returned to Morocco for the summer. Racked with jealousy and wretchedness during Houda's wedding night, he complains to his two wives (still disinclined to pity him). Problem: the handsome young groom (zoom on Houda's smile of pleasure in bed at dawn) is involved in some shady business and he returns to Belgium urgently to be safe from threatening thugs. The Haj applies for a visa at the Belgian consulate so he can finalize the divorce procedure and finally be reunited with his Houda.

Farida's scenario ends with a still shot of the Haj's face at the consulate. But Tazi has another idea (again!) and shoots another ending without telling anyone (except the male star, Bachir Skirej): in the last scene, the Haj joins a group of illegal immigrants in a smuggler's boat to reach Europe at his own risk. All humor vanishes from this abrupt, potentially tragic scene that breaks the light-hearted tone of the narrative. The shift from the matrimonial comedy to the tragedy of the *harragas* (the "burners" or illegal migrants who burn borders and papers to emigrate to Europe) is colossal and staggering.

Abderrahman Tazi casts two stars of Moroccan popular theater: Bachir Skirej (Haj Ben Moussa), and Ahmed Taïb El Alj (Haj Abdelkader, his sarcastic friend). The duo's magnificent acting combined with the authenticity of the dialogues carries the humor of the story and makes the Moroccan audience bend over with laughter. The film contains one other surprise besides its highly clandestine ending: Tazi gives a small role to his cousin Fatema Mernissi who plays the mother of one of the suitors.[17] What could be funnier than the brief (and only) appearance of the great lady of Moroccan feminism in a fiction film? The relationships between the women in the *Search* resemble those of the protagonists in *A Door, Reed Dolls* or even the one that united Moira and Touria in *Badis*. We recognize Farida in the way she imagines the solidarity shared by the Haj's wives in the house and the intelligence with which they negotiate their husband's whims. However, we are far from the tensions of *Badis*. *The Search* was a fabulous commercial success in Morocco: it stayed in theaters for four to five months instead of the usual two to three weeks for most Moroccan films at the time. Tazi recalls that it was on the marquis in Rabat and Fes for more than twelve weeks and in Casablanca between eight and twelve weeks.[18] The film is indeed so successful in Morocco that Tazi, under various pressures, goes on to make a sequel: *Lalla Hobby*, which he directs in 1996 after many setbacks. He asks Farida to write the script, but when he refuses to give her half of her (modest) fee up front, she declines. (He then turns to Noureddine Sail.[19])

Farida, however, does not stay idle. She is invited to a women's conference organized by her artist friend Khadija Tanana in Fes, where she meets, among other attendants, Judithe Bizot, who will take her on a feminist anti-globalist adventure far away from the narrow male world of the CCM of the time.

From Fes to Bamako: Aminata Traore': A Woman of the Sahel (1993)

Khadija Tanana is involved in politics and sits as elected vice-president of the administrative council of the city of Fes for nine years, the only woman surrounded by men...[20] This allows her to organize a series of conferences on women in the arts, film, poetry. One of these meetings on film convened Farida, Fatema Mernissi, and Arab women filmmakers from the Levant: Lebanese Jocelyne Saab, Palestinian Mai Masri, Egyptian Nadia Hamza, and Ines al Dighidy. Khadija and Farida recall these colloquia with joy and laughter. The next one has Judithe Bizot in attendance, who shares how much she has liked *A Door*. Because of her work at the United Nations, Bizot attended the Earth Summit in Rio in June 1992, where the contributions of the women from the South to the Women's Declaration at the Global Forum made a deep impression on her. In an article co-authored with Peggy Antrobus a few months later, she writes that poor women in the Third World "understand more clearly than policymakers that the economy and the environment are compatible" and that it is high time "to include their perspectives and institutionalize their involvement in the decision-making processes."[21] In particular, she is struck by Aminata Traoré, Vandana Shiva, Marta Trejos, and Khawar Mumtaz and what they have to say about human rights, diversity, and the environment. She commissions documentary short films (26 minutes) on the four women, produced in France by Canal+, with the intention to reach a wide international audience.[22] *For each documentary, she chose a director and a subject from the same continent to make each film. She asked me to make a film about Aminata.*[23]

We went to Bamako, we scouted location, we met Aminata, her family, her children and it was wonderful, it was really a beautiful adventure. Her admiration for Aminata Traoré grows during the film shoot, and they become close friends. *She is a really extraordinary woman, surrounded by painters, religious people. I think she is the most intelligent woman I have ever met... She gets up at five in the morning. She prays – something nobody knows, she never talks about it. Then she writes. In fact, she has written several books. From nine o'clock on, she receives craftsmen and others.*[24]

The documentary follows impressive sociologist Aminata Traoré, in her daily tasks. Born, like Farida, in 1948, the doctor in social psychology left Mali during the military dictatorship of Moussa Traoré, went to the Ivory Coast where she worked for UN agencies (e.g., OXFAM) from 1988 to 1992 and returned to Bamako after the revolution of March 1991. After Farida's film, this tireless critic of the global neo-liberal economy became Minister of Culture and Tourism in Mali (1997–2000), was a member of the Spanish socialist think-tank *Fundacion IDEAS* and appeared as a witness in Abderrahmane Sissoko's film *Bamako* (2006). The latter puts the IMF and the World Bank on trial and gives women a voice. Thus, anti-globalist Aminata Traoré appears at least twice in transnational African cinema: once in front of Farida Benlyazid's Moroccan camera, and again in Abderrahmane Sissoko's Malian frame.

In Farida's film, she stands upright, majestic, and speaks passionately in a French that is in turn calm when she describes the conditions of the men and women in Mali ("these simple people do not speak of development but truly practice development") and incisive when she denounces the outrageous enrichment of the North at the expense of the South. She vigorously turns the classic arguments of the international financial institutions against them.[25] In that, Aminata Traoré foreshadows Senegalese Felwine Saar who writes in 2016: "Africa has no one to catch up with. It should no longer follow the paths that are signaled by others but hasten its pace on the path that it will have chosen."[26] Both think that this path passes through material and immaterial resources (moral, aesthetic, political) and a local imagination (not the one broadcast on the continent by media-savvy external financial powers). Both call on Africans to "rethink progress" on bases that absolutely no longer align with those of the former colonizers or the World Bank.

Aminata is filmed in her dizzyingly numerous varied activities, committed as she is to women, unemployed graduates, illiterates, and young people. We see her set up an apprenticeship center where young people can acquire traditional and modern skills, for "production is not necessarily linked to a long and expensive apprenticeship. Training and work have only one purpose: the satisfaction of vital, social, economic, and cultural needs of human beings and of the community."[27]

We discover the restaurant Aminata Traoré has opened in Bamako, the Djenné, to the sound of water from a fountain and the music of a live kora player. Farida alternates between wide shots of this peaceful place and close-ups of the beautiful, repurposed objects that decorate it, all of which come from the cooperative Aminata created. Her voiceover explains:

> I try to draw, as much as possible, from what exists, which is essentially waste that men and women manage to transform. I am fascinated by what is often pejoratively called 'the economy of poverty', by its creativity, its tenacity, its resolve to transform metal sheets into basins, buckets, tools.

The repurposing of objects, the gift of shaping a new creation out of the discarded and giving it a new life, echoes the art of cinema practiced by Farida under constraint. Aminata's support of women's cooperatives that aim to develop education, family health, and sanitation, also resonates with Farida's commitment to education and women's associations during the 1990s in their work to bring about the reform of the Personal Code (the *Mudawana*) in Morocco.[28] They also share a common faith and a similar desire for peace, equity, and social justice. Furthermore, Aminata and Farida both make a clear distinction between the demands of "African" feminism and those of "Western" feminism—even if the nuances of the latter are somewhat lost in Aminata's occasionally reductive discourse:

> Feminism as it has been applied, is an imposition, that is, a process of de-culturation and alienation for African women. We have to get out from under it and in a way that is completely united with our men who are in the doldrums. The image of African women is shocking! I saw a poster that stated: 'illiterate, pregnant and poor'. It is not up to [Western] feminists to solve our problems for us. It is up to us, the women of the South, to throw away these lenses that were lent to us.

Western feminists had gone to Africa to spread the good word of their feminist activism in a rather neo-colonial fashion. At times, they mirrored the condescending pity of a first world certain to have in hand all the solutions and tools needed to free African women from a frightful condition of dependence and suffering at the clutches of a particularly ferocious patriarchy.[29] Aminata wishes to take the reins of feminist thought in her own country and on her own continent: putting aside borrowed thought does not mean ignoring it but rather giving it its proper place and proceeding with one's own.

Aminata Traoré affirms solidarity across genders, just as Farida had in *A Door*, in opposition to the exclusionary process of a post-1968 Western feminism. It is impossible not to grasp the dialogical dimension of the documentary. The subject and her director's meeting is almost magical in the way their political and spiritual visions align or complement each other.[30] They also share a strong taste for literature: Aminata quotes Malian author Amadou Hampaté Bâ, whom she knew well, and Farida includes a poem by the bard Albakaye Kounta of Timbuktu that she superimposes on the shot of two praying hands at the end of the film:

> Out of suffering and misery
> Out of poverty and even nothingness
> May systems be born.
> That is the bequest

In my long and thin hands
I wish to bestow upon you.

Kounta does not have the last word on screen, however, as a mini biography of Aminata Traoré pops up next to close the film. The documentary (and the poem underlines it) is an ode to the quiet strength and often silent work of women in Africa. The film also shows how Farida's feminist thinking has evolved from Nelly Roussel's socialist, feminist demands to those of equity and justice for women (*Reed Dolls*), to those of a feminism rooted in the Moroccan Muslim faith (*A Door*) to those of an anti-globalist feminism that crosses borders, ethnicities, and classes, to the freedom of choice and decision that must be granted to women worldwide. *Aminata Traoré: A Woman from the Sahel* is thus a new step in Farida's intellectual, spiritual, and political journey.

Storyteller in Morocco: *Contrabando* (1994) and *Sur La Terrasse* (1995)

Farida is then asked to make two other completely different short films: the first, *Contrabando* (1994, 13 minutes), emphasizes her political and social commitment to the voiceless in her country while the second, *On the Terrace* (1995, 15 minutes), highlights one of the major functions of her cinema. These two short films touch on themes that are dear to her.

The television channel 2M asked Farida to film a Moroccan subject of her choice in a report in images; she chose smuggling and explained why on the set of 2M as follows: *As I often travel between Tangier and Casablanca by train, I have always been fascinated by these women who carry incredible loads and who are courageous, intelligent and full of humor. I wanted these women that I had heard so many times to speak out.... We are all connected to smuggling, whether closely or remotely: who doesn't have a bottle of shampoo? A bag of cookies? It was good to learn how these women get all these goods everywhere. I'm not a journalist and it's more the human side that was of interest to me in this story.*[31]

The film begins in Tangier (panorama of the city, the port, scenes of the streets of the Kasbah with children), an historical smuggling center that requires the intervention of a whole chain of actors from the customs officer to the reseller, all of whom benefit from it. Farida films her characters with simplicity, at eye level. The film reconstructs the journey of the smugglers: from the Petit Socco market at dawn the camera follows the women as they make their way to the port before joining the passengers who take the train at the Tangier station, loaded like mules with bags full to burst. Once on the train, the smugglers are invited to speak: the subjects are middle-aged, veiled women, and young or not so young men, all from very modest backgrounds. With their faces framed in close-ups, a series of lively portraits, they tell their stories with candor, to the sound of the train heading south toward Casablanca. The film thus gives voice to the silent and makes (hyper)visible the anonymous people who support an entire economy. Once again, Farida brings to the fore the survival of the most modest in society.

The second short, the following year, is ordered not by Moroccan television but by the CCM on the occasion of the 100th year of cinema. She directs a short film for the omnibus produced by Sarim Fassi Fihri, *Five Films for a Hundred Years* (1995), dedicated "to all Moroccan filmmakers who died without having celebrated the 100 years of cinema." Farida is thus recognized as one of the five beacons of Moroccan cinema of the time, alongside Omar Chraibi (*Lumière/Light*), Jillali Ferhati (*Le mouchoir bleu/The Blue Handkerchief*), Abdelkader Lagtaa (*Happy End*), and Hakim Nouri (*Cinéma imperial/The Imperial Movie Theater*). Her short film, *Sur la terrasse/On the Terrace* (15 minutes) narrates Laila's discovery of cinema from the terrace of her grand-parents' house in Tetouan, during the screening of an Egyptian classic outside in the town square (starring the mythical couple of actors Farid Chawki and Houda Soltane). This first story frames another, just as Scheherazade had done during her storytelling marathon that lasted a thousand and one nights. This narrative mise-en-abyme mixes oral legend and the history of Tetouan and Chefchaouen and places the film in both the tradition of women's oral transmission and the local context of a legendary powerful heroine. Farida confirms with her camera (or rather with Kamal Derkaoui's) her desire to film the culture of her region in the tradition of that very region. In this, she joins the postcolonial discourse of filmmakers such as Sembène Ousmane who saw himself as a cinematic griot, talking to his community.

Her short film also contains recurring themes in Farida's cinema and writings: the world of women, Moroccan heritage, as well as the city, cinema—what Farida calls "modernity"—and the overflowing imagination of children. She even slips in a note about Islam. After filming and writing about Tangier and Fes, she now tackles two northern cities: Chefchaouen, the blue city, and Tetouan.

SYNOPSIS—We follow Laila, a little girl with a vivid imagination who lives in Chefchaouen and goes with her mother to be treated in Tetouan where her paternal grandparents live. The little girl is literally inflamed (she is overcome by a disturbing fever) by dreams featuring the legendary queen Lalla Sayda el Horra (1493–1561). Her heroine rides horses, fights wars, governs Tetouan after the death of her first husband, and sets her conditions when she agrees to marry Sultan Ahmed el Watassi of Fes for the second time.[32] When little Laila asks her father to explain how "the free lady" was defeated, he answers "because she was betrayed"—without specifying that it was by the men of her own army. Lalla Sayda was an independent woman of rare strength, who could inspire generations of little girls in Morocco.[33]

Upstairs, the grandparents' house opens onto a terrace where women come to sit behind a railing to watch a film projected in the open on a screen in the square below. The women enjoy the show without being seen, just as they used to watch the street from the shelter of their moucharabiés. It is a magical discovery for Laila (as it was for Farida, as a little girl, when her mother took her to the cinema).

Meanwhile, the oral tale of Lalla Sayda el Horra, read by an acousmatic female voice, continues to obsess the little girl who starts to role-play the antagonists of the legend in front of a mirror—her own private screen. Laila, from spectator of an Egyptian film has turned into Laila, director and actress of her own local Moroccan film, an entirely female narrative of resistance.[34]

Hasna Labbedy notes that Lalla Sayda is not the only resistant heroine of the region who appears not in the written history (by men) but in the oral tales transmitted by women.[35] These tales of powerful female figures propose models of resistant (and nationalist) proto-feminism in total rupture with the male history which, if it mentions them, describes them as exceptions. Although Farida does not tell Lalla Sayda el-Horra's entire story, she alludes to it so extensively that the women of the North recognize her. The legend is thus performed on screen and young Laila can make her story her own.

Another dimension of cinema appears fleetingly in a snippet of dialogue between Laila's grandfather, impatient for dinner and suspicious of cinema, and his daughter and daughter-in-law. "It's a new vice, invented to lure us again. At the mosque the other day, the imam said it was sinful," he says. But the young women show him that it is not sinful, that "these are only shadows" and not humans, and that they are not idols either.

They thus put an end to the possible resurgence of an outdated false debate on the prohibition of the image in Islam that some ultra-orthodox people were reviving in Algeria, in particular, during the black decade.

Kamal Derkaoui's vertical tracking shots that open up the space to the peaks of the northern mountain landscape and stimulate Laila's imagination recall the flights of fancy in *A Door*. Farida continues to celebrate the aesthetics of Moroccan heritage with shots of steep alleys, of the architecture of old Chefchaouen, its blue and white walls and the courtyards of its homes. The team is familiar: Faouzi Thabet as sound engineer; scriptwriter and journalist Fatema Loukili cast as Zoubida, Laila's mother; Farida's son, Abdelhaye Adbib as Tariq, Laila's friend with whom she discovers cinema from the terrace. This very short film thus tackles gender equality as it celebrates a heroine who is often ignored today and who did not let herself be fooled by the powerful men of her time.[36]

Finally, the location of the viewing, the terrace, is significant: a space that is at once open and closed, it allows women to be simultaneously in and out of the house since it is an extension of the dwelling that connects to the outside.[37] In this sense, the terrace is suspended beyond the reach of patriarchy (the patriarch refuses to set foot there in this film), a passage between the public world and the intimate world of the house. It also constitutes the "threshold" described by Bhabha, where the post-colonial subject stands between the space of his/her culture of origin and the space of modernity, at first foreign, then gradually turned into his or her own. It is the space, finally, from which to watch not only the world pass by under the windows, but the magic of cinema. Here, the intradiegetic spectators of the Egyptian film are women (since the grandfather boycotts the film) and children: the only little boy is Tariq. To celebrate its hundredth anniversary, Farida's cinema addresses women and children on the terrace rather than an adult male audience in the movie theater.

NOTES

1. Gille Perrault wrote: "Hassan II, a crime buff, replied to Amnesty International's complaints: 'Every head of state has his secret garden. No other has so carefully cultivated so repugnant a garden of torture. De Gaulle, who was not a softy, observed: 'He is unnecessarily cruel.' "The Mamounia-Club and the social question," *Carré Rouge*, No. 12, October 1999: 54.

2. *Réalités marocaines: La Dynastie alaouite, de l'usurpation à l'impasse.* Paris: Albatros (reprint 1987) (1st edition 1972); *Réquisitoire contre un despote: Pour une république au Maroc.* Paris: Albatros (reprint 1991) (1st edition 1972); *Chronique d'une expulsion annoncée.* Paris: L'Harmattan, 1991; *À qui appartient le Maroc?* Paris: L'Harmattan, 1992; *Mémoire d'un peuple: Chronique de la Résistance au Maroc, 1631–1993.* L'Harmattan, 1993.

3. Diouri, Moumen. *A Qui appartient le Maroc?* Paris: L'Harmattan, 1992.

4. Diouri denounces the "facade" of the makhzen's newfound openness to human rights, exposes how the parents of the young demonstrators killed in the streets of Fes in 1990 did not dare to claim the bodies of their offspring from the police for fear of arrest, and demonstrates the complicity of Europe in protecting Morocco, the world's fourth largest exporter of hashish. In this book, he also details the King's assets in Morocco and elsewhere (in France, the United States, Brazil) and meticulously documents the royal family's stranglehold on all of the country's economic sectors, from the exploitation of raw resources to banking, industry, and services (e.g., transportation).

   Moreover, the preface by Ahmed Rami in its first edition (which will disappear from later editions) challenges the religious role of the royal dynasty: "The tyrannical regime of Hassan II is not based on any legitimacy. It is based neither on the Islamic *shura*, because Islam forbids hereditary monarchy, nor on the principles of Western democracy. It is a hybrid creation of medieval despotism and early twentieth century colonialism, a kind of motorized archaism" (6) (my translation).

5. "After the Ben Barka affair, we couldn't afford to have two opponents killed in Paris... There was a contract on my father's head: 5 million francs at the time... They sent a guy to kill him, who thought: 'well, let me find out exactly who I have to kill.' He went to the FNAC [large bookstore]. In one of my father's books, he saw that Dad was telling the story of his own father, of which he knew nothing. He finally found out what had happened to his father, who had been torn to pieces: they had killed him with a machete...The guy realized that my father knew a lot of things. He said: no, I can't kill him. He went back to Morocco, took his whole

family away and went to hide in Libya." Kenza Diouri, March 20, 2018.

6. "It was in 1991. My father was a political refugee and he had just written a book that embarrassed France and Morocco. It was a shock for us. We called Mom and she came right away. She stayed with us during this whole period when we were running all over Paris to find a lawyer. We went to Gabon to see our father. We brought him back to France (because the French government lost the case). Then, she left for Morocco." Ayda Diouri, February 8, 2018.

7. Farida Benlyazid, October 7, 2017.

8. Carrée, Roland. Op. cit.: 129–130.

9. Ibid.: 130.

10. Farida Benlyazid, October 7, 2017.

11. Farida Benlyazid, February 26, 2016.

12. "Paul Bowles, sans émotion," Jean-François Clément, dir. *Morocco. Les signes de l'invisible, Autrement. Série Monde*, No. 48 (Hors Série), 1990: 118 and 121.

13. «Une journée dans la vie de Hajja Leitmeth,» in Jean-François Clément, ed. *Morocco. Les signes de l'invisible, Autrement. Série Monde*, No. 48 (Hors Série), 1990: 85.

14. «La patience est belle»/ "Patience is beautiful." Chalier, Catherine, ed. *La Patience: Passion de la durée consentie*. Paris: Autrement, 1992: 195–205.

15. "In the old neighborhoods of Fes, one always heard that so-and-so, a rich bourgeois, had just repudiated his wife for the third time and that, according to Muslim law, he could only remarry her if she first remarried another man, consummated this other marriage at least once, and then that this second husband agreed to divorce her. The rich bourgeois had to go looking for a husband for his ex-wife, a sort of straw man who would agree to marry her and then divorce her. Everyone knew about these stories." Dwyer, Kevin. *Beyond Casablanca*: 31–32.

16. At the third National Film Festival in Meknes in 1991, he approached Algerian directors Mahmoud Zemmouri and Merzak Allouache, and Tunisian directors Taïeb Louhichi and Brahim Babai, but the project did not develop further.

17. "… You know, Fatema was certainly used to audiovisual presentations, interviews and all that, but she was not used to rehearsals and

especially to having to repeat things three or four times. To relax her, we shot the scene in her childhood home, where she lived until she was a teenager." Ibid.: 46–47.

18. Ibid.: 26.

19. Ibid.: 214–216.

20. *She had organized three meetings around women's creativity, and under terrible circumstances, with monstrous difficulties, but she had succeeded.* Farida Benlyazid, October 7, 2017.

21. Antrobus, Peggy and Bizot, Judithe. "Women's perspectives: Towards an ethical, equitable, just and sustainable livelyhood in the twenty-first century," *Isis International Women in Action*, Vol. 4.92 & 1.93: 30–31.

22. After Farida's film on *Aminata Traoré* (1993), came Rhada Hola and Shazia Ilmi's film on the Indian Vandana Shiva, *A Daughter of the Earth—Portrait of Vandana Shiva* (1996); then *The Right to Dream* (1996) by Chilean Valeria Sarmiento about Marta Trejos; and finally, *Through the Veil* (1996) by Turkish filmmaker Canan Gerede.

23. Farida Benlyazid, May 3, 2016.

24. Farida Benlyazid, May 16, 2016.

25. On the stand, she declares in Sissoko's film: "Africa is a victim of its wealth! I would like us to talk about pauperization and not poverty" or again, with Césairian accents: "We do not live in an open world. It is certainly open to whites, but it is not open to blacks... If there is a need to civilize globalization, it is because it de-civilizes." And "The most serious problem in Africa is indebted African countries. People need to know this, and 70% of them are illiterate. The victims do not know that their governments are struggling to follow development policies that only push them into an increasingly tragic indigence."

26. Saar, Felwine. *Afrotopia*. Paris: Philippe Rey, 2016: 152.

27. *L'Étau: l'Afrique dans un monde sans frontières*. Arles, Actes Sud, 1999: 134 (my translation).

28. http://www.hrea.org/programs/gender-equality-and-womens-empowerment/moudawana/#11.

29. E.g., the documentary on female genital mutilation in Africa, *Warrior Marks* made by novelist Alice Walker (after the publication of her novel *Possessing the Secret of Joy*, 1992, on the same theme) and filmmaker Pratibha Parmar in 1993. The film drew the

wrath of African feminists who did not want women from outside to come and give them lessons at home.

30. For example, in her book *L'Étau: L'Afrique dans un monde sans frontières*, Aminata Traoré writes, "The only wealth lies in men and women (...) It could be that our so-called poor countries, because they are deprived of capital, technology and perspectives, have preserved this sense and concern for the human being, which fades where the market economy takes hold" (169) (my translation). A few years later, Farida echoes her, as she discusses a Bernard Stiegler's solutions to the robotization of human labor: "*Humans have resources that we cannot imagine*"—and: "*We must not forget humans: we must keep the foundation of their values*" [March 24, 2018].

31. Broadcast *Rétro 94*, introduction to *Contrabando*, December 1994.

32. "To let him know that she had no intention of giving up her political role, she demanded that the king travel to Tetouan for the wedding ceremony. It was the only time in the history of Morocco that a king got married outside his capital." Mernissi, Fatema. *Sultanes oubliées: femmes chefs d'État en islam*. Albin Michel/ Editions Le Fennec, 1990: 30 (my translation).

33. She was also a pious woman who, after her deposition, spent the rest of her life in her father's palace in Chefchaouen meditating and re-reading the Sufi theologian Mohamed Ben Abdallah el Ghazouani. She is buried in the palace which has since become the Raïssouniya zawiya.

34. The history of Sayda al-Horra has several ramifications. First of all, she played a primordial role in the history of northern Morocco at the time of the conflict between the Ottomans and the Europeans, and her deeds (barely recorded by Arab historians until very recently, according to Fatema Mernissi) have given her a legendary aura in oral literature. Born in Chefchaouen a year after the fall of Granada, she was Andalusian by her mother and Moroccan by her father, and a descendant of the dynasty that founded Chefchaouen. Elegant, refined, highly educated, very pious, she spoke Arabic, Castilian and Portuguese, and ruled alone for fifteen years, after the death of her first husband (Mandri II, of Andalusian origin) over her territory and the western part of the Mediterranean. Having

under- stood that governing meant first of all ensuring the necessary resources for the life of her subjects and for the war against the Portuguese invader, she became a pirate leader! Her famous fleet of privateers based in Martil was so efficient and prosperous that Europeans nicknamed her "The Barbarossa of Tetouan" in reference to her famous ally and neighbor in (present-day) Algeria, Kheir-Eddine, known as Barbarossa (Red Beard), who ransomed ships in the eastern Mediterranean. She agreed with him to share the piracy zones in order to resist the Portuguese invaders without going to war with them. See Mernissi, Fatema. *Sultanes oubliées*: 29–32.

35. Thus, the oral literature in Darija of the Jbala women tells of the legend of this woman who defended the village of Dar Radi by lighting many camp-fires at nightfall to make the enemy believe in the presence of a large army, thereby avoided combat and death and saved Sidi Mezouar and the village. However, this story exists only in the tales of the women of the north, and not in any archives. See Lebbady, Hasna. "Women in Northern Morocco: Between documentary and the imaginary," *Alif: Journal of Comparative Poetics*, No. 32, *The Imaginary and the Documentary: Cultural Studies in Literature, History, and the Arts*, 2012: 127–150.

36. Since this short film, 2M has co-produced a series of documentaries in 2016 with Nabil Ayouch's Ali'n Prod, *Dix Femmes de notre histoire/Ten Women of Our History*, including *Sayyida al-Horra (The Governor of Tetouan)*, by Layla Triqui, May 2016. And the mythical figure has also inspired a novel: *Le Chant de Sayyida Hurra/The Song of Sayyida Hurra* by Bachir Damoun.

37. "La terrasse: le lieu du possible," *Qantara: magazine des cultures arabe et méditerranéenne*. Vol. 18, 1996: 66–67.

CHAPTER 4

Farida's Great *Halqa* Throughout Morocco and Beyond

Abstract Context: The age-old tradition of the popular *halqa* and its revival in postcolonial Morocco. Benlyazid uses the traditional story-telling technique in three narratives: her first *halqa* is a play, *Help Thyself, Heaven Will Help Thee* (1996–1997), which she writes and produces as part of a public health campaign to lower pregnant women's fatalities. The second one is the adaptation on screen of *Keïd ensa/The Wiles of Women* (1999), and old Andalusian tale she heard as a child. The third one is an activist citizen's film: *Casablanca, Casablanca* (2002). The chapter contains large excerpts of Benlyazid's play, a transcultural analysis of *Keïd ensa*, and a quick analysis of an adaptation from novel to screen.

Keywords *Halqa* · Cunning · Transcultural · Oral literature · Corruption · Campaign · Adaptation · Bodies of words · Storyteller · Call-and-response · Qurʾān · *Ijtihad* · Bouanani · *Souffles* · Casablanca · *Boukman* · *Nia Taghleb* · Rida Lamrini · Laura Box

In Morocco, there is a long tradition of oral storytelling: that of the *halqa* حلقة—literally the <circle> of storytellers, from which, inciden-tally, the Moroccan theater of independence drew much inspiration. The storyteller—*el hlayqi*—stands on a market square, at a crossroads, at

F. Martin, *Farida Benlyazid and Moroccan Cinema*, Palgrave Studies in Arab Cinema, https://doi.org/10.1007/978-3-031-40616-4_4

the entrance of a Kasbah and first delineates his territory with water before haranguing onlookers to attract them to his show. The circle of spectator-listeners is formed. The storyteller then invokes God and His prophet and launches into his performance with music, voice changes, even acrobatics or dances, mesmerizing his audience. The spectators are not frozen in place, as Khalid Amine reminds us: no fourth wall, no fixed distance between the stage and the spectators who are invited to spontaneously approach the *hlayqi*. The duration of the performance fluctuates according to the story, the storyteller, and his audience.[1] The latter reacts loudly, laughs, communicates with the storyteller at all times. This physical call and response system sustains the structure of the storyteller's performance while the spontaneous, dynamic encounter of the storyteller and his listeners produces meaning.[2]

The *halqa* influenced postcolonial cinema in Morocco. In *Souffles* No. 2 (1966), Abdellatif Laâbi brought together ten filmmakers to discuss the function of emerging cinema in independent Morocco. It is crucial, the participants claimed, for filmic narratives to speak of and to the people, using models of transmission that are familiar to them. Thus, the first task of a filmmaker is to learn about Morocco's cultural heritage and traditions.

> BOUANANI: ... In a *halqa*, when the storyteller speaks, he first of all has to entertain, and that's his only goal: to entertain the audience. But is what he says mere entertainment? No, because people themselves get something else out of it. From a tale, one can learn many lessons. Yet, the storyteller is not there to lecture.
>
> LAABI - The filmmaker can transform this approach by using the technique of the *halqa* and storytelling. He could communicate something else. There would thus be an oral transposition in a conscious artistic creation.[3]

The listeners thus produce meaning that goes beyond the tale: a meaning that lies in its response to the call of the tale and in its extension. Farida, during the seven years to come, also revisits the *halqa*. Like the classical *hlayqi*, she defines the contours of her public, which, like that of the *halqa*, grows and changes according to her tale. First, she dialogues with a theater audience in her traveling play *Aide-toi, le ciel t'aidera/Help Thyself, Heaven Will Help Thee* (1997); then, she becomes a storyteller on screen and addresses cinema audiences with her film *Keïd Ensa/The Wiles of*

Women (1998); finally, she addresses Moroccan society as a whole when she denounces corruption in her film *Casablanca, Casablanca* (2002).

These projects will cause Farida to travel a lot in the country. The next few years will take her to Casablanca, Tangier, and then throughout Morocco.

In 1996, life offers Farida two gifts: her first granddaughter, Alya, daughter of Ayda, and a marriage proposal from Mehdi Menebhi, a Tangier aristocrat she admired from afar in her teens. *He was the most handsome man in Tangier!* A fine man, funny, who adores Farida, as she said in an interview in 1999: *My current husband, Mehdi Menebhi, an artist of great subtlety, is a watercolorist who paints for his pleasure. He is a gentle person who is not afraid to share his admiration for my work. He was my artistic advisor for 'Keid ensa', a film on which he never tried to impose his views.*[4] His watercolors, with their delicate outlines, now cover the walls of her small house in the Kasbah. Mehdi attended American school and then Cornell University in the United States and speaks French with a charming hint of an English accent. He lives in the wing of a nineteenth-century palace, a few blocks from Farida's home, a Fellini-like palace with the patina and cracks of a past splendor. She will shoot her next film there.

THE FIRST *HALQA* IN THE THEATER: *HELP THYSELF, HEAVEN WILL HELP THEE* (1996–1997)

If the economic situation of Morocco in general starts to improve in the last half of the 1990s, a number of inequalities remain, including access to education, especially for women: in 1999, the literacy rate is 62.6% for men, against 37.4% for women. In rural areas, the figures are even worse.[5] Women's lack of access to education has an impact on their economic status and their health—particularly in the area of reproduction.

Between 1970 and 2000, the U.S. Agency for International Development (USAID) had an assistance program with the Moroccan Ministry of Health (MOH) that focused on family planning, child health services, and strengthening the various institutions to support them. In 1994, the program entered its fifth and final phase, aimed at curbing one of Morocco's scourges: the very high rate of maternal mortality—during pregnancy or just after childbirth. The figures are chilling: in 1995, an estimated 257 mothers died for every 100,000 pregnancies in Morocco (compared to 112 in Tunisia and 15 in France in the same year).[6] A number of reasons (medical, economic, sociological, cultural) prevent pregnant women from accessing the specialized medical care they need.[7] In 1994, during its International Conference on Population and Development in Cairo, the UN recognized the right of women to safe motherhood. USAID and the Moroccan Ministry of Health called on the American team at the Center for Communication Programs (CCP) at Johns Hopkins University to develop health communication campaigns for populations in developing countries.[8] The agency commissioned a touring play from Farida who wrote *Help Thyself, Heaven will help you*.

Farida's mission is to address women of childbearing age and their families in order to prevent complications and possible deaths by organizing her play around the theory of the three delays that are often fatal to young mothers: (a) the initial decision to seek medical care; (b) the act (going to the medical facility often located far away); (c) accessing adequate care (in the face of a lack of medical personnel or equipment).[9] In the space of fifty minutes, the play must therefore show that pregnancy and childbirth involve risks, but that the death of mothers is neither inevitable nor predestined.

The two-act play is supposed to take place in a small maternity hospital run by two midwives: Mouï-Aïcha, an elderly midwife, and Fatem-Zahra, a young graduate midwife. Enter Mina for her first delivery, Khaddouj (with her husband Ahmed), who has repeated miscarriages, and Touda, exhausted by her many pregnancies (with her nurse neighbor and her husband who bursts onto the scene: both men remain anonymous). The dialogues in Darija are spoken for the most part by the female characters, who show what hinders women's access to medicine. Mina, whose water has not yet broken, refuses to go home: "My mother-in-law won't let me return. She doesn't want me to give birth in the hospital.... She says that I'm just doing what I want. And that women have always given birth at home." (I, 6) Khaddouj arrives too late to avoid a fourth miscarriage. Her husband puts his trust in God and says that poverty prevents him from having his wife treated in Rabat. Fatem-Zahra does not buy it:

Fatem-Zahra:
My father always quoted the example of Our Lady Mary in the Qur'ān. The angel told her to shake the tree so that the dates would fall. The dates could have fallen by themselves. God is great and He wants us to make the effort, otherwise life would have no meaning. "Help thyself and Heaven will help thee." (I, 12)

Touda, about to give birth, did not have access to the necessary care because of her stubborn husband. Tragically, the ambulance requested by Fatem-Zahra arrives too late.

The stories are shared with women but also with the men who will be part of the audience. The main characters appeal to believers and to the responsibility of everyone in these stories, as emphasized in the epilogue in which an angel gives advice on hygiene and health: "First care for the body that God has given you. Doesn't He say in the Qur'ān, 'Don't do anything that will lead you to ruin'? The play, focused on the bodies of pregnant women (in a culture where a woman's body is only bared behind the walls of the house or the hammam), tries to invalidate the believer's perspective on the female body by showing that ignoring it is an act of disobedience to God. The same is true for education: "Even if one cannot read -which is already a fault before God, for is not the first word of God in the Qur'ān 'read'? Even if one cannot read, there are other ways of knowing" (41). Finally, the text reminds the audience of the duty to use one's reason and critical sense (*ijtihad*—اجتهاد), for "God prefers the active believer to the passive believer. He likes it when you defend yourself and use all the means available to you. He does not like humans to behave like animals. If God has given humans reason, it is to use it" (43). With frontal candor, Farida denounces the interpretations of the Qur'ān by men who neglect women's health, the practices that diverge from the prophet's message, and the male manipulation of the religious word.

The playwright's vigorous writing has an immediate effect on the people in the cities and villages where the play is performed: in this, Farida joins her Maghrebi sisters who write, from the very place of the female body, the body that will be performed on stage. The author creates "bodies of words" to build the character of the female body. "Just as a woman actor uses her body in order to construct a presentation of self, the woman writer uses words. The difference is that the woman actor may not have agency, whereas the woman writer attains agency...".[10] At this point, Laura Box recalls, the Maghrebi playwright changes status in relation to her culture since she ceases to transmit—i.e., merely reproduce—it. Shedding her traditional role of passive transmitter, she actively questions her culture with her new "bodies of words" and thus intervenes in the culture. While inscribing herself in its form, she transforms its discourse from within, now an active—no longer passive—participant in the construction of Moroccan postcolonial culture. It is through this intervention that the play successfully undermines every traditional justification given (whether cultural, gendered, economic, or religious), each of them harmful to the health of the mother or the baby. The play brings two messages to its audience: death is not the inevitable outcome of a pregnancy and everyone can act to prevent it. The challenge then becomes to get the message across by performing the play in as many places as possible in Morocco.

The premiere in Rabat on March 13, 1997 under the patronage of Lalla Fatima Zohra, president of the National Union of Moroccan Women (UNFM), was a great success. With the help of the UNFM, the play toured some thirty cities and villages throughout the country, its passage announced on television, radio and on posters produced by the Ministry of Health and mobile medical teams in the provinces: JHU's report stipulates that 37,000 spectators saw the play. Farida recalls thirty-five performances. The show in a village or a small town in rural Morocco is no surprise to their inhabitants who are accustomed to itinerant forms of entertainment. And the play has a similar function to that of the very first films commissioned by the state after independence: to act as an instrument of communication and education for a population without access to the written word (whether in French or Arabic). In the text of *Help Thyself*, dialogues and stage indications signal precise moments when the fourth wall is broken: the characters then address the audience directly. Thus, in the dialogue between Fatem-Zahra, a young qualified midwife, and Ahmed, the husband of a patient who has just had a miscarriage ("It's what God wants," he declares), the young woman tells him that next time, his pregnant wife will have to go to Rabat and see a specialist to ensure that everything goes well for mother and child.

- Ahmed: But Rabat is far away, and we are poor.
- Fatem-Zarah (*getting angry, she turns to the spectators and addresses them*): Tell me, you beloved ones of God, is anything too far for this person's health?
She waits for the audience's response while the man nods, embarrassed.
- Fatem-Zarah (*turning to him*): Money can always be found for marriages and baptisms...
She turns back to the audience.
- Fatem-Zarah: We are strange. We find money for rituals, but we neglect our health. And the same goes for people: you find them ready to help you for a burial, but not for health. In the end, it's up to you: if you want

children, if you care about your wife, if you don't want to see her die, you have to do something about it. (Act I, pp. 10–11).

Similarly, in the second act, in a scene between Moui-Aïcha (the elderly midwife) and Fatem-Zohra, the latter addresses *both* women *and* men in the audience directly:

> - Mouï-Aïcha: You are lucky, you can choose to have children when you want... In my time, we didn't... God has had mercy on you, women of today. Only the one who does not want...
> - Fatem- Zahra (*nods in agreement and adds*): He's had pity on us and on men. They too no longer have to bear this burden, for feeding and raising two or three children is not the same as feeding and raising ten or twelve...
> - Mouï-Aïcha: You bet. Men are different. Very few of them even know what their children eat...
> - Fatem- Zahra: Yes, but if we want a healthy society, both parents are responsible, as God says in the Qurʾān.
> - Mouï-Aïcha (*sighing*): Who are you speaking to?
> - Fatem-Zahra: Who am I speaking to? Me, you and all the people who are listening to us.
> *She points to the public.* (Act II, pp. 22–23)

The audience here is regarded as that of a classical *halqa*. Farida thus enters in authentic dialogue with her listeners, the modest people whom she has always wanted to address since she started making films.

Once the tour is over, *Help Thyself* continues to circulate. The video of a performance is shown on national television and on the long bus rides of the Moroccan Transport Company for three months. Then the initial circle of urban and rural spectators, once enlarged to that of television viewers, expands further and crosses borders. As this awareness campaign is the only initiative of its kind in the Arab world, the Ford Foundation sends a Moroccan representative to Cyprus in June 1998 to present it in a workshop on the role of the media in reproductive health.[11] The reach of Farida's play is now working in ever widening concentric circles beyond her first (synchronic) audience all the way to women in other developing Arab countries facing similar health problems.

That's when her talent as documentary filmmaker is called upon in a completely different area. In 1998, the National Office of Fishing in Morocco (ONP) asked her to make a 15-minute public film: *The*

Sardine of the year 2000 (Morocco and Japan), followed by a second short film to be presented at the 1998 Universal Exhibition in Lisbon: *Fishing in Morocco, between tradition and modernity* (15 minutes). Farida remembers how much she enjoyed going to see the fishermen early in the morning and how hard people worked in this sector. Once these commissioned films are finished, she can devote herself to her much more ambitious project: a second feature film, based on a tale her stepmother had told her when she was a child.

THE *HALQA* OF THE TALE ON THE SCREEN: *KEÏD ENSA/RUSES DE FEMMES/THE WILES OF WOMEN*

After having seen *A Door*, an enthusiastic Chinese delegation invites Farida not only to come and present her film in Beijing, but also to make a film in China. *I told them: "Listen, I don't know anything about Chinese culture!" And they answered: "Come up with a tale"*[12] She thinks: why not a tale? not in China but in Morocco and adapts the tale *Aïcha, the merchant's daughter* into the script of a light-hearted film about women's ability to resist patriarchy through cunning. *The ruse, in this case, is a dodge. It is a defense mechanism, a life reflex. And it is thanks to cunning that Moroccan women are not martyrs. They are alive, daring, courageous. You only have to look at them having tea in the afternoon, you can't say that they are unhappy! Their universe is rich, plentiful. It's a world that frightens men.*[13] She reconstructs the mechanisms of the cunning born of the fertile imagination of women in *Keïd Ensa*. She thus picks up the words of cloistered women narrators who exchange tales of defiant escape loaded with meaning. In *Dreams of Trespass/Rêves de femmes*, Fatema Mernissi describes how one of the women of the harem appropriates the meaning of Sheherazade's tale of the peacocks: "This story is not a bird story. It is our story too. To be alive is to move, to look for places that suit you, to roam the planet in search of more hospitable islands."[14] Yet, such stories ensure the survival of the women stuck in the harem, in the house of the father or husband. The tale is thus double-edged: while sharing the dream, it keeps the patriarchal order, since physical escape is never realized. Yet perhaps not in the one Farida chooses to stage.

Farida remembers her initial surprise when her mother-in-law told her the story: *I was pleasantly surprised that this exemplary, modest and rigorous woman told me the story of this young woman in love, who will use all her cunning, let's say all her intelligence, so that her prince, who is also in love, loves her for what she is and not for what he would like her to be. She will go so far as to undermine the man's virility, to humiliate him and convince him that his power and physical strength are no match for the cunning of women and the strength of their minds... I remember feeling that I was discovering a hidden side of this woman and of other women.*[15] Farida also pursues her work on Moroccan heritage: *By adapting this tale, I seek to preserve the memory, that of the world of women, inside the houses and on the terraces.*[16]

She is the writer, producer (with Tingitiana) and director of the adaptation of the Arab tale *Lalla Aïcha, the merchant's daughter*. This time, despite the generous support of the CCM (1.5 million dirhams), the budget available to her is far below the needs of the film.[17] She turns again to Hassan Daldoul. They knock on many doors.[18] The project, co-produced by Morocco (Tingitiana and the CCM), Tunisia (Touza Films with Hassan Daldoul), and Switzerland (Waka Films with Silvia Voser), obtains French funds (production aid from the CCN, Canal+, development aid from the Montpellier International Film Festival) and Swiss support (the Tanley Tho grant). She also remembers an episode of financial rescue in extremis as miraculous. *After four weeks of film shoot, I found myself with no money. There were two weeks of shooting left. I could not receive the third installment of the Moroccan Film Center's grant in time. I wrote a letter to Mr. Benjelloun of the BMCE, who was already a sponsor. I wrote him: 'Maybe I am crazy. I am asking you for 500.000 DH that I will pay back later. I have no guarantee, only my word and I hope you will trust me. I was on the set when I was called from a BMCE agency. And to my surprise, Mr. Benjelloun had called from the United States and granted me the loan.*[19]

Farida hires an experienced French director of photography, Serge Palatsi. The Tunisian team includes Faouzi Thabet again for the sound, editor Kahéna Attia, and the prodigious actress Fatma Ben Saïdane (to play the role of Mbarka, Aisha's servant). The Moroccan team includes the composer Mohamed Charraf, and two costume designers: Larbi Yacoubi and Farida's daughter, Ayda Diouri. Kenza joins the Tingitiana production, and little Abdelhaye plays a small role in the framing narrative of the film. Farida's half-brother, Mohamed Boukaa is co-director of the production with Abderrahim Bargach. Her husband Mehdi is the artistic advisor; the film is shot in the Menebhi palace, which becomes a magical setting for the occasion. Farida's friend, Fatema Loukili (the mother in *On the Terrace*) plays two small roles: that of the mother in the framing story and that of the slave the prince offers to his bookseller. Finally, the main actress (Aisha), is Samia Akariou, star of Tazi's film, *In Search of My Wife's Husband*. The role of the prince is entrusted to Rachid el Ouali. She also hires the grip of the CCM who has accompanied her since the beginning: Abdellah Bayahia, who shares pro tips with her. This is Farida's second time shooting in the desert (after *A Breach in the Wall*), which presents several challenges: *as soon as you take a step, it shows on the dune. How to erase all that? Bayahia showed me: he took a large cable, he at one end and another person at the other and they dragged it over the dune to smoothe it out.* Once the Moroccan-Tunisian family of the film is formed, they launch into a seven-week shoot all over Morocco: in Tangier, Chefchaouen, Ifrane, and Merzouga, in the Sahara. Farida remembers the trips as an adventure through four seasons! *We left at 8 am and went from Merzouga to Chaouen in the same day. It was extraordinary, because crossing Morocco, you crossed all the climatic zones. We were in the heat of the desert, then once up in the region of Ifrane, it was snowing! Then, near Chaouen, it was raining!*[20]

SYNOPSIS—A little girl argues with her recalcitrant brother. Their mother advises her not to respond to violence with violence, but to use cunning instead, as in the tale of *Aisha, the merchant's daughter*. She tells her the story that her mother had told her when she was her daughter's age.

Once upon a time, Aisha, the daughter of a widowed merchant, lived in a house next to the Sultan's palace. Every day, Aisha watered and pruned her basil and other plants on her terrace. Every day, the Sultan's son, from the top of his castle, would stare at her through a spyglass, his curiosity piqued. One morning, the prince asked: "Lalla Aisha, daughter of the merchant, you who look after the roses and the basil, tell me how many leaves are on their stems?" To which the lovely Aisha replied, "When you tell me, you, son of the Sultan, who have studied in the book of Allah, how many stars there are in the sky, how many fish in the sea, and how many dots in the Qur'ān." Thus begins a daily sequence of repartees between the two on either side of the parting wall. Each character plays a trick on the other (the prince disguises himself as a fish merchant and manages to kiss Aisha on the cheek; she disguises herself as a slave and manages to shave his beard while he sleeps) and the prince, who loses more often than he wins at this game, ends up asking her to marry him. Her merchant father, who has locked her up in his own house, protests against this union which will deprive him of his daughter. But she begs him to accept and reassures him by suggesting that a tunnel be dug between her father's house and the adjoining palace.

Instead of marrying her, the prince throws her into a dungeon inside the palace and asks her every day:

– Aisha the humiliated, who live in the cellar, tell me which is more powerful: the cunning of women or the cunning of men?
– The cunning of women, my lord! [*Keid ensa, moulay!*]
– Well, you'll stay here. I will come every day until you recognize that the cunning of men is more powerful.

Unbeknownst to the prince and the people of the palace, Aisha spends her life between her dungeon and her father's house, with Mbarka, her faithful servant. She escapes from the palace and pretends to be someone else during three trips taken by the prince. He never recognizes her, spends the night with her and each time, she becomes pregnant and gives birth to a child named after the place where they made love: two boys, Sour and Dour, and a girl, Hmamat Laksour, who are raised in the merchant's house. Finally, tired of her resistance and stubbornness, the prince tells her that he is about to marry the woman his father has chosen for him. She brings the three little ones to the palace. The long-awaited reconciliation follows—just like in Scheherazade's last night: liberation and the promise of love and happiness for the princely couple and their children. The wedding finally takes place. The conclusion, pronounced on the bed of the loving couple gives the last word to Aisha:

– Lalla Aïcha, we are in your hands. Which is more powerful, the cunning of men or of women?
– We are under God's command. He has given strength to men and cunning to women. It is up to us to use them wisely... With understanding, kindness and tenderness. And may God guide us!...

Related stories enrich the texture of the main narrative, such as that of the pious and learned old bookseller, Haj Tahar (Mohamed Zrine, who often appears in Farida's films), with whom the prince often discusses women's intelligence and who reminds him of the existence of learned women, scholars, who had power and glory in history. He tries to educate the prince and lends him a book by Jallalo Din Rûmi.[21] The all-powerful prince presents him with a beautiful slave (Fatema Loukili) that the very wise Haj Tahar and his wife, Lalla Zahra, take in and free, thus putting an end to her treatment as a woman-object of sexual and commercial transaction.[22] Or that of Bilal, a black slave of the prince in love with his cousin Mina, who has a golden voice. She sings Andalusian airs in the palace garden while he broods: "I could have been a prince. I am also the son of the Sultan." (The accident of birth that makes one a slaveand the other a prince within the same family is a theme that Farida will explore further in a TV movie a few years later.) Finally, the claustration of women by men is depicted twice: the jealous father forbids Aisha to go out into the street, even on the terrace in broad daylight, for fear that she will be seen; and the prince, who imprisons her until she yields to his will. When Mina, defying the ban, comes to see her at the entrance to the dungeon and implores her to say what the prince wants to hear, Aisha replies: "Anyway, we women spend our lives locked up" (even if she has found a way to leave her dungeon every day!).

Through her re-reading and rendition of the tale on screen, Farida continues to expose the condition of women. *They are the most fragile in society, the most exploited. Rights and power belong to men, and yet the Qurʾān gives women the same rights.* She also keeps on fashioning images of strong women who find ways to overcome male diktats, and to convince male characters—it is a fairy tale after all!—of their rightful place in society. Farida's camera is more than a working tool to narrate a fairy tale: it is also a machine that circumvents censorship *to pass on ideas of tolerance, to show the condition of women, to tell their struggles.*[23] If the heroine of the tale is careful not to challenge the social edifice of patriarchy through her wit, her intelligence, she nevertheless silences the powerful prince by her clever way of posing riddles that are impossible to solve. The gobsmacked prince literally remains silent. Similarly, at the end of the tale, he who gives orders and is obeyed, he whose word can make or break a life, becomes speechless, and leaves the last word to his young wife. Moreover, the film shows in sound and images a great freedom of expression for the women whom we see dancing, singing, playing the Arab lute.

The dialogue between Mina and her cousin the prince, early on in the film, reveals the cruelty of the misogynistic treatment of women. "They say the merchant does not want to let her go out. He taught her to read, write and even count, but what's the point? As the saying goes: 'Who has seen in the dark eyes adorned with kohl?'" she tells him, to which the one endowed with the gender of power responds: "Fortunately I was not born a woman!" Aisha is thus educated but imprisoned by her father, then by her husband; intelligent but reduced to an exercise in seduction by the prince. Farida takes great care to present the parallel enlightened words of the only male character inclined to consider women and men on an equal footing: Haj Tahar.

> Of course a woman has children, she has to raise them, take care of them. That doesn't leave her much time to do anything else. "Woman is good, and woman is evil." And God says, "Their cunning is great." Truly we must hope that God does not make them our enemies.

The same character frees the slave the prince gave him as a gift, because he does not want to displease his old companion, his gesture thus expressing his thoughts on both polygamy and slavery. The film constantly dodges. violence from its framing narrative to the framed tale of Aisha's resistance as she fights for her right to speak. She finds tricks to escape the prince's cruelty without ever, herself, inflicting violence on anyone. *It is in fact a film that assumes its title and values the intelligence of women. Because I can't stand the violence that is usually inflicted on them on screen,"* the director confided to Nesma Didi.[24] The film is itself a form of resistance to the miserabilist filmic portrayals of women and advocates the principles of non-violence dear to Farida.

Finally, the tale follows the structure and archetypes of folk tales identified by Vladimir Propp and Bruno Bettelheim: Aisha and the prince meet, are separated (by the prince's stubbornness and cruelty); they go through a number of ordeals and are then reunited at the end of the tale in a fairy tale happy ending.[25] As for Aisha, she can be seen as the archetypal figure of the adolescent girl who leaves the world of childhood under the jealous care of her father for the home she will share with her husband. The triggering element is the famous basil that she waters every day, of which she takes extreme care: a plant known for its medicinal virtues that calm the pain of menstruation, a plant symbolic of the young girl's passage from childhood to adolescence.

The female inspiration of the film appears in the opening credits: "I dedicate this film to my mother Fatimita Amor who introduced me to cinema at a very young age and to my father's wife Aisha Diouri who amazed the little girl I was when she told me the tale of 'Lalla Aisha, the merchant's daughter.'" Thus, after the father's film (*A Door*), here comes the mother's film, although maternal characters are remarkably absent from screen until Mina and Aisha give birth: Lalla Zahra has lost her daughter; Aisha has lost her mother; Mina's mother remains off-screen. Yet, the framing story of the film points to a mother narrating a tale to her daughter, a tale that young and old viewers will recognize.

The fairy tale known since childhood in Morocco attracts a varied audience in Morocco and elsewhere: *Grandmothers went to see the film (...) to see how a tale they told their children was translated into acts and images. It was an opportunity for them to remember this story, which they were told when they were very small.*[26] In France, when the film was shown at the media library in Villeneuve-les-Salines, the audience was also very female: "Moroccan women were there, alone or with their children. *Keid Ensa* a made them laugh, they applauded Farida's film and, at the end, most of them kissed the filmmaker, to say hello, thank you and good luck!"[27] Reviews are varied in Morocco. A few negative ones come from authors disappointed not to find the magic of their childhood tale that they expected in the film. "We feel there was an effort to match the tale in the clothes and the restitution of its fabulous settings. But the film in general failed to create that atmosphere of wonder and that magical universe that characterize all the tales of the world."[28] Others bemoan a "lack of dynamism" (sic!).[29] The vast majority of critics, however, in their complimentary articles note a freshness of tone as a welcome change from the neo-realist formatted cinema of the time. Rachid Temsarani points out: "It was time to get out of the usual straitjacket of societal dramas and beautiful love stories that always end well. This time, the spectator is invited to relive a story that he or she had imagined as a child." He also praises the "Moroccanness" of the film: "... a people without cinema is only a consumer of the imagination of others. Our country is full of imaginative and creative minds. Let's help them direct and flourish."[30] Another reviewer applauds the filmmaker's wily use of ellipses both to tell the tale in a linear fashion and to annihilate the power of the prince:

> She uses ellipses and thus offers a linear tale with a mixture of rusticity and sensitivity.
> The ellipsis does not only target the events to be filmed: it reaches further as pure eloquence by truncating the existence of the higher power. There is no king, no vizier, no political force in the fiction. The prince who calls the shots is left to his own device in favor of the cunning plotted by a weaker being who counts on her wits only and who will end up having the upper hand.[31]

The film toured the festivals in Morocco: the International Festival of Mediterranean Cinema in Tetouan, the Moroccan Film Festival in Laây-oune, the Festival of Rabat, and the Festival of Ifrane. It was awarded Best Film of the Year at the National Festival in 1999 and also received an award for the costumes. It was released in theaters in the kingdom and was a hit at the box office: over 500,000 entries, a record in Morocco at that time for a Moroccan film. Farida was delighted: her film even beat the big American blockbuster of the year in Morocco: *Titanic!*

Keid Ensa *did really well: people went to see it in the cinema. Besides, I had a very small budget and I had said to the actors: here, I pay you this much, but if it makes money, I'll double it. Since it did, I happily wrote them checks. They couldn't believe it! They said to me: "You know, we never believed these stories of yours! Nobody does that!" As a result, I gained a certain notoriety: people could work for me and trust me.*[32] The film toured in international festivals on at least three continents where it won awards.[33] A German company (covering Germany, Austria, and German-speaking Switzerland) distributed the film. "This is the first time that we have considered an Arab production, of the oriental type, and we have every reason to believe in the success of this work, which presents another dimension of human culture for film lovers in Germany."[34] The film stayed six weeks at Balazs (in central Berlin), with five screenings a day and was screened at two other Berlin cinemas for two weeks.

"People expect us to show Moroccan misery," says Farida Benlyazid, "I've often been asked whether I wanted to make a film about the role of women in Islam, for which there would be money right away. But I'm not interested," she says. She has apparently had great difficulty in finding funding for her films, despite the image of Morocco that she conveys in them, evocative of that of tourist guides, beautiful books and the *Arabian Nights*. "Who cares about our fairy tales?" was the response of several potential investors.[35]

If the comments of the distributor and the journalist give off an aroma of orientalism and elitism, the fact remains: Farida's cinema can be shown in Berlin, and thus stand up to the competition of films from all over the world. Here, therefore, Farida extends her audience from the women and former children of Morocco to a diverse audience all over the planet. As a Spanish journalist points out, her film is a bridge that spans vast differences: "A bridge between modernity and tradition, between freedom and repression, between equality and the visible preponderance of one sex over the other."[36]

Now, if building bridges from one gender to another, from one era to another is already complicated when addressing one's own community in Morocco, it might be even more challenging to reach an audience (cinephile or not) far from the cultural references of *Keïd Ensa*.

The *Tale of the Basil Girl*, which is part of the oral heritage shared by the Maghreb and Spain, had already fascinated Federico García Lorca, who adapted it for a puppet show, with music (by Albeniz, Debussy, Pedrell, Ravel) transposed and orchestrated by Manuel de Falla. The tableaux of Lorca's play also broke the fourth wall and invited the spectators to intervene in the play, in a Spanish version of the *halqa*.

But did Farida transpose this *halqa* structure on screen? How did the film transpose or recreate the sharing of the tale with its call-and-response structure as well as the "aesthetics" of the tale—or more precisely, its cross-cultural aesthetics? For the tale from oral literature is suddenly transformed into a cinematic text projected to a Moroccan audience seated in the front row that recognizes it on the screen and, in the following rows, a non-Moroccan audience. For the system of the cinematographic *halqa* to work, every viewer must be able to respond. In *A Door*, the filmic narrative, which showed a back-and-forth between a secular Western modernity and a Muslim spiritual culture, relied on cross-cultural off-screen references, such as the texts of Rimbaud and Ibn Arabi. Thus, from Nadia's bicultural point of view, the audience had access to the representation not only of her return of the soul but also of her plunge into the Moroccan cultural heritage (supported by the extraordinary architecture of the zaouiya). The references to European and Arabic literature, for example, provoked a feeling in the spectator oscillating between a cultural déjà vu and an initiation. This led to the visual and auditory representation of Nadia's transculturalism that engaged the audience through particular inclusive aesthetics playing with off-screen references. This form of viewer engagement demanded by the film mirrors Bill Ashcroft's transculturalpostcolonial one:

> In the transcultural text, an implicit and constant dialogue exists between producer and consumer in which the affective and sensual engagement of the artist and the affective and sensual engagement of artist and viewer

are mutually developed. In the cultural contact zone aesthetics can no longer be seen as a quality. It is a form of engagement, of act and response opening a space for continual transformation.[37]

In the case of *Keïd ensa*, the viewing experience unfolds in a multi- dimensional transcultural space that transitions from oral literature to film, from the world of women to the world of men, from the world of the sultan to the world of the slave, from past to present patriarchal power, from Northern to Southern Morocco, from the solo of a woman to the music of a group, from spoken Darija to French or English subtitles. In other words, a spectator only savors the film thanks to what Bill Ashcroft calls the "resonances" of the postcolonial text: she lets herself be carried away by everything in the cinematographic text that resonates with her, on an affective, even sensual level, without being short-circuited by the analysis (music, mise-en-scène, acting, humor, etc.). This way of savoring film for a spectator situated outside the intimacy of the first circle proceeds from a vision coming out of the sphere of the naive, again, in the sense of R' bati and Farida, the new storyteller on screen.

At the moment when the world is changing from one millennium to the next, Farida has found the balance that we are lucky enough to reach occasionally during a luminous time that lights up the rest of our lives. Everything smiles to her: Farida returns from her second pilgrimage to Mecca with a great inner peace: *There is a euphoria that takes you and that lasts two to three months after the pilgrimage. It is exhilarating and calm at the same time.*[38] Her spiritual life has fulfilled her, her film was a success, her emotional life is happy and confident.

Meanwhile, Mohamed VI ascends the throne after his father dies in 1999, raising a great wave of hope for social justice and freedom of expression. Civil society seems to be changing. Women have strengthened their associations and demonstrated in the streets of Casablanca and Rabat.

Farida the script writer is approached by Majid Rechich to adapt François Bonjean's novel *Confidences d'une fille de la nuit* (Confidence of a Night Girl) written from the point of view of the Muslim protagonist into a feature film, *Histoire d'une rose/The Story of a Rose* (1999).[39] She writes the screenplay but *Once the product was finished, he began to transform it, so much so that it became unrecognizable.*[40] This serious attack on the integrity of her work raises the question of gender again: would a director take such liberties with a male scriptwriter? It seems that, at least at the time, this type of behavior was reserved for a woman author, still considered a subordinate, despite her success as screenwriter and filmmaker.

Next, Moroccan channel 2M asks her to make two movies for TV: the first, *Nia Taghleb* (<Good faith wins>) is broadcast during Ramadan in 2000 and the second, *Boukma* in 2001. *Boukma is about God's creatures that are silent - essentially domestic animals that man must treat well,* Farida explains. Thus she opens up another circle to her *halqa* here: TV viewers. *Once, I was waiting at the airport and a customs officer stood in front of me and said, "I really like your films, Ms. Benlyazid. I saw Boukma on TV and I really liked it." I thought: what a strange idea, here is a small film that I made for TV which is nothing extraordinary, about animals, and I ask him: "Really? You liked that movie?" To which he replied, "You know, just because you're a cop doesn't mean you don't have a sensitive heart!"* Television makes her famous outside the circuits of film festivals, outside the intelligentsia of Morocco. Fame is both familiar and strange to her. *When I am recognized in the street in Tangier, I find it normal: I am from here, I've spent many years here. We know one another as Tangerines. But when it happens in the middle of the desert?!* [Immense astonishment on her face] *I imagine that it's because of television: there is no cinema in the desert!*[41]

She watched him go by when she was young: the most beautiful man in Tangier, she says, dreamily. Then she found him thirty years later. She is told: why marry a sick man (he is diabetic)? He is so moved by her, feels so close, and so admires her that he gets drunk to give himself the courage to propose to her. She says yes. When they get married, he predicts that they will probably only have one year together, that his bad health will speed up the hourglass, and that he cannot help it. She refuses: "No! Ten years!" Finally, they *split the difference...* They will know six years of a loving, splendid tangéroise intelligence shared by two refined beings. Mehdi dies in 2001. Farida will no longer pose for the portraits in pastel tones that he composed. Farida will no longer laugh with him at the caricatures he sketched. It is a period of intense mourning that she faces now, a throbbing pain, sharp as a blade, starting right before the shooting of her next film, *Casablanca, Casablanca*, dedicated to him.[42]

THE CITIZEN'S *HALQA*: *CASABLANCA, CASABLANCA*

Farida adapts the novel by Rida Lamrini, *Les Puissants de Casablanca*, a re-edition of a serial published in the pages of the daily newspaper *L'Économiste*.[43] This is her first adaptation of a text by an author other than herself.[44] The genre of the novel is hybrid: "Is it a detective novel? a political-economic-social pamphlet? or a testimony on the life of the Casablancais?" asks a critic, giving a glimpse of its content: "The same reflexes continue to gnaw at our society: clientelism, bribes, abuse of power, cheating. The innocent are brought to justice while the real culprits continue their illegal practices."[45] A change of register for Farida, who goes from the tale of the girl with her pot of basil to a political discourse and like Aminata Traoré speaks truth to power in terms of class. Lamrini's book gives Farida *the desire to speak out as a citizen. This film is a form of commitment. In 1996, at the time of the great clean up campaign, I was staying with my brother in Casablanca. Every day he told us about the misfortunes of his employees. The psychosis was spreading all around.* The Powerful of Casablanca *plunged me back into it.* This time, she defines her spectators' circle with a sharp political gaze.

This famous clean-up campaign, ostensibly aimed at fighting corruption in Morocco in the business and drug sectors (a number of drug barons in the north of the country were arrested) but also in the administration, has several facets. The campaign launched from the palace was the first necessary step toward a neo-liberal reform of the constitution in response to the wishes of the World Bank for democratization and business transparency. Morocco wanted to attract foreign investors and business partners from the European Union, the Mediterranean, and even the United States. To do so, it needed to bring its legislative and judicial systems in line with international standards and fight corruption. As soon as the free trade agreements with Europe were signed in 1995–1996, the kingdom started a 1996 clean-up campaign, which was widely reported in the country's press.[46]

Farida has a great admiration for the novelist Rida Lamrini, whose clear writing lends itself to adaptation, according to her, on the *one hand because it is presented in the form of a detective story, with all the ingredients of the genre (plot, suspense, denouement). On the other hand, for its visual dominance. Until now, the books that were submitted to me for a possible adaptation were too intimate, too meandering, and therefore difficult to put into images, except by distorting them excessively.*[47] To adapt the book, she enrolls the help of Ahmed Boulane: *I didn't want to betray the book... But it needed a special narrative flow and rhythm for the screen. I worked on the script for a long time, and then Ahmed Boulane helped me structure it. The film seems less melodramatic than the book... I wanted to develop the female characters - men rarely think of them - and to present them as active women.*[48] To use Truffaut's term, these are only the very first "correspondences" established by the filmmaker between the original novel, the composed screenplay, and its final version. These correspondences, which are never translations but re-creations, begin with the new title. For a while, she had thought of calling it "A Man Who Weeps." Finally, inspired by Martin Scorsese (*New York, New York,* 1977), she opted for *Casablanca, Casablanca,* which "corresponds" to the Arabic title of the film *Dar el Beïda ya Dar El Beïda/*"Casablanca, O Casablanca," *that is to say: 'he who goes there does not come back'. I didn't like this literal translation and I didn't like the title of Lamrini's novel either.*[49]

She takes up this new filmic challenge: to make a politically resonant crime film in contemporary Casablanca—a world away from the spirituality of *A Door* or the dreamlike space of *Keid Ensa.* Yet, in this film, we recognize her shots, her way (truly democratic!) of sharing the screen, and the word with men and women, of giving voice to the poor and of imaging the presence and practice of a Muslim faith.

SYNOPSIS—The plot brings together three investigations that place a series of characters in the crosshairs of the 1996 sanitation campaign: (1) Aisha, the eldest daughter of Ba Lahcen (Mohamed Zrane), a vegetable vendor on a sidewalk in Derb Talian,[50] disappears. Aisha worked for Amine (Younes Mégri), who recently returned from Canada with his family out of idealism and love for his country. (2) The body of Aisha's friend Lamia is found at the bottom of a well in the yard of a farm just sold by the powerful banker Yamani to another wealthy bourgeois outside the city. (3) Amine, a good father, good husband, good citizen, good Muslim, owns a company that imports Chinese tea and is accused of fraud (packages of tea mysteriously weigh more than what was declared at customs). It takes the entire film to unravel the ramifications of the system of corruption that infects the commercial, financial, and administrative world of the city before clearing his name and realizing that nothing changes.

So the story is about how the clean-up campaign fails to bring justice (the big banker and his son get off scot-free) and the police are powerless to fight an entire system. *This campaign has resulted in show trials and many slippages. Many innocent people paid for the guilty. But I believe that there can be no democracy without justice. Sound justice, human rights are themes that pop up in the conversations between the characters.*[51]

The film opens with shots of the garbage that litters the poor neighborhoods, and follows Jamal Yamani's sports car gliding through the streets of modern Casablanca, music blaring, but also sets up a vertical shot (often found in Farida's cinema) that rises from the crowded street by night or day to the minaret of the Hassan II mosque piercing through a roll of clouds over the city and settles there for a serene breath. The director thus visually reminds us not only of the faith of some of her protagonists but also of the forgotten religious side of Casablanca. *Casablanca is not only traditional, but not solely modern either. You can't talk about only one of these two aspects while avoiding the other... the way I see it, this city remains whole. These shots also allow the film to breathe,* she tells Roland Carrée.[52] More impressively, the film dialogue gives the female characters much more say than the novel did. Thus, in a scene where three couples of friends are breaking the fast (the plot takes place during Ramadan), the women become Farida's spokespersons in the film. The psychologist declares: "without justice, there can be no democracy, that much is clear!" while Amine's wife, Alya, who works in an association for the defense of the environment, declares: "Everything is connected: you can't have a civic sense if you don't have citizen's rights." Farida's political intervention does not stop there, as she slips in one or two other messages in her film. Her viewers are reminded of the role of women in the city, of the limited life choices the poor face daily, as her camera zooms in on the loose puzzle pieces of a megalopolis riddled with corruption without ever leaving Casablanca. Farida recalls feeling an urgency to make the film, to intervene with her camera, because Mohamed VI's reign has just started. *I thought that a little door was opening, and that we had to get in there. And it's true that they made things easier for me... Look, I was able to film inside a police station for three days! I went to the police department, they read the script and they agreed!*[53] She seizes the moment and goes for it.

Her film is a Moroccan-Swiss co-production, with her own production company Tingitiana), RTM and Waka Films (with Silvia Voser, as for *Keid Ensa*) and her younger brother Mohamed as executive producer. The CCM granted her a 2 million Dirham grant in 2000. Farida assembles a team with familiar faces and a few newcomers.[54] The crew is very united, welded around its director who directs her film while experiencing great suffering. "We were all always listening to her, we really wanted to support her" recalls Younes Mégri: "she was in the midst of mourning…".[55]

The film experienced a serious mishap at its premiere at the Marrakech International Film Festival, where the screening of an unsubtitled copy led Amine Rahmouni to write a particularly negative article to which Farida chose to respond with an open letter in *Le Journal* of February 8, 2003. Her film had been sent in a hurry to the festival because Nabyl Ayouch and Abderrahman Tazi had withdrawn their films from the program and the festival's director wanted a Moroccan presence on screen. *This may sound ridiculous, but I must admit that I am like a fireman, and I cannot refuse to help those in distress. After all, the CCM is our partner, and I participated in the preparation committee of the first Marrakech International Film Festival. … The preview of the only Moroccan film of the festival had not been carefully prepared. A leaflet at least could have been inserted in the catalogs, explaining that the two films announced had been withdrawn and attaching the technical data sheet of* Casablanca, Casablanca… *The audience could have been warned that the film was not subtitled… We must learn to think about promoting ourselves!* Farida puts her finger on one of the major handicaps of the Marrakech festival which struggled until very recently to include Moroccan production in its programming. Farida also describes the following scene that tends to happen in film festivals such as this one, where local spectators are sometimes turned away to let in foreign guests: *We feared the worst. A human tide broke through the doors and stormed the hall. My goodness, these are our viewers, and this was their festival too. Despite the terrible conditions, the audience stayed until the end and applauded. One Frenchman attended the screening sitting on a step of the staircase: M. Lemoine, the owner of the Megarama in Casablanca where the film is now in its third week.*[56]

The film remained on the Megarama screen for at least four weeks but was viewed nowhere else, partly because of another stance taken by Farida on the first day of its release that did not please. The Chamber of Producers to which she belonged, had sent a letter signed by all to the King. *It was certainly clumsy because it should have been sent to the minister. All the* [filmmaker-producers] *who wanted to see their film distributed, were told that they had to resign from the Chamber of Producers. Those who resigned were distributed, the others boycotted.*[57] Once again, she finds herself in the firing line of a whole arsenal of men and has to fight to have her film seen, does not let herself be easily impressed and insists on making things clear whenever she can.

When asked where she finds the strength to keep making film given all these obstacles thrown in her way, she evokes her grandmother's patience, her own total faith in the richness of the human being and her own journey toward wisdom. *I am not a Sufi. I am on the path. I don't consider myself to have arrived and the path is long: it can last a lifetime*, she says, before adding: *well, it does last a lifetime...*[58]

After having ventured from the North to the South of Morocco, filmed the mythical time of tales and the present of modern Casablanca, she begins a new circle in her upward spiral as a filmmaker: filming the memory of the Pearl of the North. She closes the loop of her great Moroccan *halqa* and it is in Tangier that she will shoot her next film. In 2002 Farida plunges into an ambitious fiction project about a protagonist in her own city.

NOTES

1. Amine, Khalid. "Theatre in Morocco and the postcolonial turn," *Textures*, September 21, 2009. http://www.textures-platform. com/?p=556.
2. A similar phenomenon occurs with West African griots, or, in music, a jazz or blues jam session in the United States.
3. *Souffles*, No. 2 (Rabat, 1966). «Débat sur le cinéma: pour un cinéma national»: 31.
4. Interview with Didi Nesma, "Quand Farida s'entête, le succès se pointe," *Citadines*, No. 40, April 1999: 38.
5. https://uil.unesco.org/fileadmin/multimedia/uil/confintea/ pdf/National_Reports/Africa/Africa/Morocco.pdf.
6. Figures from WHO and UNICEF in 2015. https://data.uni cef.org/topic/maternal-health/maternal-mortality/. As official as these numbers are, they are probably underestimates since they reflect only the reported number of women who died during pregnancy or childbirth (sometimes their deaths were attributed to other reasons).
7. Development agencies cite the quality of medical personnel; the absence of health centers in rural areas; the prohibitive cost of medicine and of transportation to the nearest hospital for the poor; the power of decision owned mainly by husbands and mothers-in-law; the systematic use of traditional medicine; and the belief shared

by all that pregnancy inevitably leads to complications (therefore ignoring medical issues that need to be treated urgently).

8. The international team worked with local partners to develop a two-phase campaign for safe pregnancy in Morocco to spread a clear message: giving birth should not kill women. The first phase targets the country's political and medical institutions (at the local, regional, and national levels) and seeks to raise awareness among decision-makers of the urgency of the situation by sending each official an 18-minute documentary, *Khlat Eddar* (<the house is now empty>) and a booklet on the causes of maternal mortality. The goal was to mobilize the resources needed to monitor pregnancies even in remote areas and to prioritize the care of pregnant women in the medical sector. The second phase has what the research team calls an *Enter-Educate* approach that educates while entertaining, with two projects: a short documentary drama, *Bent et-tajer* (<The Merchant's Daughter>), on the danger of not identifying the problems of pregnancy in time, and Farida's play.

9. See Hatem, Marie, Fatima Temmar and Biklis Vissandjée, "Childbirth and maternal mortality in Morocco: The role of midwives," in H. Selin, ed. *Childbirth across cultures, science across cultures.* The History of Non-Western SACH, Vol. 5, 2009 (195–203): 197. https://link.springer.com/chapter/10.1007/978-90-481-2599-9_17.

10. Box, Laura. "Women playwrights and performers respond to the project of development," in Salhi Kamal, ed. *African theatre for development: Art for self-determination.* Bristol: Intellect, 1998: 148.

11. See campaign report, pp. 5 and 17. Johns Hopkins University Center for Communication Programs (JHU/CCP). *Communicating safe mother-hood in Morocco—The family planning/maternal and child health phase V, project, final report.* Baltimore: JHU/CCP, March 2000.

12. Hamid Berrada, op. cit.

13. Farida quoted in Alami, Bouchra. «Farida Benlyazid sans malice» Télé Plus, No. 170, 24–30 October 1998: 11.

14. Mernissi, Fatema. Trad. Claudine Richetin, *Rêves de femmes: Contes d'enfance au harem (Dreams of trespass—Tales of a harem girlhood,*

1994). Paris: Albin Michel, 1996; Casablanca: Le Fennec, 1997: 258–259.

15. Alami, Bouchra. Op. cit.: 11.
16. Alami, Bouchra. Ibid.: 12.
17. Berrada, Ihlam: «Farida Benlyazid fait du militantisme ciné-matographique.» *Nouvelles du Nord*, April 24, 1998: 14.
18. *Mr. Othman Benjelloun, CEO of the BMCE, has been a great support as well as the RAM, the Banque Populaire foundation and many others ... We managed to get money through foreign sponsors, such as the ACCT and the grant for the development of the Montpellier festival. In addition, my Swiss co-producer obtained funds from several foundations in her country and Hassan Daldoul helped me by taking charge of the Tunisian team, which was essential during the shooting and editing. Thus, by scrounging left and right we reached a budget of five million dirhams. As you can see, it is expensive for a Moroccan film, but it is a film that could have cost twice as much, had I not had the support of the merchants of Tangier.* Nesma, Didi, op. cit.: 38 (my translation).
19. «La confiance Farida.» *Parade*, Vol. 58, No. 2, November 1999: 46.
20. Interview with the author, November 20, 2017.
21. Furthermore, the Sufi poet's acousmatic voice is heard during a night scene, after the prince has succumbed to the spell of a talented singer (Aisha), saying: "Woman is not an object of desire. She is the light of God."
22. "As far back as I can remember, some sell to me and others give to me," says the young woman.
23. Mouysset, Françoise. «L'Obstination de Farida,» *Sud-Ouest*, November 19, 1999.
24. Didi, Nesma, op. cit.: 38.
25. See Propp, Vladimir. Trans. Marguerite Derrida, Tzvetan Todorov and Claude Kahn. *Morphologie du conte* [1928]. Paris: Seuil, 1965.
26. Farida Benlyazid, quoted in «Fatima Benlyazid à l'affiche en Allemagne,» *Libération*, September 29, 1999.
27. Mouysset, Françoise, op. cit.
28. Amzelloug, Abderrahmane. «*Keid ensa* de Farida Benlyazid: juste un conte». *Le Matin du Sahara et du Maghreb*, March 22, 1999.
29. "The narrative of this film remains delightful even if Belyazid's camera is content with and persistent in placidly filming the scenes

without aesthetically elevating the pace in framing and movement…" Belcadi, Hassan. "*Keid Ensa*: un divertissement coquet et médodieux" *Libération*, Sat/Sun 15/16 May 999.

30. Temsarani, Rachid. «Silence! On tourne!» *Les Nouvelles du Nord*, April 24, 1998: 15.

31. SOF, Mohamed. «Il sort aujourd'hui en salles 'Kayd Ensa', pour l'amour des femmes.» *Al Bayane*, April 21, 1999.

32. Interview with the author, November 20, 2017.

33. In Germany, in the International Forum of New Cinema during the 49th edition of the Berlin Festival in February 1999, at the Mediterranean FilmFestival in Cologne, at the International Francophone Film Festival in Stuttgart; in Spain, in Cadiz in September, in Portugal in Troia, where Samia Akariou won the prize for the Best Female Hopeful; in Italy, at the Festival of African Cinema in Milan, where it won the prize of the Milanese public; in Switzerland, Tunisia, Lebanon, Austria, Egypt, in the United States, at the Women in Cinema Festival in Seattle in November 1999; in France, where it was screened in Cannes, Metz, Bastia, La Rochelle, Tourgoing, and where it was awarded a prize at the Journées du Cinéma Africain de Ferney-Voltaire (Ain) in 2000.

34. Torsten Frehsen, quoted in «Un conte accueilli avec les honneurs,» *Le Matin du Sahara et du Maghreb*, February 15, 1999.

35. "Von uns erwartet man, die marokkanische Misere darzustellen," sagt Farida Benlyazid. "Ich wurde oft gefragt, ob ich nicht einem Film über die Rolle der Frau in Islam drehen möchte, dafür gebe es sofort Geld. Sie habe grosse Schwierigkeiten gehabt, Geld für ihren Film aufzutreiben, und das, obwohl sie ein Marokkobild vermittelt, wie wir es aus Reiseführern, Bildbänden und aus 1001 Nacht Geschichten kennen: "Was interessieren uns Eure Märchen, war die Reaktion mehrerer Geldgeber," sagt sie (10). Gerlach, Julia. "Keine Lust auf Ethno-Filme: in Marokko entsteht ein Neues Kino," Freitag *Ost-West Wochen Zeitung*, July 30, 1999. I would like to thank Prof. Bruce Campbell for his valuable help in translating this excerpt.

36. "Para Farida, tangerina medio española, esta antigua leyenda de tradición oral constituye todo 'un puente.' Un puente entre modernidad y tradición, entre libertad y represión, entre igualdad y distinta preponderancia de un sexo respecto a otro." Calvo, Carmen. "Dos historias de mujeres llegan al festival gaditano:

'Pecata minuta' y 'Keïd ensa' fueron presentadas ante los medios," *Diario de Cádiz*, September 13, 1999.

37. Ashcroft, Bill. "Towards a postcolonial aesthetics," *Journal of Postcolonial Writing*, Vol. 51, No. 4, 2015: 417.

38. Interview with the author, February 2, 2016.

39. Bonjean, François. *Confidences d'une fille de la nuit*. Algiers: Éditions Baconnier, 1942.

40. I.M. «Entretien avec la cinéaste Farida Benlyazid.» Le film «*Casablanca, Casablanca* est une forme d'engagement.» *Le matin du Sahara et du Maghreb*, Wednesday, January 15, 2003: 6.

41. Interview with the author, May 1, 2016.

42. The credits mention: "In memory of Mehdi, Hicham, Julie and Sextoy."

43. Lamrini, Rida. *Les Puissants de Casablanca*. Rabat: Editions Marsam, 1999.

44. This first part of the trilogy *La Saga des Puissants de Casablanca* will be followed by *Rapaces* (2000) and Le *Temps des impunis* (2004). See Valerie Orlando's clear and contextualized account of Lamrini's work in *Francophone Voices of the "New" Morocco in Film and Print: (Re)presenting a Society in Transition*. New York: Palgrave Macmillan, 2009: 35–43.

45. Zaki, Rachid. «'Les Puissants de Casablanca' de Rida Lamrini. Les crimes sans châtiment.» *Reporter*. November 11–17, 1999.

46. See Catusse, Myriam. «Chapter IV. Un État de droit pour les affaires. Les enjeux de la normalisation,» in *Le Temps des entrepreneurs? Politique et transformations du capitalisme au Maroc*. Tunis, Institut de Recherche sur le Maghreb Contemporain, 2008: 163–190.

47. Et-Taïeb, Houdaïfa, op. cit.

48. I.M. op. cit.

49. Roland Carrée, op. cit.: 134.

50. Derb Talian is the former Italian neighborhood (Talian), with wide avenues lined with white art deco buildings from the 1920s and 1930s.

51. I.M. op. cit.

52. Ibid.

53. Interview with the author, November 20, 2017.

54. Ayda and Zohra Aïcha took care of the costumes, Faouzi Thabet was her faithful sound engineer, the photo was again entrusted to

Serge Palatsi. The cast includes actors from her other films, Rachid el Ouali, Mohamed Zrine, Fatema Loukili, Samia Akariou, and new ones like Moroccan star Amal Ayouch, the filmmaker Ahmed Boulane, and the actor and composer Younes Mégri.

55. Interview by Younes Mégri with the author, Tangier, March 12, 2018.
56. «Droit de réponse: Farida Benlyazid réagit». *Le Journal*, weekly magazine of February 8–14, 2003.
57. See Bahaa Trabelsi. «Farida Benlyazid: 'Dieu n'est pas dogme, Il estamour.'» *Masculin & Résolument marocain*, No. 7, March 2003: 104–106.
58. Interview with the author, March 24, 2018.

CHAPTER 5

Tangier and the World: *Juanita Narboni* (2005)

Abstract Two elements are crucial to contextualize Farida Benlyazid's creative output during this period: the digital disruption and the repercussions of 9.11.01 on the Arab world and on Morocco in particular. The chapter proceeds from the perspective of one year (2006) through three flashbacks: (a) the making of the film *La vida perra de Juanita Narboni* (2005), Farida's adaptation for the screen of Angel Vásquez's eponymous novel, set in her home-city, Tangier. The analysis includes large excerpts from an interview with her first assistant; (b) *The War on TV* (2006), a short made in collaboration with al Gandouzi and Mounir Abbar, in response to the bombardment of Lebanon; (c) Benlyazid's feminism expressed in both her article "Women's Cinema" (2006) and in her political activism to push for a true reform the Family Code or *mudawana* (2004). Benlyazid then returns to filmmaking: she focuses on the youth as she collaborates with Dominique Caubet on the documentary *Casanayda* (2007), on the music and arts festival L'Boulevard in Casablanca which promotes the use of Darija; and on the repercussions of *Family Secret* (2009).

Keywords Multicultural · Transnational · Spanish · Monologue · Language · Nostalgia · Inheritance · Makhzen · Jihadist · Filiation · Darija · Multiple cultures · Slave · Slavery · Tangier · Svetlana Boym · José Luis Alcaine · Lebanon · Israel · IMA

F. Martin, *Farida Benlyazid and Moroccan Cinema*, Palgrave Studies in Arab Cinema, https://doi.org/10.1007/978-3-031-40616-4_5

THE SHADOWS OF SEPTEMBER 11, 2001

The shock waves emanating from the attack on the Twin Towers on September 11, 2001 and the American military response in the Middle East extend to the far reaches of the globe. More and more deadly orthodoxies furiously spread during the first two decades of the millennium, supported by the juicy contracts of the arm industrial complex and by a systematic brainwashing orchestrated by gang leaders. The absurd has the upper hand: on the one hand, access to oil and economic neo-liberalism bog down soldiers and mercenaries in wars that kill civilians; on the other hand, a small group of "enlightened" people believe that committing suicide by killing infidels is an enviable gateway to heaven.

For the first time in the history of humanity, all this is relayed in real time by quasi-simultaneous images. The result is an unprecedented collapsing of space: we are in New York, Paris, Baghdad, Tangier, Jenin, Beirut, at least visually, at any time of the day or night. During this constant spectacle, distances seem to be both abolished and curiously reaffirmed by the political and economic powers fighting one another all over the world. Intellectuals try to step back and make sense of the images of the two towers of New York "collapsed in a cloud of unbreathable dust" that are replayed in a loop until the emotion is saturated on the small screens of the globe. Abdelwahab Meddeb questions these images and "scenes of jubilation in Palestine and Lebanon, also shown on television. These humanly pornographic and politically catastrophic images were later returned to their marginal truth." He then looks at the terrorists as the monstrous products of an unexplored field in need of close anthropological examination and ends up diagnosing the murderous madness of child-like adults as a nefarious side effect of the "disease of Islam ... still inconsolable of its destitution."[1] Jean Baudrillard deciphers September 11 as the first traumatic event inscribed both in the real (of tragedy) and in the virtual that launches a war led by the Bush administration. Jacques Derrida describes the horror that the event provokes in the face of genuine anguish, i.e., fear that cannot know its object. September 11, 2001 suddenly brings to the surface a diffuse, unknown, and unknowable anxiety worldwide. The "war" that will follow will also be played out on a terrain that is both real and virtual.[2]

The Arab countries of the Gulf, aware of the power of the image, panicked by the amalgams quickly concocted by non-Muslim viewers in the West, decide to respond to these images of horror with counter images of Arab protagonists. Having no film networks in place (there were no cinema theaters then in Saudi Arabia, for example), they create film festivals in Dubai in 2004, Abu Dhabi in 2007, and Doha in 2009, funded by the region's oil reserves, and competing with the traditional Cairo International Film Festival. The Gulf powers formulate a diplomatic retort to the images of "terrorist Arabs" shown on western screens and to the filmed beheadings relayed on the web by Al Qaeda operators. In a pan-Arab move, they also support the production and distribution of Arab film stories from the Maghreb to the Mashreq.[3] The new visibility of an Arab quasi-label of film on a global scale thus stems from a primary political urgency, in the face of the hypervisibility of a series of monstrous caricatures of Muslims. The call for film production in the Arab world responds to the need to produce one's own narrative: the lion rises to write its own story and throw away those of its hunters—whether hooded or not.

The nasty waves of September 11 also hit Morocco and its inhabitants hard. On May 16, 2003, five attacks committed by twelve suicide bombers (from the slum of Sidi Moumen) kill forty-five people in Casablanca. The reaction is immediate: the frightened American majors, whose filming schedule had been planned for a long time, no longer come to film in Ouarzazate; tourists shun Morocco. The government is quick to respond.[4] Yet, on March 11, 2004, incredulous Moroccan viewers discover the images of another carnage on the news, perpetrated by young Moroccan kamikazes in Madrid who kill nearly two hundred people and injure nearly fifteen hundred others.... The enemy is unknowable and yet intimate. He is a son, a cousin, a neighbor who has become a stranger. To try to understand how the young terrorists got there, Mahi Bine-Bine publishes the story of the 2003 suicide bombers in *Les Étoiles de Sidi Moumen/The Stars of Sidi Moumen* (2010). Nabil Ayouch adapts it for the screen in *Les Chevaux de Dieu/Horses of God* (2012).

In short, unless you are a hermit on a desert island, it is impossible to escape the daily spectacle of human violence and killing during this first decade: the digital revolution has enabled everyone to relay information very quickly with disconcerting dexterity. Terrorists and government channels use the power of the image and manipulate their audience, combining power and cruelty, access to weapons and hegemony. The ancient fears revived at the turn of the millennium were perhaps prophetic: the world seems to have traded its ethical compass for a perpetual screen of brutal close-up horrors.

In Tangier, Farida follows the violent news on television. In September 2001, stunned by what she sees on television, she sends an e-mail to the cultural service of the U.S. Embassy *to express my horror at what had happened, especially since I had been invited in April of the same year by the State Department to a very nice trip that had taken me to different states to participate in meetings on cinema and Islam.*[5] Dismayed, she observes the manifestations of an increasingly divisive, watertight communatarianism. She hardly recognizes the country she has filmed with passion nor the exhibitionist violence of some of its people. Two desires seem to animate her: that of reacting, of helping, and that of finding the open alleys of Tangier's multicultural past. In this tumultuous period, she refocuses on the city of her childhood, and reacts to the sad state of the world, pen and camera in hand. She carves her own soothing way through the ever-changing chaos of our planet. From these few years will come a feature film, *La vida perra de Juanita Narboni/The Wretched Life of Juanita Narboni* (2006, 101 minutes), a short film, *Une Guerre à la télé/A War on TV* (2006), a documentary, *Casanayda* (2007), and a fiction for television, *Secret de famille/Family Secret* (2008) as well as a variety of writing projects. Farida assumes her dual role as creator and intellectual (in Émile Zola's sense of the term: someone who intervenes in society to denounce injustice and publicly takes sides). She is carried into action by her organizing talent her work power, and her spiritual practice of listening with patience. She intervenes therefore in Tangier but also elsewhere. The filmic and intellectual spaces she occupies in that period unfold in several ways according to her reflection and her sometimes simultaneous interventions. This is why finding a path to her thought, her creation, her actions in that period must follow the apparent meanders of a non-linear time, as if her life was passing through a succession of leaps forward and backward, as in her film about Tangier.

2006: A Year of Contrasts

2006 is a year of ups and downs for Farida. Her film leaves her largely fatigued but is otherwise a solid success. Her first husband Moumen returns from his political exile in France to Morocco, which will make life easier for their daughters. But one day, Fatima, Farida's free-spirited and whimsical mother, her gourmet and fabulous cook mother from Melilla does not wake up from her nap after breakfast. Her incredulous husband calls Farida: "she is refusing to breathe". Farida loses her unpredictable, funny, nurturing mother who was so generous and tender and who had first taken her to the movies.

2006, the 50th anniversary of Morocco's independence, is the year when Israel attacks Lebanon, initially targeting Hezbollah in southern Lebanon, and increasing its attacks on bridges, ports, and infrastructure (including air traffic) to cut off the Beirut-Lebanon axis and isolate Beirut and the rest of the territory. Known in Lebanon as the "July war", it signals a new stage in the hardening of the Israeli–Arab conflicts.

Finally, it is also the year when Farida publishes her article «Le cinéma au féminin» (Women's cinema), an exposé of what being a Moroccan woman filmmaker means.

Each of these events appears as the denouement of a previous story that illuminates it retrospectively. To understand that year we must therefore proceed by flashbacks.

FLASHBACK 1: *LA VIDA PERRA DE JUANITA NARBONI* (2005)

The story of *La vida perra de Juanita Narboni/La Chienne de vie de Juanita Narboni/The Wretched Life of Juanita Narboni* takes place during the period of Tangier's international status. Farida had read Angel Vásquez's novel after its publication in 1976. *I met Angel Vásquez at the home of his friend Emilio Sanz de Soto, another Tangier native who had moved to Madrid. I was a student in Paris and Jillali and I went to spend a few days in Madrid. I really got along with them and Angel gave me his book, which I devoured on the Talgo* [train] *that was taking me back to Paris. Suddenly I was neither in Madrid nor in Paris but in Tangier* .... Having read it in one go, she was so taken by its language that she thought of translating the novel into French and went so far as to contact Flammarion to do[6] so, but the project was not to be. The book delighted her, as she later confided to Michel Amarger: *It reminded me of my childhood, the world of my very Spanish-speaking mother... That is perhaps where my nostalgia lies. I had an enchanted childhood.*[7] At the time she read the novel, she was focused on Moroccan cinema, on making films steeped in the cultural riches of the independent country. However, the novel is with her when she returns to Morocco, just like the Tangier of her childhood. *Until then I was very influenced by Moroccan culture, which I was afraid would disappear. But I am reassured, it is not about to disappear. So, I went looking for this multiple identity that seems so extremely interesting to me.*[8]

Years later, therefore, she wants to return to the truculent universe of the novel and its open city. The city of the Straits, at once Moroccan and Spanish, Muslim and Jewish, Christian and atheist, the city that spoke a multitude of languages, in other words, a cosmopolitan time–space that is the antithesis of a Morocco racked with intolerance and terrorism, the antithesis of the daily news on TV.

The novel, at first glance, seems difficult to adapt to the screen. A Spanish filmmaker had already tackled it: Javier Aguirre, in 1982, who had directed his wife Esperanza Roy in 1981 in an experimental film. The resulting *La vida perra by Juanita Narboni* is the first feature film by the avant-garde filmmaker and theorist of what he calls the "anti-cinema" (*anticine*). He puts language and Juanita's constant declamations in the limelight (Roy has a breathless 90-minute-long monologue!) interpreted with a mastery that will be rewarded with two prizes.[9] But Tangier is off screen—in fact, the film was shot in a Spanish provincial town. The Juanita of this film, like the ogress Aïcha Kandisha of the Maghrebian tales, engulfs the characters and the city in her dramatic soliloquy. One can understand the temptation of such a gesture once you have read Angel Vásquez's postmodern novel. But how refreshing and enjoyable it is to follow Juanita in the city of Farida's film!

Ángel (or Antonio) Vásquez Molina, a Spaniard born (in 1929) to "Mariquita the hatmaker" in Tangier, lived there until 1965, when he moved to Madrid. He lived there during the international years, the Second World War, before Morocco's passage to independence. Recognized since the publication of his first novel in Spain with the Planeta Prize (1962), he had nevertheless lived through all those years far from Franco's rule, in a friendly land, and in his novel he restores the image—or rather the soundtrack—of a place open to others.[10] The dedication of *La vida perra* reads: "In memory of my mother and her circle of friends, Jewish and Christian, whose language Juanita Narboni has appropriated, forcing me to write this book."[11] Juanita's language is as complex as the maze of the city. Made up of Spanish, *Hakitia*, snippets of creolized Arabic, French and Italian, it is lively, colorful, and disregards the grammar of its various linguistic components.[12] Selim Cherief describes with gusto the floating of gender in the nouns of the oral Hispanic language of Tangier of the international period. *El papel* (masculine in Tarifa) becomes *la papela del telefono* (the telephone book suddenly feminized) in the mouth of Juanita.[13] "Nor should we be surprised," writes Selim Cherief, "to see Jerusalem artichokes replaced by *petinamba* or, in *Hakitia*, the Arabic word *foul* ('beans') changed into *fororo*." Not to mention "redundancy by doubling a word with its version in another language, literal translation and the invasion of one language by another (or several) were common tics of expression that are found in *La Vida perra de Juanita Narboni*."[14] Vásquez restores the variants of a Tangerine language that is, however, in decline. So much so that the pleonasms and the breathless rhythm of the very talkative Juanita are almost a written archive of Tangier's lingua franca of the past. But that's not all: "These competing and complementary registers do not exclude a specific slang, rare uses and a private lexicon, sometimes a source of hilarious comedy and unexpected wordplay."[15]

Moreover, the novel, a long monologue teeming with details of Juanita's daily life and reflections, is striking for its daring mix of analepsis and repetition. Faced with the numerous ellipses, one barely glimpses what is happening in the background. The Spanish Civil War, the Second World War, Morocco's accession to independence, and even crucial elements of the protagonist's life remain blurred, relegated to a foggy off-screen. The reader knows, for example, that Juanita has lost her parents, but she only mentions her father's death for the first time late in the novel (p. 188), when she is told to renew her parents' plot in the cemetery, due to expire a month later.

In this novel, Juanita, a film buff, constantly stages herself in the light of the stars of the time. In a fascinating doubling of the self, she projects her life onto an inner screen woven with references to the films she saw in the blessed movie-going days of her youth. The novel is full of references to cinema that spice up the most trivial scenes—one of taking a sleeping pill, for example, becomes comic-tragic: "I open my eyes: it is Monday. This Bellergal made me sleep well. It is with Lumina that Ana Maria Custodio tries to commit suicide in 'Hija de Juan Simon'" (184). Her sudden inability to remember a scene accurately reminds her of the cinematic illusion: "Images, they are only images in the shadows, as on a screen in the half-light of a cinema" (166). Not at all afraid of contradictions, Juanita also finally sees that reality exceeds fiction: "These films that I invent for myself, I'm going to put them in my pocket, with my handkerchief over them.... Reality exceeds celluloid" (253). No wonder Farida finds such pleasure in the pulp of the novel's language, in its evocative account of the city of her childhood and of cinema in the madness of a woman trapped in her memories! The heady scent of nostalgia for a lost place that emerges echoes memories of Farida's childhood neighborhood, as Juanita formulates it:

> ... God gave us birth in a city where we are not quite Christian, nor quite Jewish, nor quite Muslim. The wind decides for us. We are a mix. We had Jewish friends who prayed to St. Anthony to send them a fiancé, Muslim friends who told us about Miriam - the Virgin Mary - and the Archangel Gabriel, and Christian women, my dear, who invoked Aisha Kandisha in the hope of seeing their husbands die. So don't lecture me! (335)

How to film the "neither quite this nor that" quality of its tone? How to adapt to the screen the unique creole language of Tangier? A story of a woman in-between-multiple (hi)stories? A story that indifferently glides from the ogress of the Maghrebian tales to the Catholic Saint who finds what you have misplaced for you? How to restore the crazy verve of Juanita, exiled in her own city? *The work of Àngel Vasquez is difficult because it is multicultural,* Farida wrote in an article published in 2007. *You have to know the different cultures that traverse the work to appreciate all the facets of Juanita Narboni, splashed by all these cultures as by the waves of the seas that surround her. It is quite a unique work, a harbinger of a multicultural world.*[16] Only Farida the Tangerine would be able to undertake such a colossal and nuanced project.

She calls on the Spanish screenwriter Gerardo Bellod to collaborate on the script. Given the texture and structure of Vasquez's novel, their task is to reproduce its arc, to adapt its many ellipses, backward steps and forward leaps, in order to create an architecture that lends itself to cinematic narrative. Both are in love with the novel and do not want to flatten the thought, the voice, the vivid colors of the past that it resurrects. They take the original text as humus from which a new, intimately related text grows, that splits the original text and exceeds it at the same time, thanks to an ingenious system of equivalences at the semiotic level.[17] Farida and Geraldo rewrite the script several times over a period of four years before arriving at a satisfactory version. *We worked a lot on the script. He designed a very good structure that I took over and I introduced the voice-over. This constantly present voice is a challenge. We had to find her monologue voice, to express what was in her head.*[18] The construction of the novel is not linear—the present, the past, and the future in the past constantly collide—so setting up the skeleton of the filmic narrative is difficult, as the editing will be.

This time, Farida enters a system of Moroccan-Spanish co-production, facilitated by Medea (an exchange program between the northern and southern shores of the Mediterranean) as well as an agreement with the Spanish television channel Canal Sur, the Moroccan television channel 2M, the Consejeria de Cultura de Junta de Andalucía, and the CCM. The total budget is 1.3 million euros. The production is twofold: Farida's Tingitania with her daughter Kenza as producer, and ZAP Producciones (a Sevillian production company) with Mar Villaespesa at its head. The technical team will also be 50% Spanish and 50% Moroccan, as well as the artistic team, with the exception of the composer Jorge Arriagada, Chilean, known for his film music (in particular Raúl Ruiz's films).

Farida composes a Tangier-related family to make this film: a clan of friends of Vásquez, Juanita, and their city. The cinematographer, José Luis Alcaine, born in Tangier in 1938 and nostalgic for his city repeats "I am one of those who love Juanita Narboni," while Concha Cuentos (Bella), who had been living in Tangier at the time of the film for a dozen years, "and Paco Algora (Dede Tribly, the last survivor that meets Miss Narboni) were 'also in love' with the city of the Strait."[19] Fayçal Al Gandouzi, a native of Tangier, who at the time was studying film in Madrid, remembers more than ten years later coming to the shoot with emotion and laughter. "When she told me: 'I'm taking you on as an assistant director intern' I was dazzled! Dazzled without knowing the work that awaited me!" And the work is immense...

Immense for a thousand reasons other than those perceived by the then apprentice filmmaker: how, for example, to compose an image of Tangier and its changes between 1940 and 1970 without shooting a history lesson but respecting certain realistic details? Farida documents the city but does not want to make a simulacrum of her former city. *We didn't have a lot of money so we couldn't really do big reconstructions. And when I looked at pictures of Tangier, it always looked so decrepit. I've never seen a picture of Tangier looking brand new and beautiful. My Spanish producer told me that this had to do with the cities by the sea. Cadiz is the same. ... and then I didn't want to do a magnificent reconstruction because it's not true. Tangier remains a very megalomaniac small city, a kind of parody of life that is not real life. It is amusing.*[20] But still, the film needed characters in places of the time, driving in cars of the period, in other words models of the 1940s, 50s, 60s, 70s ... Fayçal Al Gandouzi, who knows his city well, remembers helping the production:

The production had found all the cars in Casablanca but the price was exorbitant. The first assistant then asked me to search all over Tangier to see if I could find any old cars that worked or that could be repaired with little money. A friend of mine introduced me to a very unusual mechanic who didn't want to know anything about the world unless it had to do with a film shoot. He only understood cinema, but he also knew where all the old cars were in the garages of Tangier. We went all over town looking for people who had old cars. We needed about forty of them. I ended up getting thirty-eight! And the difference in price between the cars in Casa and Tangier was such that the production expected to pay 5,000 MAD per car per day - and for a luxury car like the one in the scene in the cemetery, around 10,000 or 15,000 MAD per day! I found cars from all eras - I even went to Ceuta - at 1,000, 1,200 MAD per day, sometimes 1,500. This obviously had nothing to do with my assistant directing job, it was for the production, but well... That's how it was.[21]

The film shoot also takes place in well-known locations in Tangier (the entrance and gardens of the Rembrandt Hotel, the gardens of the Minzah Hotel, the Catholic cemetery of Boubana, the beach of Tangier), and even in the homes of friends—a scene will be shot in the garden of Elena Prentice's villa, for example, in the Old Mountain neighborhood. Fayçal Al Gandouzi's experience also shows the artisanal dimension of the film shoot. His job was to make sure that everything was in order an hour before everyone else. The actors had to be at the ready on time, the cars, the sets, and the equipment in place, before each shooting session. "We laughed a lot during this shoot!" Even—perhaps especially—in the cemetery scene, in which a woman was supposed to walk by, played by Maggie Deane. But Maggie had partied late the night before the shoot and, wanting to do the right thing, had gone straight to the cemetery at dawn, without returning home. They looked for her everywhere without finding her... until someone finally spotted her, lying on a grave in the middle of her beauty sleep!

The fact that the film was scheduled to be shot from August 23 to October 2 also had other consequences, some of them funny, such as the story of the casting director who was concerned about the... goats featured in the film! "They have a fever! Do I get them off the hill or not? They tell me that if they go down, they won't be able to come back up. But they are in the sun, what are we going to do? And I said to myself: what do you want me to do?" Summer, in addition to the heat that was detrimental to the health of the goats, also meant the return of emigrant vacationers on the beaches and in the cafes of the city. How to film and duck the last wave of *chez-nous-là-bas* still invading the scenery at the end of summer?

> It lacked silence. There is an aural silence and there is also a visual silence. The great abyss is the latter. That is to say, all of a sudden, this was a time when this silence no longer existed. It is a silence perceived in the sounds, the horns, the construction sites, but also in connection with the buildings, with the construction overload. We had to evoke something much barer, a Tangier that was still being built, so to speak.[22]

It was all the more important to know how to restore what Fayçal calls the "visual silence" of the Tangier of yesteryear, since the city is constructed as a character in the film. As the Spanish critic Javier Valenzuela noted:

> The film will be the story of a Spanish woman, Juanita Narboni, told by a Spanish homosexual, Angel Vásquez, and shot by a Moroccan woman, Farida Benlyazid. All three have Tangier in common, as if, as the filmmaker says, the film could also begin with "once upon a time there was a city where all religions and races lived together."[23]

In order to evoke the authentic Tangier of yesteryear shared by this transnational trio, the film needed a gifted cinematographer and a director familiar with the interstices of the city of the Strait. Fayçal Al Gandouzi describes the two creators, José Luis Alcaine and Farida, as "parents of the shoot," in constant dialogue during these few weeks in Tangier.

The Spanish and Moroccan co-production is not always easy, however: money creates divisions, clashes, discussions during which harsh words are exchanged and at the end of which conflicts sometimes seem inextricable. What an immense challenge to bring together two production companies from two different cultures, speaking different languages! The Tangerine (like Fayçal and Farida) have an advantage over their Spanish partners: they are used to navigating along multiculturalcurrents and know how to make connections, while seeing things differently, but their Spanish partners have no such experience. It takes a lot of patience and stamina on both sides to keep the delicate balance between the production companies during the 6-week shoot then post-production. The narrow window of the shoot also requires an extraordinarily precise preparation to avoid all missteps and disasters. The difference in the conception of cinema between the Moroccan and Spanish teams lead to disagreements and huge misunderstandings related to money. For instance, a producer from Seville grafted onto the project has demands that Farida does not expect: she orders 30,000 meters of film to be paid for when Farida has expressly asked for only 20,000 (and will, in the end, only use 17,500); and Farida does not understand. When she is told "but that's how film industry works," she replies: *no, we cannot work like 'the film industry', we work on 'artisanal cinema' and I can't pay!* Their decidedly divergent view of cinema is eventually compounded by a touch of dishonesty on the part of the Spanish co-producing team, illustrating the insurmountable difficulties that a translocal co-production (here: Seville—Tangier) sometimes generates, which allows the making of a film but weighs heavily on a director (even if Farida already has a solid experience of transnational co-production). This distressing story is beyond the scope of the film, however, and is the only shadow in the picture—but a very long shadow, since Farida the first woman producer in Morocco, traumatized, decides thereafter that she will never (co)produce her own films again. *After this film, I was nauseated. I couldn't watch a movie anymore. That's why I want someone to do the production part if I make a movie. I can't do both.*[24]

The cast is international: to play the role of Elena, Farida invites Lou Doillon (who has the advantage of being fluent in French and English).[25] For the role of Amrouche, Farida hires Salima Benmoumen (*Casablanca, Casablanca*, 2002). For the lead role, after having approached Victoria Abril, she selects Mariola Fuentes, known for her roles in Almodovar's films (*Carne Trémula/In the flesh*, 1997; *Hable con ella/Speak with her*, 2002) and comedies by Miguel Albaladejo. Once again, Farida immediately recognizes in her chosen actress the incarnation of her protagonist. *It's Juanita. She has the same slender legs as Miss Narboni, the main character of the novel, admits to having!* she declares to Joaquim Mayodormo.[26] This physical detail is not insignificant: it is her legs, precisely, that support the impeccable physical play of the actress in her way of representing the entire arc of a life: we see the character walking the streets of the Kasbah with a determined gait; we see her sketch a few steps of a nostalgic dance under the temporary euphoria of alcohol; we follow her more hesitant, heavier step, toward the end of the narrative. The actress's performance is brilliant: she delivers Juanita's endless ratiocinations with the right linguistic accent and tone in which dull frustration and explosive anger alternate, as well as a rich range of emotions from regret to constantly repressed desire and from shared friendship to the most brutal envy. The character of Juanita is extraordinarily complex.

SYNOPSIS—We follow the constant monologue of Juanita Narboni throughout her solitary life in Tangier, during which nothing happens to her... nothing! The time-line of the filmic narrative stretches from the interwar period to the early 1970s, in three acts dated on screen.

- Act I (Tangier 1938): the youth in Tangier of Juanita, daughter of an austere Spaniard mother and a bon vivant English father from Gibraltar. She comments on every event in her life in a colourful language punctuated by often hilarious hyperbolic expressions. She goes to the ball, lets no boy approach her and is jealous of her sister, Elena, who is more "modern" than her. In 1939, she loses her mother and finds herself de facto housewife while her father works at the British consulate and goes out a lot.
- Act II (June 14, 1940): the entry of Franco's troops in Tangierchanges the situation according to the father; Elena leaves with a lover for Casablanca and never returns (nor sends any news of her whereabouts). Juanita's father dies, as we learn during a visit to the Boubana cemetery where Juanita and her maid, Amrouche, come to clean and put flowers on the twin graves. Juanita often comes to share the latest tidbits of Tangier gossip with her (buried) mother. We see Juanita's friends, the closest of whom is Esther.
- Act III (1965): Esther leaves the country. After having seen the city of her childhood disintegrate with the departure or death of others, Juanita, alone and aging, sinks deeper and deeper into the fog of alcohol. At a chance meeting, she reconnects with Dédé Tribly but he is murdered shortly thereafter. Amrouche disappears and Juanita realizes that she knows almost nothing about her, despite their forty years together. In the 1970s, Juanita wanders through the streets of her city, which she no longer recognizes.

In the first two acts, the chronology mixes the time of the story with older memories, as in Vásquez' novel. Thus, Juanita's stream of consciousness moves from one era to another without warning. The film then makes visual transitions that indicate the passage of time, with the vintage cars, fashion, the presence or absence of certain characters (the mother, the father, Elena, Amrouche). Any past or contemporary event is related with theatricality. In the third act, Tangier has become an empty shell for the protagonist, haunted by the less and less tangible presence of the ghosts from an increasingly distant past.

The film thus proposes the pictorial representation of nostalgia from an individual point of view (that of the protagonist who speaks non-stop) and from a collective point of view (that of Tangier), the latter being the one that Farida insists on more than Vásquez. Nostalgia (from the Greek *nostos*, the house, the home, the familiar, and *algia*, pain, suffering) was first an illness, as Svetlana Boym reminds us in her seminal essay, before becoming an emotion that is increasingly common in modernity.[27] Juanita performs her memories of past Tangier and laments her crumbling past, as if her development and consciousness had freeze-framed around the event of her mother's death. She seeks to resurrect the moments of a Tangier forever lost in what Svetlana Boym calls "reflexive nostalgia." She holds on and replays the episodes of her past, tirelessly, in a loop on her inner screen. Her compulsive reruns lead her to a pathological and dangerous nostalgia that arrests her development. She doesn't grow up, continues to confide in her dead mother, and persists in longing for every past moment belonging to the Tangier of "before." But that Tangier is hers alone. The memory of the city, revived by her soliloquy, belongs to her, her family, her friends, her church with its pretty priest, the films she has seen, but clearly not to Amrouche, her Moroccan maid, for example. Juanita's nostalgia is reflexive in that it focuses on describing the pain that comes with the (reiterated) realization of what no longer exists. Nostalgia usually arises after a break in time and space—it is the song of Ulysses who longs for Ithaca throughout his journey home. But Juanita has never left the city of the Strait! The protagonist's languid retrospective glance toward her past resembles that of Lott's anonymous wife in the Bible when she looks back to contemplate the ruins of Sodom and Gomorrah, in spite of the divine prohibition, and immediately turns into a statue. Juanita does not turn to stone, but she becomes stuck in the persona of a cantankerous old woman who stubbornly rambles and stammers about her past, unable to move on. "Nostalgia, like progress, depends entirely on the modern notion of unrepeatable and irreversible time."[28] Ironically, Juanita the nostalgic, does not hold still. She walks in the streets, forever on the go, spies on people, and resists the passage of time in her constant whirlwind of words and cantankerous recriminations.

Once on screen, Juanita's nostalgia acquires another dimension, however, as filmed and filtered by the director. Farida brings in the other

side of nostalgia, a collective nostalgia for international Tangier, by recre-
ating its spirit and some of its characters in her film. This "restorative"
nostalgia as Svetlana Boyn would call it, makes it possible to honor the
past and to soothe the pain that comes with the feeling by staging all
sorts of elements in order not to reconstitute a historical international
Tangier, but an identifiable international Tangier nonetheless. She recre-
ates its languages, its accents, its music, its landmarks (Madame Porte's
pastry shop, the Fuentes Café, the Café de Paris), its modes of dress,
the films that were shown there, the different characters that walked the
steep streets of its Kasbah and the wide avenues of its European quarter.
And then, of course, the film is structured, as we saw above, along the
temporal axis of history: the interwar period, the occupation of the city by
Franco's troops, the independence of Morocco in 1956, the end of Tangier'sinternational status and the departure of Morocco's Jews for Israel,
Europe, or the New World (including Juanita's close friend Esther, who
joins family members in Canada) in 1965. The temporal division is under-
lined by the changes in Juanita's dress, her hairstyle, the acid comments
she makes about the long-haired men of the 1970s, her own hair turning
grey, her pace slowing down.

   The Tangier of the film is not a city set in the sepia toned palette of
memory: on the contrary, it is a city that moves with the years, lively and
warm in Alcaine's photography.[29] Farida directs a haptic film here, calling
for the intervention of the other senses besides the primary two (sight and
hearing). It is the scents, the tastes of the food prepared, the caress of the
sea wind, and the slap of the chergui (the east wind) that Farida films
as closely as possible to restore not the city but its affects. For instance,
during the scene of Juanita's lunch with her father in the gardens of the
Rembrandt Hotel, Juanita, who is afraid of spending money, orders an
omelet while her gourmet father asks for prawns as an appetizer, then
a fish-dish and a chilled white wine. The camera lingers on the dishes
served, the wine glistening in the glasses, as well as the drunken exas-
peration with which Juanita swallows her omelet and the quiet pleasure
with which her father shells his prawns. In the same way, in the ball scene
where we see Driss (Muslim) invite Esther (Jewish) to dance, a close-up
shows the discreet gestures of infinite tenderness shared by the clandestine lovers. Farida chooses scenes in the novel that appeal most to an array
of senses: in a nightmarish scene after her mother's death, while Juanita
is rummaging through her mother's closet, two black evening gloves fall
around Juanita's neck, and she thinks her (dead) mother is strangling her

(close-up of her face and neck under the grip of the gloves): "I'm still a virgin, I'm untouched. Don't strangle me, Mom!"; or again, much later in the film, in an apparent delirium tremens crisis, Juanita feels something going up her legs and communicates her terror to us. The soundtrack, too, restores the auditory diversity of international and then Moroccan Tangier: Spanish, French, and English songs from the various eras of Tangier follow one another, as well as traditional Moroccan music (in the scene of Driss's daughter's wedding reception) performed by the Andalusian orchestra of Haj Abdelkrim Raiss from Tangier, while non-diegetic music (by Jorge Arriagada) bathes the film in a melancholic atmosphere that reflects Juanita's solitude.

The fictional film also evokes, in passing, actual personages of Tangier. Farida readily recounts that she knew Paul Bowles, was friends with Mohamed Choukri, that the people of Tangier saw Burroughs and Beckett pass by, that she once even met Jean Genet on the train... These individuals were part of the Tangier landscape at the time of its international status. In the film, we see the silhouettes of Bowles and Mrabet pass by, while the characters also evoke female figures such as the pious Englishwoman Emilie Keene, a convert to Islam and the first European cherifa of a Sufi zawiya at the turn of the twentieth century[30] or the wealthy American Barbara Hutton who gave extraordinary parties in her palace Dar Sidi Hosni in Tangier in the 1940s.

Finally, there is an aspect of the film that is both part of the nostalgic evocation of the Pearl of the North and a certain meta-cinema that is not without irony: Farida evokes the cinema of the time which Juanita delights in quoting. The scenario of the film remains faithful to the novel in which Juanita often interprets the events of her life through the medium of cinema. Thus, the departure of her sister: "For me, it's as if she were dead, and I often wonder if she wasn't taken to Tiznit or Tafraout, to the legionnaires, as in *Under Two Flags* !" (163) Or again, inveighing against herself: "My dear, I'm sorry to tell you this, but your imagination is a real disease. The alleys! There you are, right in the middle! (...) You could already see yourself in the heart of the Casbah, like in *Pépé le Moko*" (218).

In the film, Juanita says: "I am Andalusian, serious, I am not modern. Sometimes I think cinema has hurt me. When you sit in the cinema, everything seems possible." When she and Dédé Trilby, both fans of old films, meet again after years of not seeing each other, he shows her his late mother's costume, a dress copied from the one Raquel Meller wore in *The Imperial Violets.*[31] He even gives it to Juanita after hearing her sing the film's tune, "*Doña Mariquita de mi corazon.*" Juanita then exclaims, "movies are not what they used to be!".

Juanita doesn't just quote films at every turn to comment or even understand what is happening to her—or, more exactly, what is not happening to her. She puts herself on stage, in front of her mirror which becomes the surface on which to screen her next scene. Farida films her face in close-up as she puts on lipstick, runs her fingers through her hair to make sure her hair is perfect and declares: "Impossible to improve on perfection! It's good, Juani! Go for it!" Later, when she notices the departure of her sister by entering her room where the bed has not been slept in and the closet is empty, she looks at herself in the mirror and rehearses her role before sharing the news with Amrouche. She perfects her gestures, her asides, her declamation of the news. "This is your best scene, Juani. Dignity!" She turns around with panache and shouts, "She's gone...." The camera then zooms in on Juanita's two faces: that of the actress/director of the (constant) narrative of her own life and that of the (admiring) spectator in the mirror. This double shot of the protagonist, visible through the mirror, which, as is often the case in cinema, high-lights the duality of the character, recurs several times in the film. Here, Juanita seems to address Amrouche, who speaks rudimentary Spanish, listens to her or doesn't, and occasionally laughs and dances with her. Or she seems to be addressing her mother during her visits to Boubana. One day, for example, she confides to her mother, "I've always wanted to be alone, but wanting it is one thing and living it is another." Throughout the film, it is mostly to herself that the narcissistic character confides her real or imaginary setbacks according to a script that she alone composes, day after day. The film exceeds the novel in that it mischievously frames Juanita in close-ups, thereby granting her character her dearest wish: to become a movie star! She occupies the screen constantly throughout the film that retraces most of her life: we constantly see her. We constantly hear her!

Finally, Farida's nostalgia also has to do with her mother and the multicultural and multi-faith period in Tangier: ... *it reminded me of my childhood, of my mother's very Hispanic world. She used to sing Carlos Gardel... Maybe that's where the nostalgia lies. I had an enchanted child-hood. It was a party all the time.*[32] She could have made Vásquez's dedication of his novel her own. Juanita, in the ball scene at the very beginning of the film, explains to her date that her father is English, her mother Spanish, and declares, "I am Juanita from Tangier." Given her parents, Farida could state her identity in a similar way. Farida can't resist putting into Juanita's mouth a variation of a phrase from her own mother, Fatimita. "*Dios es bueno*. God is good and the rest are tales," whether they be the "tales of the Moors" that Fatimita spoke of or the Holy Trinity of the very Catholic Juanita. However, one character remains apart: Amrouche. Juanita's maid only has a narrow subordinate role in the novel. In the film (as in the novel), Juanita never asks her about the life she might have outside her own home. Thus, when she doesn't come to work for several days in a row, Juanita, worried, ventures into a neighborhood where she has clearly never set foot and realizes that she doesn't know her address or her last name, and that she has forgotten the names of her two sons who have gone to Germany. "They all die in silence" is her only racist *miserere* for the loyal servant who has been at her side all these years. Véronique Bonnet describes the difference between Amrouche's literary character and her incarnation in Farida's film in terms of speech: "the director grants her a language, both verbal and corporeal, of which she had been robbed."[33] Instead of her speech being "swallowed up" in the monologue of Juanita who speaks for others in the novel, it resonates in the first person on screen. The rare scenes where both women dialogue or dance are located on the terrace of the house, that in-between space, that "neither quite" outside—"nor quite" inside, the space of women that differs from yet adjoins that of segregation, whether of gender or class. By recomposing the character of Amrouche, her voice and the place from which she responds to Juanita Farida gives her a dynamic presence that she did not have in the novel and denounces the dialectic of master and slave that was rampant in the former Tangier.

At the end of the film, the voice of international Tangier disappears while the postcolonial Arab voice takes over. The story highlights the transformations of language that come with decolonization. The film contrasts a woman who refuses change and ends up dying alone with a city that survives. Farida uses the phrase from Vásquez's novel to end Juanita's monologue as she roams the streets through the decades ensconced in her own bubble of ignorance: "The scenery hasn't changed: it is the same streets, the same sky, the same trees... But the operetta is over. Now a tragedy is being performed in the same settings. I do not seek to understand" (327). The modernity so dreaded by Juanita is now enunciated in Arabic in Morocco and no longer in the variegated plurilingualism and creative creole of the past. The last images show the Kasbah at the time of independence: we follow the heroine, alone, sad and aged, through the alleys where the passers-by are all Arabs, dressed in djellabas. The images go beyond the still vista of Juanita's Perla del Norte to show Farida's vibrant city.

Juanita is shown in several European festivals. In Spain, the film receives a warm welcome. At the 53rd edition of the San Sebastian film festival it is nominated for a Golden Shell in 2006. In France, the film is screened at the Toulouse Cinespaña festival in September 2006 where it is nominated in three categories: the Golden Violet for the best film, the "Coup de Coeur" of the jury of the Dépêche du Midi and the Audience Award. In Paris, at the 8th Biennale des Cinémas Arabes, it is nominated for the Grand Prix of the Institut du Monde Arabe in July 2006.[34] However, the box office in France indicates a limited commercial success with only 7,797 tickets sold.[35]

In Morocco, it is nominated for and wins awards: Salima Benmoumen receives the award for Best Supporting Actor at the National Film Festival in 2005. At the 2006 International Women's Film Festival in Salé, *Juanita* receives the award for best screenplay (Farida is honored twice: with a tribute to her work as a filmmaker and with the award for best screenplay for *Juanita*). The film is previewed in Tangier in February before being screened in theaters in Rabat, Tangier, and Tetouan. The press extolls the "cosmopolitanism" of Tangier portrayed in the film through its diversity of characters and "a realization that confirms Farida Benlyazid [as one] of the best Moroccan directors."[36] However, it does not enjoy wide distribution in the kingdom, perhaps in part because exhibitors shun an undubbed film, perhaps because it is not "Arab" enough? *Shooting in Spanish was seen as real transgression. The Moroccan public has become somewhat accustomed to French, although most of them prefer films in Arabic.*[37] However, the film has since then become a cult in Tangiers. *It has hardly been seen in Morocco, except at the Cinemathèque of Tangier, where every year—and now it has become a tradition—Juanita is shown. Tangiers and those who are passing through are delighted!*[38]

The film is also screened at the Dubai film festival. In Morocco (and in Dubai) it intrigues the public, given its choice of language. It is shown with subtitles (Farida refuses to have it dubbed) because it precisely gives voice to a language that risks being lost in the teeming and changing texture of the Moroccan culture of the north. In this sense, it is as crucial to the documentation of a plural Moroccan culture (local or not) as, for example, will be in 2014 *Adios Carmen* by Mohamed Amine

Benamaraoui, a film in Rifian Tamazight with subtitles. In both cases, the Moroccan directors film the diverse cultural components of their country that manifest themselves in the material of the language: the creole of international Tangier and the Tamazight of the Rif. In this, both films challenge the traditional official discourse of the makhzen, which, before the Arab Spring, defined the identity and language of the Cherifian kingdom as strictly Arab and Arabic.

FLASHBACK 2: *THE WAR ON TV* (2006)

In the summer of 2006, despite a punishing heat wave in France, Farida celebrates in Paris: the Arab Film Biennial which starts on July 22 at the IMA (Institut du Monde Arabe) has nominated *Juanita* for the grand prize and Mariola Fuentes receives the award for best actress. *Juanita* is in good company, with an array of top films by Arab women, such as *Khochkhach or the flower of oblivion* by her Tunisian friend Selma Baccar and *Barakat!* by the Algerian Djamila Sahraoui; women's documentaries, such as *I'd like to tell you* by the Moroccan Dalila Ennadre, *Beirut: truths, lies and videos* by the Palestinian Mai Masri, or *El Banate Dol/These girls there* by the Cairo Tahani Rached. First short films by then emergent directors are also screened, such as *Your Black Hair, Ihsan* (Moroccan-Iraqi Tala Hadid), *Me, my sister and the thing* (Tunisian Kaouther Ben Hania), *The Ball of wool* (Algerian Fatma Zohra Zamoum), and *The beautiful days* (Tunisian Meriem Reveil).

But the news is sobering: Lebanon is once again bombarded. In response to Israel's attack, the filmmakers present at the IMA launch an appeal for solidarity with the attacked populations and invite film-makers from around the world to react to this war by making short films. This urgent appeal is heard by many Lebanese and Palestinian refugees caught up in the turmoil, but also by filmmakers from the Arab world and beyond. Some thirty films gathered in a collective project, "Cinesoumoud," will result from the shooting of a wide range of directors, from the most established (such as the documentary film-maker Monica Maurer) to emergent directors.[39] Farida Benlyazid and Fayçal Al Gandouzi join the movement and produce a short, entitled *Une guerre à la télé/A War on TV*. It will be shown, along with the others, on November 6, 2006 in one hour and twenty minutes sessions in Beirut, Paris, Ramallah, Gaza, Athens, Cairo, Tunis, Casablanca. It will then be uploaded on the platform of the collective movement

"Cinesoumoud" ("ciné-résolution" or "ciné-tiens bon!"/resolute cine/ resisting cine). Fayçal and Farida film the viewers in the cafés of Tangier riveted to their TV screens. The diegetic spectators follow the firing of rockets on Aljazeera or other channels from Morocco, France, or Spain, and discuss what they see in the cafés of Tangier's Petit Socco neighborhood. The double vision feature a little blurred one of the war framed by the lively oral debates it generates. This little film, which could tell us so much about the perceptions of the conflict in the western part of the Arab world, has unfortunately vanished. Its making nonetheless illustrates Farida's political use of cinema whether it be in solidarity with women, Palestine and Lebanon, or to rescue Islam from the exegesis of a rigid orthodox heteropatriarchy. Unfortunately, the disappearance of Farida's short points to a real problem in her filmography. That year, for instance, she is also tasked with filming a documentary on *Dar el Bacha*, the former palace of the Pasha Glaoui in Marrakech with Mounir Abbar. *Patti Birch offered her collection to the museum, which the Ministry of Culture had promised to restore. We filmed the work on the palace. Patti passed away* [on February 15, 2007] *and her foundation did not want to send the collection without seeing what we had shot... Then the tapes were stolen from Mounir, and someone dropped our hard disk. To repair it, we needed astronomical sums... So we don't even have the images ....*[40] To paraphrase Rithy Panh, the number of "missing images" in Moroccan cinema seems to be as astronomical as the amount of money needed to recover the memory of a hard disk.... Unfortunately, "disappeared images," either by accident (as here), by lack of adequate conservation, by a censorship never clearly articulated, or because they are on hold somewhere in an untraceable place (like the film *La Guerre à la télé*) are legion.[41]

The production of a film, an expensive undertaking that depends on a web of multiple components, is, by virtue of its very complexity, incredibly fragile from conception to release. How can we ensure that the hard drive of Farida's and of Moroccan cinematography endures?

FLASHBACK 3: "LE CINÉMA AU FÉMININ"—THE MOROCCAN FEMINIST FILMMAKER AND THE *MOUDAWANA*

That same year, Farida publishes "Women's cinema" in *Quaderns de la Mediterrània*, in which she thus defines her work: *I would simply say that I work on time, memory, the world of women, civic engagement and that I give space to my multicultural imagination.*[42] She puts on paper the major steps of her career in the Moroccan cinema as well as her feminist civic commitment. She traces the great steps of the history of women behind the camera in Morocco to better honor the new directors of the 2000s in a burst of female solidarity:

> ... *for some time now, we have been witnessing the arrival of new young women who are making very beautiful films that have been noticed at the international level. Narjis Nejjar has made a name for herself with her beautiful film* Les Yeux secs (Dry Eyes); *Yasmine Kassiri has won more than forty prizes with* L'Enfant endormi (The Sleeping Child); *Layla Marrakchi has raised a great deal of controversy with her film* Marock, *which upset the Islamists; Zakia Tahiri, who directed* Controlled Origin *with her husband, is preparing a new film, by herself this time:* Number One; *and Fatema Zemmouri Ouazzani made the highly acclaimed* In My Father's House.
> *All of them live abroad and have made co-productions with France, Belgium and Holland. I will point out Layla Triki, who is fighting to make her first feature film in Morocco. Many like her started by making short films --- Dalila Ennadre, Salma Bargach and Lamia Naji. Others have made films for television.* (222)

While the pioneer cites young directors and their films and is pleased with the number of their first works, she also suggests that women directors in Morocco can only rely on international co-production networks with a European or northern country. Otherwise, they have two solutions: "fight" and/or produce short films on their own in the hope to build on them later. Farida is thrilled the place of women in Moroccan cinema has finally expanded. Pen and/or camera in hand, she proclaims her solidarity with women directors who have defended other women in their films in a professional extension of her activism for women in her country. To better understand the latter, we need to open a fourth flashback leading to the *mudawana*.

During the first years of the second millennium, the King had led a program of democratic reforms, in parallel with a tightening of the police regime to counter terrorism. This period also signaled a retrospective examination of the exactions of the previous regime with the creation of the Equity and Reconciliation Commission (CIER, 2004–2007) and the creation of the *mudawana*, a reform of the personal code that grants more rights to women in Morocco (2004).[43] The result is an anthology of novels and autobiographical accounts, such as *Tazmamort: 18 ans dans le bagne de Hassan II/Tasmamort: 18 Years in Hassan II's Penitentiary*, by Aziz Bine Bine, released in 2009, and also films in the 2000s, as evidenced by Leïla Kilani's moving documentary, *Nos Lieux interdits/ Our Forbidden Places* (2008), which records not the words finally spoken by the former prisoners but the silences in the living rooms of the families who have waited for years for news of their detainees.[44]

The makhzen also tackled a reform of women's rights which led to the 2004 *mudawana*. It was not without a struggle, however, given the new turn the political arena took in the elections of September 27, 2002. On the one hand, thirty-five women acceded to the Parliament and on the other hand, the Islamist PJD (Party of Justice and Development) became the first political force with its forty-one seats to oppose such a reform. Farida, with her experience as an MLF activist in France and her practice of patience, committed herself to women on both sides of the ideological socio-political spectrum. Her idea has the elegance of simplicity: to bring together women from both sides—the Islamists and the "modernists"— to debate. In March 2000, a few months after the advent of Mohamed VI, the two groups had each organized demonstrations: the modernists in Rabat and the Islamists in Casablanca. In the latter, the thousands of men and women who marched held banners in Arabic and French that read "Against the Westernized Elites." The Islamists who adhered to the main lines of the project of the *mudawana* (especially women's literacy and insertion in the working force) disapproved of the measures passionately defended by "the modernists," namely: the increase of the minimum age of marriage for a woman from 15 to 18 years; the abolition of polygamy; new laws governing divorce. Some mosques started to foment an organized resistance against the new family code project. Farida panicked. The neighboring country, Algeria, had just come out of ten years of civil war between the Islamists and the government, ten years of relentless massacres of men and women. She felt it urgent to prevent the Moroccan women from taking part in these dangerous games.

I had been alarmed by the two women's marches: one in Rabat that I had filmed for a Canadian director who made a film about women's marches around the world; and the other in Casablanca, which had been organized by the Islamists to counteract the one in Rabat... I called Naïma Beniïch, who was teaching theology in one of the mosques in Tangier and who still had some influence in the PJD to which her husband belonged. I offered to collaborate and convene an informal group to see if dialogue was possible at all. We worked for a year, meeting weekly, and it was fascinating. One of the issues we brought up was to give shelter to single mothers. They felt that it would encourage women to have sex outside of marriage....

I remember telling them that it was not about housing them in palaces but just to save them from the street; that Islam could not be against it...They finally agreed and even founded an association for single mothers, and they named me Honorary President. The listening center created afterwards worked very well to reintegrate women into their families. They had no qualms about getting to the fathers who did not want to recognize the children. They even built a reception center in Tangier and we went to see Aïcha Chenna, a pioneer in this field in Casablanca, who explained to us how it worked. There was a crèche and a professional training center for the mothers... For thirteen years, we worked together: we found adoptive parents for children who could not be kept by their mothers, etc. The association still functions today but without us secularists, because of a change in its statutes: they used to forbid all affiliation with any political party, but when its president, Ouafa Benabdelkader, ran for regional elections under the aegis of the PJD, she refused to leave her position. It was a very painful moment for us who had to resign and drop what we had worked so hard for....

But the work we had done and the different points we had raised were submitted to the commission constituted by the King for the elaboration of the new mudawana.[45]

Her activism ultimately has an impact. The dahir signed by the King in February 2004 sets the minimum age of marriage for women at eighteen (Article 19); establishes their right to a monogamous marriage if they so desire; and imposes limits on polygamy (Articles 40 to 46); it also legislates on divorce, repudiation, and the obligation to pay alimony (Article 45). Although it is a personal code for all members of the family and society, it is primarily women's rights that are thoroughly revised (with the glaring exception of inheritance, which remains untouched). Scholars of Islamic feminism agree that the new Moroccan *mudawana* is one of the few codes that establishes the Qur'anic notion of gender equality in law by instituting the notion of co-responsibility of the family, for example.[46] The need is then to organize a vast communication campaign in order to reach illiterate women and/or women living in remote areas. Some women filmmakers set to task immediately: Dalila Ennadre with her documentary *Je voudrais vous dire.../I Would Like to Tell You* (2005), Zakia Tahiri with her mainstream comedy *Number One* (2008), Laila Marrakchi with her dramatic comedy *Marock* (2005). Thus, while the makhzen hunts down and dismantles the jihadist networks on its territory, it also seems to be making room for wider changes and acting on the reforms long awaited by its people, in particular its women.

CASANAYDA (2007)

Her voice, a voice of justice, becomes a voice of solidarity when she decides to film the young musicians of the independent festival L'Boulevard (The Boulevard of Young Musicians) in Casablanca. This documentary project is a new collaboration, commissioned by the French sociolinguist Dominique Caubet who wrote the script and did the location scouting. It will be called *Casanayda* (2007), a portmanteau: "Casa" for Casablanca and "*nayda*" (Darija for 'it moves' or 'on the move'). This annual festival, inaugurated in 2000 (which only the COVID-19 pandemic of 2020 will have the power to interrupt), signals the emerging part of a mutation at work not only in the youth culture but also in the Moroccan civil society as a whole. Its author, Dominique Caubet, analyzes the production of new musical expressions in Darija that characterize L'Boulevard festival. She also follows the development of the "nayda" as an underground phenomenon that gradually rises to the public stage and contributes to making things happen.

The four intertitles that punctuate it deliver a lapidary abstract of the documentary: (1) Nayda: breaking down barriers; (2) Nayda: Morocco on the move; (3) Nayda: the whole society vibrating; (4) Nayda: a phenomenon made in Morocco. A wide range of subjects appear: rappers, metalheads (metal rock artists), hip hop singers and dancers, graphic designers, video editors, an urban fashion designer (Amine Bendriouich), as well as journalists and writers (including Driss Ksikes and Mohamed Tozy), a documentary filmmaker (Ali Essafi), a scriptwriter/journalist (Fatema Loukili), a theater director (Hicham Akbari), but few members of the public. The film begins with a question about the name given to the Moroccan underground music and graphic art movement: the foreign press calls it "Moroccan movida,"[47] or "Moroccan Woodstock." Such Western labels highlight the surprise at the emergence of this movement that has nevertheless been brewing for a while, and the apparent impossibility to think about it in Moroccan terms. The songs that unfold, if they borrow forms from models elsewhere (rock, rap, slam), are in Darija (and not in French or classical Arabic) and mix Moroccan musical instruments (e.g., the qraqeb of the Gnawas) with the electrified instruments of pop and rock. The result is an alternative musical fusion of not only Moroccan but global pop and hip hop. In this sense, the music produced by *Nayda* is in line with Nass el Ghiwane, the mythical Moroccan band of the 1970s that combined the cultural and musical traditions and language of Morocco with the pop music styles of the time. Likewise, Nass el Ghiwane's visibility had increased around the world thanks to Ahmed Maânouni's documentary just as Farida and Dominique's documentary will do for *Nayda*.[48]

The sung or rapped texts are thus expressed on stage in the language of everyday life, addressed to all, literate or illiterate, children or adults. One of the hip hop performers is a little boy, MC Ano, baseball cap coquettishly screwed on backwards, large floating sweatshirt, who raps: "I am Moroccan. I came to sing for my friends and family." Although the vast majority of the rappers in the film are boys, a few young girls dressed in hip hop fashion can be seen slamming and dancing. We can even spot a young girl wearing a black veil in the middle of a jubilant audience at the C.O.C stadium in Casablanca. *I saw veiled girls dancing at L'Boulevard. I filmed them, but I did not seek to collect their testimonies. I didn't want to stigmatize them for their unusual look in this space.*[49] The audience cuts through social strata, says the founder of the festival L'Boulevard, Mohamed Merhari, known as "Momo," because the singers claim a Moroccan identity redefined on their own terms and in darija, a language that is changing status: "long associated with illiteracy and backwardness, [darija] is now called in the definition of a Moroccan identity revisited and is a carrier of plurality." It is therefore positioned at the antipodes of the Arab and Muslim identity advocated by the Makhzen, "while the country has always lived in plurality: plurality of origins (African, Berber and Arab), linguistic plurality (Moroccan Arabic, Berber, classical Arabic, French, Spanish ...), religious plurality (Muslim, but also Jewish)."[50] In short, L'Boulevard celebrates a blossoming "Moroccanity" that can only express itself after the breaking down of the mental barriers to the blossoming of the Moroccan individual (erected during colonialism and held up during the regime of Hassan II). The rappers declare: "I am tired of being underestimated." "Let's stop being afraid!" Documentary filmmaker Ali Essafi picks this up in the filmmaking workshops for young people he leads during the festival: "we must first help them get rid of their inferiority complex that prevents them from creating." That's exactly what Momo is thinking about when he wants to "give hope to these young people."

The texts are funny, direct, about work, unemployment, the tempta-tion to "burn," life and its difficulties. By pointing out what is wrong and by using the Moroccan spoken language, this alternative artistic practice is subversive.

Shot in May–June 2007, the film shows the *nayda* once it has gone from being underground (or barely surfacing in the public space) to the general public space of the concert stage from 2000 onwards. We follow the transition from the space of the Fondation des Œuvres Laïques—or F.O.L.—in Casablanca (which Momo opened to young people for rehearsals in 1998) to the stadium of the Club Olympique de Casablanca—or C.O.C. (to which the stadium of the Racing Universitaire de Casablanca—or R.U.C.—was added in 2007). As the groups rehearse in the available venue, they gain in professionalism. Their performance in front of the 30,000 spectators of the C.O.C. displays great mastery, especially in 2001, remembers Dominique Caubet, "even if it was still considered marginalized and alternative music."[51]

But they also attract undesirable attention... A few months after the election of the PJD (in February 2003), members of a metal rock band find themselves accused of undermining the Muslim religion and prac-ticing Satanism. The story is picked up by the progressive press in Morocco (by *Tel Quel*, in particular) and abroad, and the fourteen metal-heads are released and exonerated a few months later. The Islamists in power then target the use of darija and the enjoyment of rebel music to settle their ideological (rather than strictly religious) score with the country's plural and young society.

Finally, the film comes at a time when speaking in darija is beginning to appear on free radio and television. *An-nayda* reaffirms a great pride in a national cultural heritage through the requirement to say aloud—and in rhythm—what one thinks, in the language spoken and understood by the people from the humblest to the most sophisticated. At the same time, it gives musical groups the opportunity to meet their peers from abroad and to tour outside Morocco. The film, which remains to this day the only film to have been made about the *nayda* phenomenon at that time, was broadcast on 2M at the end of 2007 and screened at film festivals in France.[52] Here, Farida, in close collaboration with her friend Dominique Caubet, captures an important episode in the current social and cultural history of her country. After having plunged into the interna-tional Tangierof her childhood with a retro spyglass, she changes the lens of her camera to focus on present-day Casablanca, seen from the perspective of its rebellious youth. In both cases, she films the personal history and the many cultural expressions of a Morocco that decidedly resists a unified definition.

FAMILY SECRET (2009)

Next, she is invited to make a TV movie. Thanks to a combination of circumstances (including a crucial reform of the Moroccan audiovisual institution and the fact that Noureddine Sail is now president of 2M— from 2000 to 2003), the television channel has started to produce fiction films *made in Morocco* with the country's great and emergent filmmakers. The directors can finally film without having to be their own producers and can also make a living in between two cinema projects of their own. Farida writes a scenario close to her heart, with an intersectional feminist vision of the condition of black women, often from Sub-Saharan lineages, who used to be the slaves of Moroccan wealthy families. Farida focuses on the descendants of slaves from the southern part of the Sahara who remained in Morocco and followed the condition of their parents in their essentially domestic functions. According to historian Chouki el Hamel, although slavery became illegal in Morocco under French occupation (with the 1920 closure of the Marrakech slave market), it was never abolished by royal decree. Slavery thus became both illegal and tolerated.[53] But the Qurʾān, say both the historian and the filmmaker, contains no reference to the practice of slavery as an acceptable phenomenon, quite the contrary. Slavery would therefore be born from a misinterpretation of a couple of more or less reliable *hadiths* by certain theologians (male, it goes without saying).

Farida knew descendants of slaves in Tangier who shared the lives of the family to which they were attached. In *Family Secret*, she explores the mixture of intimacy, power, and submission that she has witnessed. The secret in question is as much about the survival of slavery in twentieth-century Morocco as it is about the filiations that the sharing of life between slave descendants and masters can produce.

SYNOPSIS—The story's breadcrumb trail follows a young Malian student, Awa, who is researching slavery in Morocco, and who is introduced to Haja Radia, the grandmother of a Tangier dynasty. Haja Radia, a widow, lives in a large house with a former woman slave, Aznass, the latter's husband, Si Mokhtar, and their son Slim. Haja Radia's two children come to visit her: Mohamed, married to Yamina, a volunteer lawyer for a women's rights association, and Sara, a divorcee. Mohamed and Yamina have two children: Karim and Maria. The latter leaves to study in Spain. Sara has a daughter, Hind, married to Marc, a non-Muslim Frenchman.

Slim directs The Children Theater Group of the Arc-en-ciel (Rainbow) Association, which is managed by children. Several secondary characters cross the narrative to illustrate the causes defended by both associations. Slim is in love with Maria, Mohamed's daughter, who returns from Spain for the vacations and finally decides to fall in his arms. But when they tell Aznass about their plan to marry, the former slave reveals the secret of their consanguinity that makes their marriage impossible: Radia, Maria's grandmother, could not have children, so Aznass bore the children of her husband. Aznass is therefore the biological mother of Mohamed and Sara, Maria's father and aunt respectively—and, of course, also of Slim.

Meanwhile, Karim and the researcher Awa fall in love with each other and get engaged toward the end of the film.

The very economical narrative nevertheless allows us to glimpse a lot in a very short time. Awa discovers that some of the slaves in the Moroccan harems in the past were white (Radia gives the example of a blonde Turkish woman with green eyes); that none of the women could leave the house; and that the male slaves were not allowed to enter the house; that "parents sold their children in times of famine in Morocco" to ensure their survival.

Aznass, the family nanny (the grandchildren, Karim and Maria, call her Dada) has raised two generations of children who are very attached to her and confide in her as they arrive at Haja Radia's house. Gradually, a complex picture emerges of the relationship between masters and slaveswithin the same family, a painting of a multifaceted form of hereditary servitude in the realm of the intimate. Farida also shows the racism that continues to divide: Awa has trouble making friends with fellow students during her 3 years in university and she is perceived and described as "an olive" by lighter skinned Moroccans.

To make *Family Secret*, Farida uses her film family again, with a couple of additions.[54] The actor who plays the role of Slim, for example, is a musician Farida met when she was filming *Casanyada* in which he performed under the name L-Tzack. He appears in the credits of *Secret* under his civilian name: Abderrazak Ezzahir. We see him perform a few steps in one scene and admire two break dancers on the floor in another. Farida thus feeds her TV movie with a few touches of *Casanayda*. The film also contains references to her own filmography and biography.

In the opening scene, at Lalla Raida's house, *A Door* is playing on television. In Slim's room, a poster of *Casanayda* is pinned to the wall. The association for the defense of women—Association Hajja Mina Amor—bears Farida's mother's maiden name as if to inscribe the latter in her film. Karim, who is played by Farida's son Abdelhaye, wants to make a documentary with children to counter the violent films they are constantly subjected to. In it, he wishes to use NVC—non-violent communication.[55] This corresponds to a fundamental ethical principle of the filmmaker: to make films that are neither mortifying nor violent, films that incite no hatred and no dangerous behavior, devoid of any aestheticization of violence. Farida's deep-rooted cosmopolitanism and rejection of colonialist violence are also reflected in the epigraph opening the film: "I want all the cultures of all the countries to be blown about my house, as freely as possible; but I refuse to be blown off my feet by any - Mahatma Gandhi."

This is not one of Farida's greatest films, but it is deftly crafted for a general audience. In this sense, the film for TV is the continuation of a dialogue with her Moroccan audience on a screen a little smaller than the one on which she usually likes to project her world. Although it was shot in Tangier, it speaks to Moroccans all over the kingdom, perhaps even to those she will film next: the people in the south, in the desert.

NOTES

1. Meddeb, Abdelwahab. *La Maladie de l'Islam*. Paris: Seuil, 2002: 10, 18.
2. Baudrillard, Jean & Derrida, Jacques. *Pourquoi la guerre aujourd'hui?* Paris: Nouvelles Editions Lignes, 2015.
3. See, in this regard, the interview of Abdulhamid Juma, President of DIFF (Dubai International Film Festival) on December 4, 2015 in *Variety*. The festivals indeed offer competitions for grants to Arab directors (for script rewriting, or post-production, for example), including those from the Maghreb. However, this enterprise is also focused on the Gulf countries: under the cover of red carpet and glitter, the ultimate goal was to attract established filmmakers from around the world to train Gulf filmmakers. Meanwhile, these

festivals also offer Egyptian, Lebanese, Mauritanian, Palestinian, Tunisian, Algerian, and Moroccan productions a rare access to a global showcase. They are even sometimes placed in A-list festivals such as Cannes or Venice by the network of producers and programmers of international festivals invited to these events.

4. Parliament passed an anti-terrorist law on May 28. Ten members of the *Salafia Jihadia* were sentenced to death on July 11 and a hundred others in August. The margin of freedom of expression is shrinking in other countries and being severely curtailed in Morocco. Amnesty International and Human Rights Watch denounce torture and arbitrary arrests by the thousands between 2003 and 2005.

5. Email, December 9, 2019.

6. Carrée, Roland. "Farida Benlyazid: Se tourner vers le ciel" *Répliques*, No. 12, 2019: 120.

7. Michel Amarger. "Le Maroc regarde ses identités plurielles." *Africiné*, 10/07/2007. http://www.africine.org/entretien/le-maroc-regarde-ses-identites-plurielles/6969.

8. Ibid.

9. Esperanza Roy received two awards for best actress in 1983: Fotogramas de Palta and Sant Jordi.

10. Emilio Sanz de Soto. "Pièces d'un possible portrait d'Ángel Vásquez" Afterword by Vásquez, Ángel. Selim Chérief, *L'Homme qui avait été amoureux de Bette Davis*. Lyon: Rouge Inside, 2011: 105–126.

11. Vazquez, Ángel. *La Chienne de vie by Juanita Narboni*, Selim Chérief, trans. Lyon: Rouge Inside Éditions, 2009.

12. "... in Tangier and in most cities in the protectorate, Tetouan, Larache, Chefchaouen, Azila, Alcazarquivir, there existed a hybrid mixture deserving the name of authentic language: *hakitia*; this term comes from an Arabic root 'h-k-y' which is used in the sense of talking or conversing about anything unrelated to the religious domain. The creation of idioms specific to a given situation seems to be a constant of the Jewish genius. Hakitia is in fact a North African branch of *ladino*, which encompasses all the dialects born after the expulsion of the Jews from Spain to other Mediterranean regions as far as Turkey. Selim Cherief, "Le monde sonore d'Àngel Vasquez". *Itinéraires*, 2012–2013: 145.

13. Selim Cherief, Ibid.: 143.

14. Ibid.: 147.
15. Philippe Di Meo. "Langage tangérois (Un): Ángel Vásquez—*La Chienne de vie de Juanita Narboni*," *La Quinzaine Littéraire*, July 2009, Vol. 995: 7.
16. Farida Benlyazid. "¡Lhabiba Tanja! [Tangier darling]," *Al Jamia*, December 2007 [82–86]: 85.
17. « La création procède par mutation du code et par déplacement sémiotique. » Alexie Tcheuyap, "Chapitre 1, Littérature à l'écran: approches théoriques et limitations," in *De l'écrit à l'écran : les réécritures filmiques du roman africain francophone*. Ottawa, University of Ottawa Press, 2004 (17–34): 20.
18. Farid Benlyazid, interviewed by Michel Amarger, op. cit.
19. Joaquim Mayodormo. "Juanita Narboni vuelve a Tánger para contar su 'vida perra'," *El País*, December 17, 2004.
20. Farida in her interview with Michel Amarger, op. cit.
21. Fayçal el Gandouzi in an interview with the author, op. cit.
22. Fayçal el Gandouzi, ibid.
23. Javier Valenzuela. "La Segunda vida de Juanita Narboni," *El País*, Sunday, October 13, 2002.
24. Interview with the author, Tangier, May 1, 2016.
25. She had made her début in Agnès Varda's *Kung Fu Master* (1987) and already played several roles for her father Jacques Doillon (in *Trop peu d'amour*, 1998 and *Carrément à l'ouest*, 2002).
26. Joaquim Mayodormo. "Juanita Narboni vuelve a Tánger para contar su 'vida perra'," *El País*, December 17, 2004.
27. Svetlana Boym, *The future of Nostalgia*. New York: Basic Books, 2002.
28. Idem, p. 29.
29. Carrée, Roland, op.cit.: 133.
30. Emily Keene (1850–1944), a British traveler who arrived in Tangier in 1872, then met and married Sidi Haj Iarbi Ben Abdeslam, Cherif of the Sufi order of Ouazzane. She later became the first European Cherifa of Ouazzane.
31. By Henry Roussel, 1932.
32. Interview with Michel Amarger, op.cit.
33. Véronique Bonnet, "*La Vida perra de Juanita Narboni* de Farida Benlyazid: une réécriture filmique postcoloniale?" *Itinéraires: Lire les villes marocaines*, 2013: 91.

34. On the other hand, Doillon received the Award for Worst Annoying Actress in Paris on February 23, 2006—an unenviable distinction, certainly, but one that clearly indicates that the film did not go unnoticed!

35. See Benchema, Abdelfettah. "Les fiilms maghrébins dans les salles en France," *La Circulation des films en Afrique du Nord et Moyen Orient, Africultures,* Nos. 101–102 (26–53): 34.

36. Hamrouch, Mhamed. *Aujourd'hui le Maroc,* December 15, 2005.

37. Cecilia Fernández Suzor. "Interview with Farida Benlyazid," AFKAR/IDÉES, Spring 2005: 109.

38. Interview with Hamid Berrada in *Mais encore? With Farida Benlyazid* 2M: January 20, 2012?

39. *Starry night,* Mazen Kerbaj

> *Drawing the war,* Lena Merhej
> *Kan ya zaman:* Nicolas Damuni, Karim Boutros Ghali
> *Chère N /Dear N* ., Chantal Partamian
> *Khan Younis Camp/Camp de Khan Yunis,* Dominique Dubosc
> *La grand-mère et l'olivier /Grand-mother and the olive tree,* Dominique Dubosc
> *La vieille femme/The old lady,* Futur TV animation workshop
> *Les fiancés du checkpoint /The checkpoint finances,* Dominique Dubosc *The kid and the bomb,* Futur TV animation workshop
> *Il y a quelqu'un/Someone,* Samir Abdallah
> *Pluie de missiles /Raining time,* Futur TV animation workshop
> *Once again,* Monica Maurer
> *Une femme résistante/A woman freedom fighter,* Jean-Yves Croizé
> *Supper hajja,* collective namla at3a, Tarik Kandel
> *Une histoire de farine/A flour story,* Dominique Dubosc
> *Le pêcheur /The fisherman,* Futur TV animation workshop
> *Avant-après /Before-after,* Elie Yazbek
> *Lendemain du cessez le feu/The day after the ceasefire,* Rania Stephan
> *Genocide,* Collective
> *Une guerre à la télé /War on tv,* Faycal el Gandouzi (under the name Bentahar) and Farida Benlyazid
> *Split cities,* namla at3a collective; hapsitus team collective
> *La corde à linge/the laundry line,* Dominique Dubosc
> *Walls and bridges,* Abraham Segal
> *La station/The station,* Futur TV animation workshop
> *Mariam,* Maher abi samra, Collectif cinemayat
> *Le pont /The bridge,* Futur TV animation workshop

Pont banlieue sud/Southern suburb *bridge*, Rania Stephan
De Beyrout à ceux qui nous aiment / *From Beirut to those who love us*: Collective Beirut DC.

http://www.babelmed.net/article/1758-cinesoumoud-des-films-courts-pour-le-liban-et-la-palestine/.

40. Farida Benlyazid, interview with the author: Tangier, April 28, 2020.
41. I am thinking here of the story of Ahmed Bouanani's documentary *Mémoire 14* (1971) made during the reign of Hassan II: the film was transformed into a 24-minute short film after a number of editing sessions...
42. Farida Benlyazid. "Le cinéma au féminin," *Quaderns de la Mediterrània*, No. 7, 2006: 224.
43. The CIER aims to investigate 20,000 cases of disappearances, arbitrary arrests, and torture between 1956 and 1999, that is, during the reign of Mohamed V (until 1961) and especially during the "years of lead" of the Hassan II regime after 1961. For the first time, the words of surviving prisoners released from detention camps by the Sultan toward the end of his reign are heard in public.
44. Among the films from this period that offer striking images of the inhumane conditions of detention are: *Ali, Rabia et les autres/ Ali, Raba and the others* by Ahmed Boulane (2000); *Le Spectre de Nizar/Nizar's Ghost* by Kamal Kamal (2002); *Mona Saber* by Abddelhaï Laraki (2002); *La Chambre noire/The Dark Room* by Hassan Benjelloun (2004), based on the eponymous autobiographical story by Jaouad Mdidech (2000); *Jawhara* by Saad Chraibi (2003); *Mémoire en détention/Memory in detention* by Jillali Ferhati (2004). In contrast, by filming around the absence of the beloved prisoner with an intimate approach, Lila Kilani highlights the consequences of the years of lead on the daily life of the anguished families, to which responds, in a surging wave, the anguish experienced by all of Morocco.
45. Farida Benlyazid, email: December 9, 2019.
46. See Margot Badran. "Le féminisme islamique revisité," *Genre en Action*, 2006. https://www.genreenaction.net/Le-feminisme-islamique-revisite.html.
47. In reference to the transgressive post-Franco Spanish cultural movement of the 1980s made famous by Pedro Almodovar and

Victoria Abril, for example; but the analogy can only remain superficial between the reign of Juan Carlos and that of Mohamed VI.

48. *Transes*, by Ahmed el Maânouni (1981) is famous for having attracted the attention of Martin Scorsese who had it restored by the *World Cinema Project* Foundation in 2007.

49. https://www.bladi.net/maroc-marock-pjd-jeunes.html.

50. Dominique Caubet. "La 'nayda' marocaine et ses espaces: De la scène musicale underground à la scène publique": 212–213.

51. Ibid.: 214.

52. Interview with Dominique Caubet: July 11, 2020.

53. "The slave trade was officially abolished. But the protectorate's officials were forbidden to interfere in the homes of Muslims. The colonial authority thus tacitly consented to slavery, used mainly for domestic purposes. It only took administrative measures against those aspects of slavery that shocked, in cases of obvious excess and abuse. From 1935, the royal Moroccan establishment cooperated to combat the clandestine sale of slaves. It should be noted that French traders took advantage of the slave trade and boarded Senegalese women as passengers on French ships, who were then sold to wealthy Moroccans on a private basis." https://www.lemonde.fr/afrique/article/2019/07/28/racisme-anti-noirs-au-maroc-le-coran-ne-soutient-pas-la-pratique-de-l-esclavage-mais-son-abolition_5494395_3212.html.

54. Her daughter Ayda Diouri is the costume designer, her son Abdelhaye plays the role of Karim, her granddaughter Alya is among the children who play in the film; and Fayçal el Gandouzi is assistant director. Farida also shoots a scene in the sewing workshop of her friend and cousin by marriage, Zoubida Mnehbi. To this first family were added newcomers. Thus, Rokhaya Niang, a Senegalese actress (*Madame Brouette*, by Moussa Sene Absa, Senegal 2002; *Un Ange*. Belgium: Koen Mortier, 2018) whom Farida had met a year or two earlier at the International Women's Film Festival in Salé, plays the role of Awa. Rokhaya has such respect and love for Farida that she calls her "my Moroccan mother" (Rokhaya Niang, interview with the author: Dakar, May 27, 2016).

55. "Nonviolent communication is based on a practice of language that strengthens our ability to maintain the qualities of our heart, even under trying conditions," says Karim/Abdelhaye in a scene from the film.

CHAPTER 6

The Sahara, the Atlas, and Tangier

Abstract Context: a larger access to the web facilitates the sharing of digital information and plays a crucial role in the Arab uprisings and revolutions. In 2009 prescient Benlyazid writes "The Opening of the Maghreb is also cultural." During the "Arab spring," she contributes a short story to an Arab collection of essays and short stories in which she shares her hope and optimism for Morocco and its youth. The makhzen starts to modify its official view of an Arab, Muslim monolithic identity in Morocco to include Imazighen and celebrate diversity. Benlyazid makes several films: ashort for a campaign against corruption, *The Bag* (2011); a docu-fiction, *Frontieras* (2013), on Western Sahara; and a series of documentaries on Amazigh music and culture with Dounia productions for the Meziane foundation. She is therefore giving her latest output a museal function. She also receives multiple honors in Morocco.

Keywords Borders · Culture · Corruption · Web · Propaganda · Censor · Sahara · Colony · Wassyla Tamzali · Odette du Puigaudeau · Tamy Tazi · Dounia Benjelloun · Fatima Tabaâmrant · Laura Marks

© The Author(s), under exclusive license to Springer Nature Switzerland AG 2024
F. Martin, *Farida Benlyazid and Moroccan Cinema*,
Palgrave Studies in Arab Cinema,
https://doi.org/10.1007/978-3-031-40616-4_6

143

THE CULTURES OF MOROCCO
AT THE DAWN OF THE ARAB REVOLTS

In 2011, revolutionary tempests are blowing through neighboring coun-tries—especially in Tunisia, Libya, and Egypt. The makhzen seeks to protect itself from them and becomes fully aware of the urgent need to give voice to the different components of Moroccan society: the Imazighen, women, the unemployed, and the inhabitants of the regions outside the Tangier—Rabat—Casablanca—Marrakech urban axis.

As often, artists feel the wind rising before the storm and antici-pate social political changes in their work, as Farida does in her article "L'ouverture du Maghreb passe aussi par la culture"/The opening of the Maghreb is also cultural.[1] In it, she describes the profusion of cultures that have coexisted in Morocco and analyzes the specific manifestations of such diversity in the space and history of the Maghreb. She explores the idea of a unique form of cosmopolitan multiculturalism over a Braudelian *longue durée* in a double movement. She unfolds an ark that extends from the personal to the regional (the Maghreb) and reflects on the multicul-tural shimmer of Tangier. The director, a self-described foody, opens with her mother's cooking:

> *She exchanged recipes with her friends and made us a foie gras with truffles at Christmas, a paella when she felt like one, a 'dafina' when she decided to or a couscous with zucchini and turnips when she found fresh ones.*
>
> *Thus, it has instilled in us a culture of the palate, which means that wherever I travel, I am fond of local recipes. I feel like I get to know cultures better through their flavors.* (15)

She even adds a note to explain the "dafina" to the uninitiated.[2] The flavors of her childhood that emanate from Sephardic Jewish, Mediter-ranean Muslim, and French or Spanish cuisines, in the image of interna-tional Tangier, open the appetite to the dishes of the other. Opening up to the other starts at lunch time: by eating at their table, learning about their taste, being granted the honor and pleasure (in the most intimate way) of savoring a shared meal, which opens the door to a new world. Yet, such doors were shut in the feudal past:

> *The gates of the cities were closed at night and Christians could only travel beyond Tangier with a safe-conduct. They could wait for years to obtain it...*

Our inward-looking feudal societies had forgotten the principle of justice at the foundation of Islam. Women were broken and the poor were treated like slaves who were still being bought and sold. The Maghreb needed a new breath of fresh air, of ideas that would make people think. "Pacification" could have been a good thing if it had not led to colonization. (16)

In her rapid sketch of the Maghreb at the dawn of European colonization, Farida does not defend her people at all costs. Her analysis, delivered from the position of "close distance" that she has always tried to occupy, provides a vision definitely on the fringe of the conventional narratives of the dominant discourse in Morocco. She records the patriarchal practices of the powerful who exploit women and the poor and denounces the closing of minds and municipalities. She gives a glimpse of the sad reality of a fragmented, divided society that was therefore easier to conquer and oppress. *Culture is the expression of human dignity, and imposed culture feels like an aggression that leads to a withdrawal of identity* (17). The question of the (re)discovery of a culture rooted in the Maghreb means looking at all its dimensions.

... In time, the Maghreb has opened to Eastern and Western cultures. Due to its geographical situation it is at the crossroads, torn, it suffers from the denial of its own identity. Western for the Easterners, Eastern for the Westerners, it is neither this nor that and both at the same time without forgetting its Berber and African origins as well as its Andalusian past. (16)

Morocco is not the only one questioning its identity. At the time Farida writes this text, Algeria and Tunisia feel a similar identity tug since the European influence (Spanish, French) now competes with that of the Wahhabites of the Gulf in a region where Maghrebi identity (so rich, so variegated) sees itself reduced to a Sophie's choice between two geopolitical, cultural trends: Arab or European.[3] The question arises with a burning acuteness after the decade-long Civil War in Algeria that decimated the population, including dozens of intellectuals and artists. The issue of culture and identity thus becomes brutally existential.

Farida advocates exchange, education, and decompartmentalizing society.

After independence, Bourguiba's Tunisia opened up to modern culture, so that there are almost no illiterates left in that country, which opened up very early to the theater and the cinema (...) Morocco, with its traditionally based dynasty, was more cautious, but this did not prevent the elites from being educated and cutting themselves off from the rest of the population.

Welcoming the policy of openness in terms of culture led by Mohamed VI (attested by the multiplication of film, art, and literature festivals in the kingdom) and the role of civil society, Farida proposes to further update the characterization of the kingdom's culture, by conducting social and cultural work together across society: *I remain convinced that this must go hand in hand, it is through culture that the prospects of openness are possible* (17). When she wrote this, a supplementary cultural layer was being superimposed on the previous ones: that of a globalized culture conveyed by the Internet, both a powerful platform for the education of the oppressed and exchanges on a planetary scale and, as the recent past has amply illustrated, a mendacious, vulgar, dangerous platform... *There is good as well as evil on the net, it is necessary to cultivate taste by encouraging creativity.* She wishes to participate in film workshops with young people.

> *... I regret that today's children do not have opportunities to meet and play with children from other cultures. We need to create opportunities for meetings, workshops, between schools from different countries. I participated in a workshop organized by ONE MINUTE MOVIE that brought together teenagers from Casablanca, Algiers, and Tunis in a cultural center in a suburban neighborhood of Casablanca. It was really interesting to see the creativity of these young people. ... Lastly, we need political will and funding for youth projects, because they carry our hopes for openness.* (17)

Evoking the social and political dimension of culture, Farida defends her vision turned toward the future. She is committed to giving jobs to young people in the film industry, to help them become technicians, actors, producers, scriptwriters—she regularly leads writing workshops. In fact, she has given so much to students in film studies that the class of 2020 at the Abdelmalek Essaadi University of Martil-Tetouan is named the "Farida Benlyazid" class.

Riffing on Mehdi el Mandjra, she makes a distinction between the trade of ideas and cultures and the economic trade of goods and products before concluding on the importance of culture for humans: *Culture means leaving aside one's certainties and marveling at the other possibilities of thinking, communicating, and living that other humans may have* (17). Her generous vision of culture in harmony with her spiritual conception of the world stands against the fractures of religion, geopolitical borders, ethnocentrism, and self-importance; rejects identity-based tribalism and the narrow deadly Wahabi orthodoxy that threatens the Maghreb and Europe at the dawn of the twenty-first century. She is also deeply opposed to the cult of money and has always refused to shoot commercials for private companies.

THE BAG (2011)

In 2010, Transparency International, the non-governmental organization that measures the perceived level of corruption in 180 countries around the world, published its 2009 report card: Morocco was ranked 89th, with a score of 3.4 out of 10 (with 10 as the highest score in the honesty test, which no country ever reaches!). Clearly, Morocco has done poorly from year to year on this NGO's Corruption Perception Index (CPI).[4] Yet, this is not for lack of legislation: articles 248–250 of the Penal Code tie severe penalties to acts of corruption in the public and private sectors, in particular influence peddling.[5] By the turn of the millennium, whistle-blowers, notably among the FAR (Royal Armed Forces), had already alerted the authorities to endemic corruption.[6] By 2007, other images of corruption had reached the Moroccan public: those of the "Targuist Sniper," who posted his first video on line on July 8, 2007. The digital film shows the gendarmes in the region of Targuist (known for growing cannabis) grab the bills handed out by the drivers whose vehicles the police are supposed to control, but instead let them through the various roadblocks. Other videos followed on YouTube, showing in broad daylight a practice hitherto only known to locals.[7] Such citizen initiatives expose the extent to which *baksheesh* is an accepted, routine practice.[8] Finally, on October 22, 2010, the government unveils a two-year plan to fight the chronic corruption which consumes 2% of the GDP, undermines moral values and hinders both foreign investment and the drastic fight against poverty and unemployment.

Transparency Maroc approaches Farida to make a (very) short film to raise awareness about corruption (4 minutes 57!) to be released in 2011. Having resolved to no longer produce, she calls on Latif Lahlou to be her producer. She casts a fine group of Moroccan actors who include Mohamed Bastaoui, Mohamed Khuyi, Zoubida Akif, Mohamed Choubi, Mohamed Rzine, Mohamed Marouazi) to participate in the project. Farida (unlike the "Targuist Sniper") won't touch the army or the police to show the endemic dimension of corruption in her film. She follows the path of money passing from one hand to the other, the sum growing exponentially with each transaction, culminating in the purchase of an imported designer bag, motivated by a frivolous and expensive rivalry. Her camera focuses on the banknote(s) in close-ups: the filmmaker puts on display the repeated gesture of corruption—so discreet usually—smack in the center of the screen. Money increases as corruption climbs up the ladder of society. Thus, the twenty dirhams in the initial scene gradually grow into a briefcase filled with cash once it reaches the heights of financial and political power.

The camera first focuses on the hands of a woman in a dispensary who uses 20 MAD to bribe the employee who blocks the access of patients to a doctor; then on the employee's hand passing 50 MAD to a bureaucrat for an official permit; the civil servant's hand then doles out 200 MAD to a teacher to ensure his offspring pass his exam, and so on and so forth. Society operates like a clockwork mechanism, well-oiled by the circulation of the baksheesh and by the assumption that every service is up for sale. The civil servants on screen are all corruptible: from the dispensary porter to the teacher, to the lawyer, to the politician. The ironically sober last scene closes on the Parisian designer bag bought by the wife of a powerful man for a staggering sum in a garbage can through which a starving man rummages. This last character finds the bag of the title and throws it onto the road, preferring an apple he fishes out of the trash and eagerly devours. The bag, once a shiny orange luxury product, is now a dirty piece of rubbish, angrily rejected by the hobo who lives on the fringes of a wealthy, depraved society to which he never has access. This final twist takes the form of an abrupt return to the brutal reality of the abyss that separates the haves from the have-nots. The symbolic denouement also denounces the commercial temptations of a materialistic society governed by snobbery and global consumerism, to the sound of a nocturnal feline's heartbreaking meows.

A discreet extra-diegetic music with a constant dynamic beat (composed by MOBYDICK, in capital letters in the credits) accompanies each vignette. While the final credits roll, that score is the base of a rap by the singer-composer belted out ten times as loudly. Here again we recognize Farida's practice of calling on members of her film family, which expands from film to film: she had met Mobydick—who sang that he was not against the system, but that the system was against him—during the shoot of her documentary *Casanayda!* Other people will loudly echo Mobydick's belief on the streets of the Arab world.

THE ARAB REVOLUTIONS—2010–2011—AND FARIDA

On December 17, 2010, a small film on social networks ignites the Tunisian and Egyptian revolutions, as well as major uprisings in Bahrain, Yemen, Syria, and elsewhere in the Arab world. Yet, protest had been smoldering for a long time before Mohamed Bouazizi set himself on fire in Sidi Bouzid, Tunisia....

The ensuing digital videos filmed and posted on the internet by those left behind by the Tunisian regime, who seize their phones or digital cameras as weapons of resistance, have an immediate impact. Like the Targuist Sniper's resistance films denouncing corruption in Morocco, the film of the successful Tunisian revolution, relayed on screens, triggers movements ranging from turmoil to convulsion in the Arab world. The democratic use of the web to disseminate the words and images of those who had previously had no voice or access to cameras, signals both a radical gesture in repressed societies and the sharing of a collective and transnational awakening of political and social awareness.

Wassyla Tamzali, an Algerian-European feminist, a lawyer who ardently defends women's rights for UNESCO (notably via the International Forum of Mediterranean Women), calls upon forty-one Arab intellectuals, authors, and artists to write short texts, mostly fictions, about the revolutions in the Arab world. Each text can be read as a freeze frame to fix in writing "the fleeting moment of the present" of this Arab swell, as Behja Traversac indicates in her beautiful preface to the collection of *Histoires minuscules des révolutions arabes/Tiny Stories of the Arab Revolutions.* Farida writes "JUBILATION. Ce n'est que le début"/"JUBILATION. It's only the beginning" with glee.[9] In her fiction, she imagines the meeting of Latifa, a Moroccan poetess who has come to read her poems and her French friend Michèle, who has invited her to a reading session in March 2011, in the North of France.

Her short story (finished on September 17, 2011), written in the moment, expresses Farida's political views through Latifa: "Mubarak is gone! He had seemed even more monstrous when we saw him defend Israel during the war in Gaza ...." Like Farida, Latifa and the demonstrators of the February 20 Movement in Morocco are against corruption: "Like them, she wanted the corruption that gave her nausea to stop;" like Farida, Latifa defends the young people on the street who "don't ask for power" and "say aloud what everyone else is thinking." The author also highlights the transnational dimension of the revolutions that spill over the borders of the Arab world: Latifa is offered French author Stéphane Hessel's essay *Indignez-vous!/Time for Outrage!* and, once home, watches "the *Indignados* movement which claimed to be the Arab Spring in Spain" on television. "It's Only the Beginning" shows the protest movements of 2011 as symptoms of a much larger human revolution. Latifa first expresses her astonishment at the political activism of the young, hitherto accused of passivity: "We thought they were caught up in the virtual world, and now they are bursting into the real world, ready to die to stop the unbearable" (186). She follows the progress of the revolt in the media and on the screens of social networks:

> "The people want the fall of the regime!" This phrase, which was displayed on placards and broadcast on televisions around the world, gave me goose bumps. Explosive as a powder trail, it had spread from mouth to mouth, abolishing fear, prohibitions and borders. The youth had appropriated globalization... They had succeeded in internationalizing their revolution! (186)

The systematic occupation of the web and television by the young transforms these media into a transnational forum, a tool of unprecedented power. Here, Latifa-Farida attributes to the rebels a capacity for global imagination that is beyond her. Yet, she already fears it might all be illusory:

> On Facebook, their freedom of speech made her jubilant. She envied their carefree attitude, and felt they were part of another world. Was it an illusion? They looked like mutants connected across the world by invisible streams. It was not a conflict of generations, it was more than that, they lived in another world, they had an imagination that she found difficult to grasp at times (...) it was like two parallel societies living side by side, agreeing to ignore each other. (188)

Latifa already senses what will happen next when she describes her return home: "the tone had hardened... The young people were called extremists by the media... And they had become suspicious, they did not want to be taken over..." (189). But this reality cannot break the surge of the revolutionary wave, Farida-Latifa continues with optimism. "Yes, this time, things were different, authentic globalization was on the move... it was only a beginning..." (189). Her vision gives back to the term of "globalization" cannibalized by a devouring late capitalism, its sense of openness to the circulation of ideas, to sharing on a planetary scale. She predicts a possible new cycle in globalization different from the one initially triggered by the power of money. If "it is only a beginning," then what comes next is the end of the exploitation of the poor that is the mainstay of the current cycle. In a luminous flash, Farida delivers a hopeful image of what the web could become under the skillful fingers of the young revolutionary Internet users.

In 2011, the makhzen reacts at first by letting its people march in the streets of the big cities but changes course on March 13.[10] The demonstration of the M20F (Movement of February 20) in Casablanca is repressed with violence. However, M20F keeps organizing weekly peaceful demonstrations in several cities on Sundays (unlike in other Arab countries where people march on Fridays) demanding reforms until the makhzen offers a few of them.[11]

Farida is asked to write, to consult, and to make films for television. She still makes her living as writer and filmmaker even if she no longer produces her films. 2012 is a busy year for her. She composes a small text of memories for a publication celebrating the centenary of the Regnault high school, *Nos années lycée*.[12] With a nod to Ettore Scola, the film-maker titles her text "A Special Day" about her very first day at the French high school. She also returns for a moment to the world of Garcia Lorca, as a consultant for the adaptation of one of his plays for television. Two theater actresses, Samia Akariou (the star of *Keid Ensa*) and Nora Skalli have decided to rework *Bnat Lalla Mennana (The Daughters of Lalla Mennana)* into a serial for Ramadan. Nora Skalli is a member of the Takoon Theater Group, a troupe composed exclusively of women; its name refers to both the traditional headdress of women in northern Morocco and the stiletto (the extreme top and bottom of a woman's attire). Takoon combines modernity and tradition, and has already produced the play derived from Federico Garcia Lorca's, *The House of Bernarda Alba* (1936) on stage. The plot, transposed to the blue village of Chefchaouen, revolves around Lalla Mennana and her four daughters (instead of the original five in Lorca). Just as the original, austere and tyrannical Bernarda Alba had cloistered her daughters for several years of mourning in order to protect their virtue, Lalla Mennana forbids her daughters to go out. Lorca's Spanish drama was adapted into Darija for the play performed in Morocco, then into a thirty-episode comedy-drama for a series directed by Yassine Fennane, with the same actresses. The success of the first season is such (an audience of 62% the first season) that 2M produces a second season for the following Ramadan which is so appreciated by the viewers (58% ratings) that some of them boycott the channel after it announces that there will be no third season!

She shoots a fiction for television, the TV movie *Koul Ouahed or Ryou* (to each his opinion), produced by CinéTéléma. She appears in Hamid Benamra's documentary on painter Mustapha Boutadgine *Bouts de vie, bouts de rêve/Life Snippets, Dream Snippets* (Algeria, 2012). The artist makes portraits of activists from collages of photos cut exclusively from magazines in order to "recycle the scraps of the bourgeoisie for more committed images." We see, alongside Farida, her famous communist compatriot Abraham Serfaty, the visionary filmmaker Djibril Diop Mambéty, poets Mahmoud Darwich and Adonis, authors Assia Djebar and Henri Alleg, musicians Myriam Makeba and Marcel Khalife, and many others. The political and global dimension of her work are thus recog- nized and honored in this gallery of formidable individuals who have impacted the arts, literature, and politics transnationally. It is precisely the very notion of borders (necessarily political and plural) that she is now about to question with *Frontieras*, her next project, shot in 2012 and released in 2013 to counter Àlvaro Longoria and Javier Bardem's film *Sons of the Clouds: The Last Colony* (Spain, 2012).

FRONTIERAS (2013)

This controversial docudrama is unusual, and certainly more so for foreigners than for Moroccans, because it has to do with the "historical," "national" borders that delimit the territory of the Western Sahara, an area of 266,000 square kilometers, 80 % of which is occupied by Morocco in one of the oldest conflicts on the African continent.

A quick reminder: when Morocco became independent, Western Sahara was divided into three parts, administered respectively by Mauritania, Algeria (under French occupation until 1962), and Spain (since the nineteenth century). In 1975, the International Court of Justice, at the request of the United Nations General Assembly, opposed Morocco's claim to the Spanish territory called Rio de Oro. Hassan II, a genius in communication, eager (after several attempted coups) to unify his people around the monarchy, seized the opportunity. He invited 350,000 of his subjects from all regions of Morocco to go and liberate their "Sahrawi brothers" from the Spanish yoke. The famous Green March he orchestrated led a peaceful procession of citizens to the southern border of the kingdom between Morocco and the Rio de Oro, which they crossed on foot. The Spanish army could, of course, not attack the crowd of civilian men, women and children. The tripartite agreement of Madrid was signed by Morocco, Mauritania, and Spain in November 1975. The rest is known: the makhzen declared Western Sahara part of Greater Morocco (*Maghrib al Kabir*). The UN called for a vote on self-determination for the Sahrawis, which has been regularly blocked by France and the United States. Relations between Morocco and Algeria deteriorated in successive stages: Algerian President Houari Boumediène, who supported the Polisario Front created in Algeria in 1973, was angered by what he considered a takeover of the region and expelled most Moroccan citizens living in Algeria.[13] The Polisario proclaimed the Sahrawi Arab Democratic Republic (SADR) on February 27, 1976. Hassan II broke all diplomatic ties with Algeria and closed the border. The Polisario led an intense armed guerrilla and media war against Morocco until the 1991 cease-fire. Meanwhile, the makhzen sent thousands of Moroccans from the north to settle in "its southern provinces" and invested in the development of the region, which happens to be rich in phosphates and bordered by fish-bearing waters. Since 1975, this region has been the site of armed confrontations (with the Polisario), exodus, occupation, non-resolution at the UN and development. The makhzen also forbids anyone to question the kingdom's "territorial integrity," i.e., the borders of Greater Morocco with its "southern provinces." Finally, in 2020, the United States, under President Trump, recognized Morocco's sovereignty over Western Sahara in exchange for normalizing relations between Rabat and Tel Aviv. But we are not there yet when Farida makes her film....

Briefly, there are two opposing perspectives on the situation: the outside world says—with Longoria and Bardem—that the Western Sahara is "the last colony"[14] while Morocco maintains that it has freed the south of the country from Spanish colonialism and reintegrated the territory into the Moroccan kingdom to which it has historically belonged. In the first case, one could object that Western Sahara is not the "last colony"—what about Palestine?

In the second case, one cannot deny that Morocco has liberated the Sahara from the Spanish yoke. But the question remains: is Morocco's occupation of the Sahara another form of colonization? This overview is undoubtedly an oversimplification and does not pretend to do justice to an eminently complex situation.

Why does Farida tackle such a controversial topic? When I ask her, she answers: *It's a film in response to the Spaniards, to Bardem in particular, and to the Algerians, to the Polisario, in particular. I wanted to say: "The Sahara is historically Moroccan. Come on! Stop telling us that we are colonizers!* Explaining her position as that of a postcolonial filmmaker eager to defend the values and history of her nation to the exclusion of all others would be reductive in the extreme and does not account for her political and ethical principles, her freedom of spirit, and quite simply the finesse of her critical mind. Her goal is to make a film that transcends clashing opinions about what constitutes a Sahrawi identity by diverting attention away from the two contradictory political discourses that define it. She wants to hand the microphone to the Sahrawis of the region who are never heard and whose voices disappear under the words spoken by others in their place—the rantings of the Polisario, the edicts of the Makhzen, the narration of Javier Bardem (to which I probably subscribe, I confess here for the sake of transparency). *The film is not propagandistic. The Sahrawis said to us: "you talk about us, but we don't have the right to speak..." So I gave it to them... But, as you can see quite well in the film, many retracted, did not want to speak on camera.* How to make the voice of the Sahrawis heard who do not recognize themselves in any narrow national space? Neither Moroccan nor Algerian nor Mauritanian? *I think that the Sahara goes from Tindouf to Egypt.* Borders have therefore divided up a large territory of nomadic, seasonal migration and the recent colonial history of these borders needs to be weighed against the long history of the Sahrawis.

But, as she herself says, the stakes are too high and even a discreet filming apparatus cannot turn into a megaphone for people afraid of possible reprisals from one side or the other. She films—almost literally, as a matter of fact—in a minefield.

Latif Lahlou produced the film, with Cinetéléma, the television channel 2M Soread, the SNRT (Société Nationale de Radiodiffusion et de Télévision) in partnership with the Agence du Sud, with an advance on the CCM's film production assistance fund.[15]

Her spare, professional team includes Spanish actress Romina Sanchez (Carmen in *La Vida pera by Juanita Narboni*), transnational Moroccan actors Ismail Aboulkanater[16] and Mohamed Merouazi.[17]

The film's plot uses a classic trick to introduce viewers to a complex reality: Maite (Romina Sanchez), a young Spanish journalist, comes to investigate the region, convinced that Western Sahara should be neither

Spanish nor Moroccan but Sahrawi. Her Moroccan fixer, Dahmane (Mohamed Merouazi), helps her find subjects to interview, places to film, stories to (re)build. Thus, the extra-diegetic viewer is given two guides who are spokespersons for two distinct versions of the Sahrawi situation and identity: a native guide (Dahmane) who knows the terrain from the inside and a foreign guide (Maite) who has an outsider's perspective. As soon as Maite arrives at Layoune airport, we hear Farida in the words of Dahmane: "Everyone is interested in the separatists! It's as if we, in Morocco, didn't exist!" Her film clearly aims at also providing the Moroccan side of a challenging narrative.

The film immediately professes an historical perspective as its opening credits scroll over a map with a caption in Arabic and French stating "Kingdom of Morocco in its natural and historical borders," while Sahrawi music is performed by a singer supported by a string instrument. A visual fade-in gives way to a second map—"Border division of Western Sahara during the Franco-Spanish colonization"—while the music fades out and into the sounds of cannons and guns. A quote from the French ethnologist Odette de Puiguaudeau follows: "A complete study of the Moorish ethnic group could not be stopped by modern boundaries, incompatible with the necessities of pastoral life, trade, family, religious and cultural ties."[18] The rapid succession of these three texts signals an odd retrospective narrative from the nationalist myth of today's "national borders" to the artificial borders of colonization to the total erasure of borders in the Sahara. Is Puigaudeau/Farida canceling the "historicity" of Moroccan borders here?

This is a telling choice on Farida's part on several levels, since Odette du Puigaudeau, a French proto-feminist, fought against the French establishment in the 1930s to explore the Sahara and gain the same access to journalistic and scientific recognition as her male colleagues in France (and to live her life freely away from her father's disapproving gaze—about, among other topics, her love story with a woman). In addition, there is a cinematographic legend about Odette and her partner Manon, a painter and illustrator, who illuminated the ethnologist's writings with magnificent images and photos: rumor has it that they also made films which sadly, have all disappeared. Farida's film could therefore fill in the blanks of the lost female filmic archive. When she quotes Odette de Puigaudeau at the opening of *Frontieras*, she therefore pays homage to a powerful woman and takes over Odette and Manon's camera, resuming their journey in the desert of men.

SYNOPSIS—The filmic narrative tells the story of Maite's journey in the Moroccan Sahara from beginning to end. Having come to make a documentary film about this region—with no prior location scouting—Maite is a moutpiece both for Polisario propaganda and a Spanish leftist credo. "We are against the Francoists who gave the Sahara to Morocco instead of giving it to the poor Sahrawis" she explains to Dahmane. She asks him to take her to the shantytowns in which she intends to film the problems of the "poor Sahrawis." "It's a colonialist attitude to want to see misery everywhere" he retorts, in the first of several skirmishes between them.

The first half of the film, a series of interviews with religious leaders, anthropologists, historians, teachers and activists is peppered with Maite's blunders, whose prejudices Dahmane systematically points out. The journey from Laâyoune to Dakhla ends with an invitation to a party in the desert, a narrative pivotal point. The second part of the film opens with Maite meeting M'Barek, who works for a development NGO, and to whom Maite feels deeply attracted. M'Barek (Kanater), a former Polisario activist, has recently returned to Morocco from the United States. He knows the ins and outs of Western Sahara and can speak knowledgeably about both sides of the issue. He is also a lucid lover of the desert: "It is the desert that controls us," he says softly. And, resisting her advances, he confides: "Believe me, Maite, it's like a sandstorm in summer. The magic of the desert makes us see mirages."

The word "border" announced in the credits—and title—recurs like a refrain in the various interviews and discussions among the characters throughout the film.[19] All of them state that the desert knows no borders yet also provide historical accounts of the allegiance of the desert tribes to the Sultan of Morocco. Meanwhile, the tribes are rivals, as Maite discovers during her investigation. As an example, the head of the Reguibat tribe is so offended by the fact that the head of another tribe was interviewed before him that he simply cancels the appointment with the journalist. The filmic investigation actually mirrors some of the difficulties Farida's team encountered during the film shoot, whether it was a diplomatic incident impossible to anticipate or a plain refusal to speak on camera after having promised to do so.

In the second part of the film, we hear Sahrawi men talking politics under a tent in the desert. They discuss present-day Spain (2013) and the new economic powers of globalization that have supplanted the colonial powers of the previous two centuries that had drawn curious borders in the sand… "Today, the nations are paying the price of exploitation. And the price of their leaders' failure with the financiers."

The notion of territory in the desert—and of frontier—is blurred in various ways. First, the notion of a map disappears (as does that of a "road"—never traced). The caravan composed of two 4-wheel drives loses its way. The drivers do not use GPS, and the script (by anti-robotization Farida) explains the lack of GPS as "not to depend on a machine." Maite is told: "At night, the stars guide us. During the day, the winds have blurred the tracks." She finds herself out of network and unable to phone her boy-friend Nacho in Madrid. The desert has its own ways of redefining both the physical space where brown camels still roam and the virtual space of the twenty-first century relegated off-screen.

There is another dimension to this film, especially in its second half. Farida fell in love with the desert a long time ago, not only with its changing dunes but more importantly with its culture, especially the culture of the desert women in their f lowing, brightly patterned attire. They enjoy great autonomy, compose poetry as well as men, and are considered their intellectual/artistic equals, as her memory of a magical evening near Nouakchott illustrates. *Everyone, sitting around the fire, was saying their poems. Very simply, without making a show of it. It was a true moment of sharing: tea and poems. The evening went on all night, under a starry sky. It was beautiful. That's what made me want to film the desert.* With this initial impulse came the desire to understand what the Sahrawis feel. But the very notion of their territory is such a minefield that even a talented director like Farida may not be able to get a nuanced message across. The conflict in the region (outside Farida's film) keeps on being framed in terms devoid of any nuance: only in terms of national borders.

In an interview in Spain, Farida explains her vision for *Frontieras* as follows:

> *There are many films about Tindouf and the separatists and none about those who live in Morocco. The film puts history on the table, it is said that Morocco is colonialist, but this is not true, because* [Western] *Sahara was part of the country before the colonization of this territory. Hence the title* Frontieras, *which is a play on words, as Morocco was divided between two colonial powers, the French and the Spanish, a fact illustrated in the film, a very hard situation for the Sahrawis who had family on both sides of the border.*

The journalist asks her what colonization and occupation mean when referring to the Palestinian conflict. Her answer is immediate:

> *The Palestinian case has nothing to do with the Sahrawi case. (…) I can defend the position that the Sahrawi people are free, okay, but then their territory goes from the Atlantic to the Red Sea, it's a territory reserved for nomads, and you don't give part of it to Algeria and say no to Morocco; that territory is only for the Sahrawis. Ideally, all this territory should belong to the Sahrawis, because Tindouf was once Moroccan and is now Algerian.*[20]

Farida reiterates her deep belief that the Sahara has no borders, that the descendants of the Sahrawi nomads whose caravans once crossed great expanses have a vision of their world that does not coincide with the mosaic of small geopolitical squares cut out by others on their dunes. The African puzzle inherited from colonization does not correspond to their "cosmos" in the original dual sense of the Greek term— the world and the perception of the arrangement of the world. The film is paradoxical: on the one hand, the Saharan cosmos knows neither borders nor GPS, on the other hand, the Saharan cosmos is divided. On the one hand, part of the Sahara is historically Moroccan, on the other it is not since the territory of the Sahara exceeds the geopolitical limits of each of its present states. By affirming the artificiality and fragility of geopolitical borders that contrary winds can erase at any moment, Farida suggests half-heartedly that the Sahara in its integrity belongs to the Sahara—therefore to the Sahrawis—and to no one else. Logically, the paradox leads the viewer to conclude that none of the artificial territories in the Sahara have the right to wave national Moroccan, Algerian, Tunisian, Lybian, Egyptian, or Mauritanian flags. *Frontieras* thus provides an examination of history from a Sahrawi perspective that coincides with none of the other national narratives available.

Upon its release on April 2, 2014, the film has the usual two titles: one in Franco-Spanish, *Frontieras*, and one in Arabic, *houdoud wa houdoud* (borders and borders) which expresses what Farida experienced in colonial Morocco: *we had borders at different levels of the country. Thus, to enter or leave Tangier for the interior of the country, we had to have a passport. I was therefore very sensitive to the narrative of borders from my childhood on.*[21] However, viewers who interpret the film through their own prior understanding of the conflict judge this vision of borders in two opposite ways from the very beginning:

1. Filming Western Sahara can *only* be an attempt at propaganda to better serve the makhzen (and if they stick to the map in the opening credits, who can you blame them?).
2. The makhzen and its followers recognize neither the discourse nor the Moroccan nationalist narrative they expected in the film.

As a result, the film is censored in a devious way. *When the film was released in Marrakesh, people came to see it and the theater was already full: children had been brought in... Even the owner of the Megarama could only see the film sitting on the stairs! Well... I told myself that it was a programming error, something poorly managed... But when the same happened in Oujda, I said to myself: Something's up! For them, it was not propagandistic enough. I want to tell a truth, not the truth. Besides, listen to what the people in the film say. They say: "We are Sahrawis."* The film has an abysmally poor distribution: "There was almost no promotion. It was released in a few theaters simultaneously, but there was no communication, and that's a shame. It's a film that has been stifled."[22] It is a disaster at the box office: 1,222 admissions for the year, according to the CCM's 2014 report.[23]

When you see it as documenting history, the docu-fiction is controversial. When you see it as an ode to the desert and its people who share poems into the night, *Frontieras* becomes a piece of the opus that she composes, film after film, documentary after documentary, with the obstinate patience of a weaver.

DOCUMENTARIES FOR THE MEZIANE FOUNDATION AND DOUNIA PRODUCTION

This new chapter in Farida's career coincides with an era of increased professionalization of production in Morocco, thus a fresh dynamism in Moroccan cinema in general. Production companies are often based in Casablanca, run by men (such as Nabil Ayouch, with Ali'n Productions) and women (such as Lamia Chraïbi with La Prod, Souad Lamriki with Agora Films, or Khadija Alami with K-Films) who move between Morocco and abroad, to set up sophisticated transnational co-productions that benefit from transnational financial arrangements, transnational teams and increased visibility, especially in the international festival circuit.

This is a new chapter for the makhzen as well, as Mohamed VI and his government proclaim several edicts that demonstrate further interest in a plural and inclusive Moroccan culture. Morocco's Amazigh and Jewish cultures are being honored. For instance, the CCM has supported Simone Bitton's documentary *Ziyara* (2020) on "visiting the saints," a custom shared by Maghrebi Muslims and Jews who go to worship or pray to a saint or marabout to intercede for them with God.[24] Morocco now celebrates its multiple identities by opening the door to work on a diverse heritage hitherto largely overlooked.

For Farida, it is a godsend! It is the opportunity to continue and deepen her excavating work on Moroccan culture and to compose documentaries on women and other disenfranchised subjects. Her cousin, Leïla Mézian Benjelloun, an ophthalmologist and philanthropist, has created a foundation, the Benjelloun-Mezian Foundation, to restore old buildings and, above all, to promote the Amazigh heritage. She underwrites the International Chair of Amazigh Studies at the IRCAM (Royal Institute of Amazigh Culture founded in 2001) in Rabat. As President of the foundation, she also starts to build a museum in Casablanca, a future home to collections of arts and crafts from the various Amazigh communities living in Morocco. Her foundation commissions Farida's work: this is where the director's documentaries on Amazigh music that she makes between 2014 and 2015, will be housed and curated.

Farida now works with Dounia Productions (also underwritten by Leïla Mézian-Benjelloun). Ayda happily describes this change in her mother's career:

> Since she met Dounia, everything has changed: she is paid; she travels and is housed in good conditions and therefore she has a great deal of freedom to create. Before, she would be interrupted in the middle of a shoot: "Farida, tomorrow we are running out of money. We have to stop". So she would stop, phone around, get money and then start again. Then, there were other crises: this actor doesn't want to play for so many days, he wants more, he wants less, he has to be paid. That actor has an accident with a car on the shoot. You can't imagine what it's like: it never stops![25]

Dounia Benjelloun Mezian also has a transnational background and touches on many areas of cinema. Influenced by her grandfather (Haj Abbas Bejelloun), a distributor for Columbia and United International Pictures in Morocco and owner of a chain of movie theaters, she graduated from American University (Washington, DC) with a degree in communica-tions in 1983, and then began working as a production assistant for United Pictures, first in New York City and later in Casablanca. In Morocco, she became a producer, exhibitor, distributor and director of commercials, communication films, and documentaries, thus acquiring a wide knowledge of the inner workings of the cinema industry in her country and a wide array of skills.[26] She founded Dounia Productions in 1986 and has since then produced and occasionally directed films that range from advertising to the preservation of Moroccan cultural heritage. Farida describes her as *extremely meticulous, a perfectionist.*

Farida and Dounia's first project for the foundation is *Tamy Tazi: Créations au fil du temps/Tamy Tazi: Designs Through Time* (2013), a documentary about the celebrated aristocratic Moroccan fashion designer who draws on the know-how inherited from previous generations, from embroidery to traditional kaftans (not to mention sarouels and djellabas), for her contemporary designs. The short film (26 minutes) illustrates the richness of this heritage with a fashion show of kaftans. Tamy Tazi shares her enthusiasm for traditional embroideries and their variations from one region to another and teaches viewers to recognize them and spot their origin—the city embroideries on silk from Fes are monochrome and those from Tetouan are colorful; if they appear on linen, then they probably come from Chefchaouen. Her passion for collecting fragments of history is highlighted by close-ups of the embroidery designs alternating with the filming of their rhythmic, dynamic execution on the garments.

Tamy Tazi then takes up haute couture and updates the traditional kaftans worn by women at ceremonies. An erudite stylist, she designs Ottoman-inspired embroideries and lightens the heavy fabrics of the kaftans of the past to give today's women greater freedom of movement. Farida films the superimpositions of fabrics and their dance around the body during a fashion show in Marrakesh, alternating between long shots and haptic close-ups.

Farida's collaboration with Dounia Benjelloun then focuses on the production of ten, 26-minute-long documentaries commissioned by the Dr. Leïla Mezian Foundation.

Farida's first musical films for Dounia Production are gathered in two boxed sets of five DVDs, containing a small booklet with an introductory text by the filmmaker and a succinct presentation of the producer and the foundation. They constitute a dive into a musical universe often unknown in Morocco, despite some important works such as the recordings of Paul

Bowles (1959) or the series *Corps et âmes/Bodies and Souls* by Izza Genini (1987).

The first set, *Amazigh Music and Dance*, contains documentaries organized a long genre and time: *Women in Amazigh Music, The Little Maestros, Through the Valleys in Bloom, Amazigh Music of Yesterday and Today* and *Introduction to Amazigh Music and Dance*. The second, *The Anthology of Amazigh music and dance* organizes the documentaries according to their geographical region: *Middle Atlas, High Atlas, Anti-Atlas-Souss, At the Edge of the Sahara* and *Oriental and Rif*. Two other films on the traditions of Amazigh weddings were also produced: *Noces Amazigh dans la vallée d'Anzergui/Amazigh Wedding in the valley of Anergui* (2016) and *Noces nomades in Merzouga/Nomads' Wedding in Merzouga* (2017).

Even with careful location scouting and a light team, it is difficult to avoid causing disruption in the villages high in the Atlas Mountains or among the itinerant musicians gathered for a traditional jam. The social fabric of a community cannot always absorb the daily presence of a foreign group with ease. Farida, now in the position of participant observer known to anthropologists, proceeds with tact, aware of the tensions, the socio-economic-cultural differences, and the distinct expectations of each. When she directs her documentaries, she pays attention to the individuals she films, to the ways in which the filming affects them, and to how they will be perceived by future viewers. My favorite example is that of the marrying couple in *Nomads' Wedding in Merzouga* consisting of a tall young peasant woman and a much smaller shepherd. An orphan, the groom lives far away from the village with his herd and has grown unaccustomed to the world of humans. Farida realizes that he doesn't look happy at all in the wedding shots, shy as he is to the point of abruptness. How is this gruff figure going to be perceived on screen? She figures out that, being used to the company of his goats, his link to the world is through his relationship with the animals in his care. After shooting the wedding, she sends an assistant to join him and film scenes of his daily life. He brings back shots of a goat eating from the smiling shepherd's hand. Once inserted in the film, they endow the shepherd with *a tender heart*.

She researches her subject thoroughly and finds fixers whom she trusts to introduce her to her subjects. *For the documentaries on music, it was Fatima Tabaamrant who is a friend. She founded an association, and she organizes a festival every year. Hence, she is in contact with many musicians.*

We also had access to a researcher working on the Middle Atlas. At times, her network of fixers extends beyond the music scene: a resourceful young man in the south; a filmmaker friend in the north.[27] It is thanks to this careful work upstream that her subjects have such freshness in tone and impressive candor in front of the camera. *It's true that they need to feel confident, but they also have a great spontaneity.* Farida also pays close attention to the ethno-musicological dimension of her films, as attested by the text she composed for the boxed sets of her films for the Mezian Foundation.

To introduce the collection, Farida quotes ethnomusicologist Philip Schuyler who defines a practice common to all Amazigh music: their "exceptional gift for collective performance."[28] The emphasis on collective performance, with its call-and-response structure, guides the listening and viewing of each film. Farida's film focus on musical groups: bands, orchestras, lines of dancers, and groups of *zamar* (a kind of double clarinet) or *bendir* (drum) players, more often than soloists. Thus, the *Ahidous* or *Ahouaches* (in Tamazight) are songs and collective dances bringing together the populations of scattered villages for a festival or a ritual. The thousand-year-old Amazigh culture is performed and transmitted through oral jousts, poetry (poets answer one another from one mountain to the next by improvising verses), song, music, and dance.

Both anthologies work to identify and preserve Amazigh music and customs all over Morocco while they do not claim to be exhaustive. Rather, they capture performances by musicians with a representative repertoire.

In order to bring us closer to the filmed performance, Farida alternates between close-up and long shots and uses aerial shots (by drone) to locate the setting. Each hamlet or village appears remote, far from the cities. The camera also emphasizes the rural character of the music-making space by intercutting low-angle shots of tree branches in bloom and mixing the chirping of birds in the soundtrack. The documentaries thus show a music scene that extends from tiny hamlets to festivals in cities (in Nador, for example, in the Rif). Two films are particularly enlightening on the subject: *Women in Amazigh Music* and *The Little Maestros*.

The latter's note of intent, written by Farida, reveals an optimistic vision of the future in the hands of new generations:

The film Les Petits Maestros *represents the next generation and in a way the rebirth of the Amazigh culture. From their birth, we could say, the children*

participate in it with their parents. Some of them get involved very early on,
like the little maestros that we filmed.
    That in the age of television and computers, children and teenagers want
to perpetuate these dances and songs from another age seemed significant to
us. (Booklet, 8)

The first little maestro, Marwan, thirteen years old, sings with a male
troupe at the Aïn Leuh festival. He learns Ahidou (music and dance of the
Middle Atlas) from Mr. Jeddoubi at the age of five. This first scene and
Farida's comment call to mind the tradition of oral transmission of the
griots further south, in West Africa, who teach the epics of their ancestors
to their children so that the story is passed on from generation to generation. Mr. Jedoubi puts his full confidence in Marwan: "I hope he will
continue to be able to replace me so that this art persists as it was in the
past." Furthermore, just like in the griot dynasties, the little maestros are
not all boys. In the poetically named Happy Valley of the High Atlas, we
are invited to an Ahidou show outside a primary school: a group of girls
musically responds to a group of boys. In another scene near Ouarzazate,
girls and boys perform the Ahouach, first in two concentric circles (in a
wide shot): the small inner circle is composed of boys (later men) with
bendirs, surrounded by the larger circle of girls (later women) executing
an undulating dance (in a medium shot).[29] At one point, the dance splits
into two groups that call and respond to each other. The music and dance
follow a structure that unites the community in the sharing of the dance,
the music, the song, the poem, once again reminiscent of the performance
of griots in Sub-Saharan West Africa.
    The film brings a new understanding of the gendered organization of
dance and music to viewers outside the Amazigh culture. For having a
career as a female dancer and/or musician in rural Morocco has long
meant being the object of both passionate admiration (for the star) and
contempt (for the individual). The *sheikhates*, these free women (who
live without men, and are therefore suspect!), who sing and dance at
weddings, parties and festivals, occupy this dual social position of stars
and women of ill repute. Farida's *Women in Amazigh music* underlines a
similar duality:

Women have always sung and danced in the Amazigh culture. But making
a living out of it is not well seen in some regions. We have made a selection of
those who seemed to us the most representative of the genres through different

regions of Morocco. We see them sing and then they talk to us in interviews about their choices and their path in this profession. (Booklet, 7)

The film begins with an interview in Ain Leuh with the oldest female singer in the Middle Atlas, Fadma Oulthdidou, who began singing in the 1960s. Her family did not want her to sing—it was frowned upon to perform in public. But she followed the artist Hammou Lyazid for three years to learn everything from him. She now lives in Rabat, gives recitals on stage, has recorded albums, and sings in the film with a young girl, Aïcha Maya, with whom she shares her knowledge and joy of singing.

The public reluctance to let women sing is reflected in a later sequence in the film when we meet Tifyur, a young artist who sings in Arabic, Tamazight, and French with her band in Nador, and reworks old songs to modernize them. Tifyur reminds us that singing in a conservative society is far from easy. Her determination and freedom—qualities that are front and center in every singer interviewed—come in part from the need to share her ideas. "We use art to convey ideas and messages that are very important."

A political figure wrapped in a scarf printed with Amazigh symbols and colors suddenly appears on screen: Fatima Tabaâmrant, from Ifrane Saghir, an elected representative known for her militant songs. The poetess and singer who composes her lines in Tifinagh declares: "In reality I did not want to get involved in politics. I could have entered the field of politics in 1997 but the recognition of Tamazight as an official language in the 2011 constitution is what pushed me to enter politics." The identity and political purpose of Amazigh songs is fleetingly mentionned in another sequence of the documentary, when Batoul Maourani and his orchestra perform on stage in Laayoune. In a counter shot, the camera pans a very enthusiastic audience waving Amazigh flags. Politics is not the only theme in the women's songs: faith plays a large part in their repertoire, as witnessed in Tiznit by the sacred songs of the *agraw* (the community circle) of women in traditional costumes, sitting on the floor of a house, singing, and beating the bendir.

In the end, then, how feminist is Farida's documentarian project?

When Farida is asked about what is happening to women in Morocco these days, she mentions Fatima Tabaâmrant in these terms:

Look at Fatema, who went from being a sheikha to a member of parliament. She is an intelligent woman, who never went to school - but she is the first one who wrote in Tifinagh because she had no other alphabet! She learned Tifinagh, she now writes her poetry in Tifinagh, she takes things in stride! She is an admirable woman.[30]

Laura Marks in her study of Arab women video makers provides illuminating parallels. Farida and her sister videographers share a high degree of freedom to film—Farida is no longer dependent on the CCM (except for permissions), and her funding is secure. They adopt a light structure that allows them to sneak in anywhere and especially in the least public, least filmed places—Farida's subjects live in remote hamlets, accessed by unpaved roads. Their audience is neither that of the cinema nor that of commercial TV channels—Farida's documentaries, when they are broadcast on national television, are part of cultural programs with a small audience. They reside in museums as installations (for the Arab video artists) and as cultural archive in the forthcoming Mezian Foundation Museum (for Farida). Their conceptualization of gender sometimes deviates from an exclusive type of feminism in that it does not film gender front and center: "Arab video artists adopt a contextualized perspective in which the question of gender, if it ever emerges, remains linked to other questions." In Farida's work, women are filmed in the performances of musicians, singers, dancers, and in their daily lives, at their parties. Farida also seeks to capture the lifestyles of her subjects and lingers on the children's dreams of the future (*The Little Maestros*). The filmmaker's feminism thus extends into her solidarity with and empathy for the poor, the forgotten of the mountains and seeks to highlight neglected parts of the Moroccan musical repertoire. Laura Marks also describes Maghrebi women filmmakers who started out as writers, like Farida (whom she mentions in her text), and now use their cameras as activist pens: "the camera claims the activist past of the pen: an agile, portable and, if necessary, disposable instrument, it condenses and expresses political situations in a personal tone." Seen through this lens, Farida becomes a committed activist creator who is intent on making room for the enormous cultural contributions of Morocco's indigenous population to the kingdom's culture(s). As she records and shares the spectacles of the hinterland, she also saves from oblivion ancient cultures that predate the Arab occupation of the land, overlooked because they are Amazigh, and far from urban centers, rural, often economically disadvantaged.

These films do not have a national or international "release." However, they are crowned with a number of awards. Some have been shown on

2M, in Cannes and in Edinburgh, for instance, in November 2018 in the presence of the director.[31] The future location of these films that await their place in Leïla Benjelloun Mezian's museum also leads us to reconsider the film object in its archival (rather than entertainment) function in the age of post-cinema.

THE LAUREL SEASON IN TANGIER

Farida does not talk about her laurels; she does not talk about what she has done for others, does not mention those she has helped, tirelessly. The late photographer Leila Alaoui remembers seeing her at the beginning of her own career, in 2008, to include her for her project at the time: a book of portraits of artists. "We sat down and talked. I took a picture of her without posing, in the moment. She was sitting in front of me. It's one of my favorite photos by the way.... What really touched me was that at the time, nobody knew me. (…) For me, an artist who accepts to receive in her home a stranger, with no references, who accepts to play the game, that really made me happy. And it shows the generosity of the person, of the artist." It is this black and white portrait that will appear in Leila's posthumous exhibition "Moroccan women at the forefront" and also illustrate Roland Carrée's beautiful interview of Farida.[32] A stunning portrait that has captured one of the frequent expressions of Farida's: her absolutely complete attention to the other (here off-camera) that visually translates her immense capacity to listen.

Farida does not talk about her fame. Her friends do. Fatema Loukili speaks for her and of her with emotion and boundless admiration in private and in public—especially in two tributes: one at the 18th edition of the National Film Festival, in Tangier in March 2017, and one at the Marrakesh International Film Festival in November 2022. Noureddine Lakhmari narrates with verve how she and he were decorated with the Wissam Al Moukafaa Al Watania of the Order of Commander by His Majesty Mohamed VI on the occasion of the Feast of the Throne, on August 21, 2013. Her work is celebrated in Morocco and abroad (at the International Film Festival in Salé in 2006, at the Oriental Film Festival in Geneva in 2007, in Tangier in 2009, in Berlin in 2012, for example). She is invited to sit on juries of national and international film festivals. Among many others, we find her in San Sebastian in 2003, Cairo in 2006, Marrakesh in 2011, Malmö in 2014, Abu Dhabi the same year, Granada in 2015, Tunis in 2016.

In 2017, I was given the privilege to sit on a jury with her at the International Film Festival for Students (FIDEC) in Tetouan. What a treat to see her evaluate films with professionalism and empathy and discuss them with passion and humor. For, as serene and spiritual as Farida is, she is also as deeply passionate about filmmaking today as she ever was.

Notes

1. Benlyazid, Farida. "L'ouverture du Maghreb passe aussi par la culture," in Fatima Lahnait, ed., *The role of bi-national entrepreneurs as social and economic bridge builders between Europe and North Africa*. Amsterdam: IOS Press, 2009: 15–18.
2. ... "or Skhina in the rest of Morocco, a dish that the Jews of the Maghreb prepare for the Sabbath. It cooks over low heat for nearly 24 hours" (18).
3. See Ibrahim Letaïef's short film, *Visa (la dictée)* (Tunisia, 2004, 26 minutes) whose humor denounces the sad choice of emigration candidates: France or Saudi Arabia.
4. It will drop to No. 91 in 2010, for example, before recovering and staying around 80 until 2019.
5. The penalties provided for by the law range from 2 to 5 years' imprisonment and a fine of 5,000 to 100,000 MAD. Fines are doubled for a judge, elected official, or senior civil servant....
6. Captain Mustapha Adib had denounced his superiors to the press as early as 1998, later followed in 2002 by the Ibrahim Jalti and Jamal Zaïm affair denouncing how corrosive corruption was in the military.
7. "Smugglers and other 'khattafa' (literally, 'seat thieves,' illegal transporters), who make up the bulk of their 'clientele,' seem to be just as well versed in the exercise. They readily pay a right of passage of about 20 dirhams." Ziraoui, Youssef. "Sur la piste du Sniper de Targuist," *Tel Quel* (6–12 October 2007).
8. So much so that corruption is a favorite subject in both Arabic and Amazigh proverbs ("For a loaf of bread, he left his family") and French proverbs ("Marteau d'argent ouvre porte de fer"/A silver hammer opens an iron door), which can be found in the collection of "proverbs against corruption," published by Transparency Maroc during its 2010–2011 awareness campaign.

9. Wassyla Tamzali, ed. *Histoires minuscules des révolutions arabes.* Montpellier, Chèvre Feuille étoilée, 2012: 185–189.
10. See Desrues, Thierry. "The February 20 Movement and the Moroccan regime: contestation, constitutional revision and elections." *L'Année du Maghreb* VIII, 2012: 359–389. https://journals.openedition.org/anneemaghreb/1537#tocto2n1.
11. (a) The King recognizes the Amazigh cultural and linguistic heritage of Morocco. A (very nice) tifinagh writing system, completely artificial, is even introduced to fix the language in writing (despite the fact that several branches of Tamazight differ from region to region). (b) The reformed constitution prohibits torture, inhumane, or degrading treatment of prisoners, arbitrary detention, and "disappearances." While it advocates a parliamentary and greater freedom of expression, it still prohibits "false rumors" about Islam, the monarchy and the integrity of Moroccan territory. (c) The makhzen moves the legislative elections scheduled for 2012 to the fall of 2011. On October 28, the Islamists of the PJD (Party of Justice and Development) win a decisive victory in the elections (107 seats out of 395).
12. *Nos années lycée: Les 100 ans du lycée Regnault* Tangier, Litograph, 2013.
13. See in this regard Narjiss Nejjar's film, *Apatride* (2018), on the plight of bi-national Moroccans in Algeria.
14. Javier Bardem produced, narrated and starred in a documentary on the subject, *Sons of the Clouds: The Last Colony,* directed by Àlvaro Longoria (Spain, 2012).
15. *I did not have the aid to cinema on the Sahrawi culture. Moreover, it is thanks to my film that this fund was created: we had to offer the other side of the story!* The fund that Farida mentions here, created in 2015, supports film production in the southern provinces (today's Moroccan Western Sahara therefore) with two functions: encouraging producers to support films that document "culture, history, and Sahrawi Hassani space" and the training of film professionals from the region. *Frontieras* will, however, get a contribution from the King's brother, Moulay Rachid (who supports Moroccan cinema and presides over the Marrakech International Film Festival)—*money from the palace,* as the end credits point out. The Agence du Sud is the Agency for the Promotion and the Economic and Social Development of the Provinces of the

South of the Kingdom (APDS) created in 2002, and to which one must apply for film shoot authorizations, etc.

16. This dual career actor has a varied filmography both in Morocco and in the United States where he is known as Sam Kanater. In Morocco, he appears notably in *The End* by Hicham Lasri, 2011; *Femme écrite/Written Woman* by Lahcen Zinoun, 2012; *Larmes de Satan/Tears of Satan* by Hicham el Jebbari, 2015; *Lhajjates* by Mohamed Achour, 2017. In the US, he is featured in a series, TV movies, and films as varied as the biography of Gertrude Bell (*Queen of the Desert* by Werner Herzog, 2015), a horror film (*Out for Blood* by Richard Brandes, 2004) and a romance between a Palestinian and an Israeli (*David and Fatima* by Alain Zaloum).

17. In Morocco, he played in *Ali, Rabiaa and others/Ali, Rabiaa et les autres* by Ahmed Boulane, 2000; *Memory in Detention / Mémoire en détention* by Jillali Ferhati, 2004; *Burned Hearts/Les Cœurs brûlés* by Ahmed Maanouni, 2007. He also stars in *The Harem of Madame Osmane/Le Harem de Madame Osmane* (Nadir Moknèche, France, 2000) and more recently, in TV series, such as the American series *Jack Ryan*, in 2018, or the Canadian series *Toute la vie/The Entire Life* by Jean-Philippe Duval, in 2019.

18. The ethnologist Odette du Puiguaudeau (1897–1991) had traveled through the Western Sahara in 1933–1934, 1936–1938, then again in 1950 and 1951 with her partner Marion Sénones, a painter. She had brought back writings illustrated by her partner and published them in France. She authored over two hundred articles and seven books. Her doctoral thesis in ethnography titled *Arts et coutumes des Maures/The Moors' Arts and Customs,* from which the quotation comes, was published posthumously by her director, Théodore Monod.

19. Historian Bachar Ould Haidar dates the allegiance of the Sahrawi tribes to the Kingdom of Morocco to 116 (of the Hegira, i.e. 734 AD) and recalls that long afterwards, Europe had divided the Moroccan territory that extended from the Mediterranean to Senegal, drawing "imaginary borders" (aren't all borders imaginary?). The teacher Aziz Naimi, for his part, recalls the locals saying: "the Sahara extends from Khal Argan to Adrar" and explains the organic "natural connection" that unites the North to the South of the Sahara, understood as ethnic, tribal, historical, and cultural, across all borders. Anthropologist Tamin M'Bare explains

how tribes have pledged allegiance to the Moroccan monarchy over the centuries and resisted the Spanish and French occupation throughout today's Moroccan territory.

20. Cappa, Gonzalo. "El velo y el piercing son dos cosas mortiferas"— inter- view with Farida Benlyazid. *Granada Hoy*, June 13, 2015.

21. Interview with Roland Carrée: 136.

22. Interview with the author, February 22, 2016.

23. In comparison, *Road to Kabul* (by Brahim Chikri), also released in 2014, achieved 92,211 admissions according to the same document.

24. More recently, the normalization of relations between Morocco and Israel orchestrated by the United States partly supports the Makhzen's policy: new direct airlines have opened between Casablanca and Tel Aviv, in order to allow Moroccan Jews (the Mizrahis) to return to the country whenever they wish.

25. Ayda Diouri, interview with the author: February 8, 2018.

26. It ran in seven movie theaters in Casablanca, Rabat, and Tangier between 1991 and 2000, and had exclusive distribution rights for Columbia and United International Pictures films throughout the Kingdom.

27. Interview with the author, Tangier, February 4, 2016.

28. Philip Schuyler, a former professor of ethnomusicology at the University of Washington in Seattle, had recorded Moroccan music from 1970 to 1980 (now in the Library of Congress and awarded a Grammy Award in 2017) and wrote his dissertation on the music of the Rwais, from southern Morocco.

29. The Ahouach is a Chleuh ritual that mixes music and dance in the Souss region, often at night, around a fire of branches. The Ahouach performers are diverse across age and gender: poetry, song, and dance on a background of bendirs are performed by men and women, boys and girls on the stage.

30. Farida Benlyazid, Round Table on Women in Moroccan Cinema, AHRC Conference, Edinburgh, November 2018.

31. In 2016, *Women in Amazigh Music* won several Certificates of Creative Excellence at the *US International Film & Video Festival* in Los Angeles (One in the Documentary category; one in the Editing category; one in the Directing category) and the Silver Screen in the Cinematography category. That same year, *The Little*

Maestros also won Certificates of Creative Excellence in the categories of Cinematography, Documentary, Editing, Directing, and Music; *A Travers les vallées en fleurs* won the Silver Dolphin in the Ethnology and Sociology category at the *Cannes Corporate Media & TV Awards*; *Noces Amazighes dans la vallée d'Anergui* won the Silver Screen in the Documentary category at the *US International Film & Video Festival* in Los Angeles; and *Noces Nomades à Merzouga* as well as the aforementioned films were awarded the Award of Merit at the Impact DOCS Festival in 2019.

32. Carrée, Roland. "Farida Benlyazid: Se tourner vers le ciel," *Répliques*, No. 12, 2019: 120–145.

CODA—TANGIER

A Political Play in Three Acts

1. The CSMD

Farida embarks on a new, unexpected, citizen adventure. On July 29, 2019, Mohamed VI announced the formation of the Special Commission on the Development Model (CSMD), tasked with creating an innovative development model adapted to the strengths and weaknesses of Morocco in the twenty-first century. Mohamed VI also appointed a 35-people commission, including Farida, in the fall of 2019. Farida was enthusiastic: *great people, with a great passion for Morocco, some who live here, others who are in France, Korea, Amsterdam …* The task was immense, and the "approach" derived from the theory of collective intelligence: the Commission would draw ideas for new development from the ground up.[1] The filmmaker brought her perspective as a woman[2] and as an artist concerned with education and cultures in Morocco: *it was necessary to make people understand that economy and culture work together.*[3]

Farida reported that the participants *were incredibly open-minded, even when they were part of the system.* The ideas flowed—*they spoke without being censored*—and eventually came to agree on a process, thanks to their appointed chair, Chakib Benmoussa, who *had the elegance to let everyone express themselves.* The members of the Commission then spread out in small groups throughout the kingdom to conduct field trips in order to interview Moroccan subjects across gender, class, and age. Their participatory, grass-roots approach allowed them to record the opinions and analyses of local actors on local issues. The data, once integrated into a group reflection, led to the informed articulation, broad, detailed, and *consensual*[4] (Farida insists on this trait), of a thoughtful, democratic development. For Farida, it was an opportunity to meet experts in many fields, and also to take an active part in designing the future of her country. When she describes her work at the Commission, she expresses a mix of curiosity, enthusiasm, and erudite thinking reminiscent of her documentary on her Malian friend Aminata Traoré.

In the report and annexes delivered to the King, I note two points that I attribute in large part to Farida's participation: gender and culture— and in particular, cinema. The CSMD wants to address gender inequality through, among other things, education, employment, wages, non-tolerance of underage marriages, and the status of children born to single mothers.[5] Among the many strategies outlined in the document, the CSMD proposes to bring together people who are not usually in dialogue, by opening inclusive fora to theologians, doctors, sociologists, lawyers, activists.[6] How can we not read this invitation to dialogue between prac-titioners of medicine and practitioners of religion as one of the extensions of Farida's play *Help Thyself*? This is what Farida has been arguing for years in her writings, in her films, in her participation in civil society: we hear the accents of Nadia's revolt against the law of inheritance in *A Door*; we see Aisha's incomprehension in court when the (male) judges rule that she lost custody of her children in *Reed Dolls*.

The second point, culture, is equally revealing for the artist who has witnessed the various changes in the identity of 'Moroccan culture' throughout her career as a filmmaker. The reformed constitution now describes it as plural (Amazigh, Arabic, Jewish, etc.). Yet, it is also double: an elite culture for a privileged segment of the population and a popular culture for the less privileged, often expressed in different languages. The report proposes to integrate the teaching of the Moroccan rich and diverse heritage culture from the kindergarten up. Again these themes recur in Farida's corpus: in *La Terrasse*, in which a little girl discovers a legendary queen and the cinema from her grandparents' terrace; in the children theatre group under Slim's empathetic direction in *Family*

Secrets. Who, more than Farida, "values memory and history" in her films from *A Door* to *Juanita?*

The CSMD's diagnosis of the ills of cinema in Morocco also seems to come straight out of Farida's playbook, this time out of her writings and interviews over the years, namely: cinephilia and movie theaters have been in serious decline for thirty years; Moroccans know neither their history nor their cinema; financial difficulties linked to production lead to a low national production; film needs to be (better) promoted.[7]

> Film culture requires education and support for the public. We need to promote cinephilia among all profiles, make the Moroccan film heritage known, create film libraries throughout the country, support the existing film clubs and encourage the creation of new initiatives in this sense... It is necessary to move from occasional, intermittent, and precarious production to an organized market, with human and financial means for quality and quantity production... and the accompaniment of films in their post-production career. (*Annex 2,* 164)

Farida here plays another political role in the sense that she is now able to intervene, once again in the *polis,* in society. As we know, this is not her first time: she fought for the *mudawana,* and she has raised social justice issues in her work, time and again. She reminds me of her friend Selma Baccar, the Tunisian filmmaker who, after the revolution of 2010–2011, put her camera in a drawer and ran for election so she could sit in parliament and help write the new Tunisian constitution. Both postcolonial film pioneers, whose filmic work has always sided with the disenfranchised, share a deep commitment to a feminist political vision in her respective countries.

2. Tamayouz

In December 2018, Farida joins forces with fellow filmmakers Narjiss Nejjar and Simone Bitton, and with producers Lamia Chraibi and Dounia Benjelloun-Mezian to create the Tamayouz (<distinction, excellence>) Foundation in support of young women filmmakers. The foundation, entirely funded by various philanthropic sources in Morocco, seeks to provide talented young women filmmakers with the means to acquire a high level of expertise and increased visibility nationally and internationally. To do so, it has designed three complementary actions. The first one is to offer scholarships to undergraduates who do not have the financial means to complete their studies at ESAV (a fairly expensive private film school in Marrakesh); the second consists in accompanying young graduates financially, chaperoned by a professional producer to guide them on film projects for which they have no funds; the third includes invitations to writing residencies, as well as financial aid for film development and post-production. The hiatus of the pandemic affected the time line of Tamayouz, but the first protégée they coached, Zineb Wakrim, a graduate from ESAV, won third prize for her first short *Ayyur* (moon in Tamzight) at the CINEF competition in Cannes in April 2023. Thus, Farida, a committed feminist filmmaker, acts on all possible fronts, as she looks toward the future: that of the Royal Commission, that of a foundation headed by four powerful women in today's transnational Moroccan cinema, and finally that of her art as scriptwriter who writes and films... a Moroccan feminist!

3. Fatema Mernissi and Films

Tazi asks her to write the script for a film on his cousin Fatema Mernissi, based on his personal memories of her—and of himself with her. Farida happily wrote the script from A to Z, taking great care to meet with him several times and honor her fellow filmmaker's vision. However, as was the case for other film projects in Morocco in 2020–2021, the shoot was delayed, due to a string of shut-downs to try to counter the spread of Covid-19. The biopic, *Fatema, the Unforgettable Sultana* was finally released in 2022. The great feminist was played by Meryem Zaïmi while her cousin Abderrahman was played by Brice Bexter el Glaoui. Once again, the director modified the script with no real warning.

After Mernissi's death, Farida had thought of making a film about her friend and had started her own documentary project titled *Sur les pas de Fatema/In Fatema's Footsteps*—another project postponed by the pandemic. It was born out of Farida's close, in-depth re-reading of the feminist sociologist's work, in particular *Les Sindbads marocains: voyages dans le Maroc civique/Moroccan Sinbads: Journeys in Civic Morocco* (2004).[8] The latter is a polymorphous essay in Mernissi's vein: it contains multiple references to Moroccan, Mediterranean, and European history, a joyful narration of factual and imagined situations, and a social scientific investigation of the young, inventive Moroccan nomads of the High Atlas and of the desert. Her findings offer, as always, a delicious cocktail of social scientific scholarship, humor, and, above all, optimism. For her *Moroccan Sinbads* are not in a state of failure, of despair, quite the opposite.[9] Farida traveled to the Atlas to scout locations and find some of the young Sinbads who were involved in her friend's initiative, so that they could later appear as subjects in her documentary.

The filmmaker could have made her own the words of Fatema Mernissi on the place of crafts in the future of Morocco: "On our digital planet, the future will belong to the artisans, these self-taught people who freely cast their emotions and their dreams into the objects they create."[10] This film project does not signal a "return" to feminism, since Farida has never ceased to be concerned with the world of women and their rights. Her tribute to Fatema Mernissi, in progress at the time of writing, is at once an homage, an act of love, and a powerful political act.

The Renaissance of a Classic

For a long time, *A Door to the sky* was visible on a subset of the Youtube channel called Cinemaghrebia. Farida had thus made her film available to people for free—a blessing for the Moroccan diaspora and for students and researchers of Moroccan film across the world. The image was fuzzy, the sound occasionally off and the French subtitles not always accurate. Thanks to the AHRC grant that allowed this manuscript to be researched and composed, three members of the team (Will Higbee, Stefanie van de Peer, and I) were able to coordinate the renovation and digitization of an original copy held at the CCM in Rabat. This entire process was transnational in the extreme, for the laboratory we used was Dragon DI, located in the UK. (I won't go into the details of how we navigated the many twists and turns of various bureaucratic systems of different countries. Suffice it to say that it was quite a transnational adventure!) The result was well worth the collaborative effort: the new copy is stunning in its vivid colors and definition. Will Higbee and I saw Farida discover her film anew at the National Film Festival that took place in Tangier, right before the pandemic hit the world, in March 2020. She was enchanted, her face beaming with delight at the screening of her film. Since this initial public screening, the renovated version of *A Door* has toured, literally, the world: it was screened in Morocco, Europe (France, Germany, Switzertland, the UK), South America (Brazil), North America (Chicago and Los Angeles). Its rebirth and visibility occur at a point in history when the reception of the film differs substantially from what it was upon its release at the end of the 1980s.

Although the film occupies the place of a classic in the Moroccan and Maghrebi filmogaphy, its vision of women and Islam still address and distribution of roles, a shoot can be disastrous. Finally, she warns today's questions on the topic, as Algandouzi's interview of Farida below illustrates.

Fayçal Algandouzi's Interview of Farida Benlyazid For the Block Museum (Chicago) Tangier, October 2022[11]

Hello, Farida! If memory serves me right, *A Door to the Sky*, your first feature, was made in 1988–89 and is dedicated to Fatima al-Fihriya, who founded one of the world's first universities. It's a movie about spirituality, religion, feminine and feminist approaches to these questions in Fes. So, my first question is what inspired you to make this movie at the time?

Well, in the early 1980s, I experienced a full mystical crisis myself. I was looking for spirituality and I read a lot of books, Sufi texts, and I was most drawn to a religion where love is the most important thing. But at the time, all around me in Tangier, I was witnessing the development of a strict kind of Islam imported by young people who had been indoctrinated in Belgium. They would come and tell their families "You are not practicing Islam correctly!" "You are not good Muslims!"—which of course shocked people a lot. I also noticed that they lacked compassion, that they set themselves as agents of justice. I realized that Wahhabism (practiced in Saudi Arabia) was beginning to spread across the Arab world through a form of corruption: the poor were given money and told to follow this particular kind of Islam… I talk about this in the movie, by the way: Kirana, one of the characters tells Nadia: Islam is one, but it has multiple interpretations.

However, this political and violent interpretation shocked me a lot and I thought something absolutely had to be done to prevent young people from following this movement. I wanted to talk about the Islam I was brought up in, a form of Maliki Islam. It has been practiced in Morocco for centuries and does not have this violence. It is an Orthodox form of Islam based on sunnah, but it is not violent. Moreover, in Islam it is said that there is no obligation to religion. God wants us to come to Him of our own accord, wants our faith and our belief to be really profound. Forcing someone to become Muslim is not desired.

At the beginning of the movie, there is a flashback scene where Nadia's dad is dying. He remembers coming home to his pregnant wife who was told by his mother to recite the shahada. Nadia's mother thought [her mother-in-law] had just spoken words of superstition. When he tells her "Ah, you've become a Muslim!" she is shocked. He reassures her by telling her that no, she is not, that one becomes Muslim only if one really wants to. You cannot force someone to be Muslim.

1. A FIRST FICTION FILM

At the time, you had already written screenplays for other directors, but you had never made a feature film. What made you feel you wanted to make this movie, turn this particular screenplay you had written into film?

In truth, even if I had already made a documentary on women immigrant women, right after I finished school in Paris, I considered myself more of a screenwriter than a director. Yet, I also wanted to direct a film. But once I finished this script, I realized: who will actually be interested in directing it? It's too personal. So it was up to me to do it and I embarked on the journey!

2. FILM TITLE

Where does the movie title come from?

The title of the movie comes from a song by Farid al-Atrash who says in his song that the door is open for the wishes of victims or of those who suffer from injustice… That's where the title comes from.[12] And then, I was also interested in Fes. The architecture of the houses in Fes with their openings to the sky, is also a sign! Fatema Mernissi used to say that when she was a little girl she could travel sitting down: she would watch the stars and the moon enter the house. That's the reason I absolutely insisted this movie was to be shot in Fes where the walls talk. You feel like you're traveling through time on the streets of Fes and might run into Ibn Arabi or Maïmonides who walked these streets.[13]

3. **SCREENWRITING**

Tell us how about the writing of the screenplay, how the writing of the script unfolded...

It was done with a sense of urgency. I was really very inspired. I didn't understand it myself, because sometimes ideas would come to me just like that. I remember thinking: wait a minute! These ideas are right on, some of them are truly amazing! Take, for example, the sequence in the garden of the zawiya: the young woman who is one of the first to join the zawiya, and who comes and goes at night, tells Nadia, 'I'm waiting for a prompt,' 'nothing is lost, nothing is created'. She tells her about the Big Bang and even says: "I think that if we had the right kind of equipment we would be able to see the end of the world, see it go out like fireworks."

Well, I'm no astrophysicist, not even a theologian, I am an artist who draws inspiration from whatever comes to me. Yet, I recently discovered that this theory about seeing the end and the Big Bang, was published in 2014 by astrophysicists! That's when, you realize that, sometimes, our inspiration is beyond us.

4. **THE CITY OF FES**

You were born in Tangier, you grew up in Tangier. But you are no stranger to Fes. It is a city to which you traveled as a little girl...

Actually, I have few memories of Fes. I am really a daughter of Tangier, I was born in Tangier, and I grew up in Tangier. My parents are of Fassi origin, and I just have one memory from early childhood. I was struck by the way the water came out in the houses: there was something like a small fountain [in the patio]. I threw a handkerchief that danced on the water. There was no need to turn on a faucet: the water just spewed out. When we were children, we were usually prohibited from opening faucets, from playing with the water. And there, it was possible! Well, it's quite a vague memory...

Then, I remember that when I was around ten or twelve, my father took us to Fes, and he toured the entire Medina with us, telling us about the places where he had lived as a

child. He left Fes as a very young man. I was struck by the
way we entered houses. To enter the houses, they were small
doors and we thought, well, we are going to another poor
family's house. Yet, once we had gotten through the door, it
was a palace! We kept exclaiming, "Well, no, hold on, this is
something else!" We were dazzled. I also kept the memory of
Fes's secret beauty.

5. FEMINISM

**Do you consider yourself a feminist? If so, what feminist
approach does your film reveal?**

Yes, I am a feminist if it means recognizing the rights of
women. Indeed, in the 1970s, I was a student in Paris and
I participated in the women's liberation movement. I went
to general meetings at the *Mutualité* [the name of a famous
hall downtown Paris where women met to discuss women's
issues]. I joined neighborhood groups, and we had great
discussions aimed precisely at promoting women's rights, but
there is something that left me a bit surprised, let's say. It's
that the women I saw didn't know how or were not used to
managing things amongst themselves; whereas I came from
a culture where we, women, actually lived together all the
time. As Fatema Mernissi put it: we know the harem! So, for
us, feminism is not about rejecting men. Feminism must be a
struggle led by both women *and* men. It is about recognizing
human rights. That's why I thought it was important for men
to get involved with us in this fight. It's a fight against a
system in our home countries and everywhere else for that
matter. The prophet—salvation be unto him—was a feminist.
His most significant 'restriction' was rejected by the Arab
aristocrats of the time: to them, the point that was beyond
the pale was the liberation of women and slaves. Unfortunately, as soon as the prophet died, they went back to their
old ways. We are also told that, during the Jahiliya [the "age
of ignorance" before the advent of Islam], people used to
bury little girls alive with impunity when they wanted no
more girls, who, they deemed, would only bring them problems. Islam prohibited this practice. Fortunately, that ban has
remained. Apart from that, though, women haven't enjoyed
freedom although, in the Qur'ān, God addresses both men

and women: there is no difference, whether in faith or in practice. So, if you grant rights even to animals like she- camels,
how can you not grant rights to women? [This reading of
the Qurʾān] is... astonishing!... I support the movement of
Islamic feminism. I really like the work of Asma Lamrabet[14]
and other women around the world who are calling for a
more appropriate and fairer reading of the Qurʾān. This is our
fight because things need to change from within. You can't
superimpose the reality of one society onto another. It's true
that women around the world have always had their rights
violated, but women of each culture have their own ways of
freeing themselves.

6. **MULTIPLE APPROACHES TO ISLAM**
**In the movie, Farida, there are different women, and each
of them in some ways embodies a distinct spiritual and
religious approach. Could you tell us about them?**
I wanted the movie to show Islam as it is experienced by
women, because in the West people think that Islam is
forced or imposed upon them. And that is absolutely not
the case. Often, women have a much stronger faith than
men without really studying the texts—although there is
a very important oral culture that must not be forgotten.
Hence the women knew the Qurʾān, perhaps not all but
enough of it to learn the prayers and pray. Remember that
a woman, Fatima al-Fihriya, created the world's first university in Fes before Salamanca, for instance.[15] So, I wanted
these women on screen... Even afterwards, throughout my
cinematic work, I have shown how these so-called illiterate
women are extraordinarily knowledgeable.

I wanted to show a distinct facet of Islam through each
character in the movie. Hence, through Kirana explaining
things to Nadia, you see Orthodox Islam; through Nadia you
see Sufi Islam, a spiritual quest; and then through the other
women of the zawiya, you see peaceful Islam for some, and
a more violent form of Islam in others. For me, each woman
represents one of the many facets that Islam can then take.

7. **CONTRAST OR DIVERSITY?**
**Nadia, played by Zakia Tahiri is picked up at the airport
by her sister dressed in conservative European clothes.
In contrast, Nadia arrives in Fes in a punkish outfit and**

refuses at first to wear the traditional white clothes for the funeral. Can you tell us about the conflict a woman may experience between two cultures? Between two worlds?

Sure. It does not happen to women only, but to men as well. For me, frankly, it's not a real issue. I think that tomorrow's wealth resides in cultural diversity; that we must be free to choose what we want in each culture, to pick from the human potentialities that emanate from different cultures based on geography, climate and location. It is beautiful to see how humans develop a culture that is splendid in its distinctiveness, for, in the end, we are all the same: we have to eat, sleep, make children. But we all have our own rules and codes. I think that anyway, whether we want it or not, 'interchangeability' exists. Humans have always crossed boundaries, have always mixed. Therein lies the beauty, I believe, of humanity.

8. FILM RECEPTION

The movie poses a burning question on faith, religiosity, spirituality, but the context of the time was anything but ready to face such a question. In the 1980s, under the Marxist influence of the left, talking about religion seems to some, almost like taking a step backwards, a topic to avoid or sweep under the carpet. How was your movie received?

Indeed. I too had embraced this Marxist way of thinking, imagining that it would bring more justice amongst humans, of course. At the same time, however, I kept [critically] thinking about it. And then, I became overcome by this sudden inspiration as well as by my own spiritual quest.

The first screening took place at the Carthage festival, where the movie generated a lot of controversies, questions, fights. Many Egyptians were in attendance. Since they are the first ones in the Arab world to have made film, they have always felt that they were always right! Then, there were those who told me that I was not authorized to speak about Islam and that women's voice is 'awra [should be kept covered, hidden]. In other words, we should not be listened to. They faulted me for having the Qurʾān recited by a woman. So I told them: but Umm Kulthum, the great diva of the Arab world started chanting the Qurʾān before becoming the famous singer we know now.

In the film, I used a voice in playback, that of Aziza Tazi—may she rest in peace—while the actress Chaibia Laadraoui took on the role of [Kirana], a great *fqiha*, theologian. Aziza Tazi, the woman who performs the *tajwid*, who sings the Qurʾān in the movie, was renowned in Morocco. She hosted religious soirées, even at the royal palace; she had even received an award at the Kuala Lumpur festival that hosts a competition for the best voices of *tajwid*. I did not make anything up.

And then, there were those who were supposedly progressive, modern, and who felt that Islam no longer had a place in the world to come, that it was the opium of the people... In fact, I referred to this in the movie... In the quote I borrowed from Angela Davis, she cites Karl Marx, who adds that the greatest violence that has been done to the people is to have diverted their faith and manipulated them.

As far as I am concerned, the film had to be done the way I did it.

It's true that the movie specifically irritated those people who had a progressive, modernist, way of thinking, such as Leïla Shahid, for example, whom I liked a lot. At the time, she was the Palestinian representative in Rabat where she lived with her Moroccan husband. I was told she hated the movie and criticized it. However, when I met her years later, she said: "Farida, you were right! We threw out the baby with the bath water!".

And then, in all the juries, there were really big fights between those who loved the film and those who hated it. The movie still traveled around the world, it still appealed to people. For example, at the National Festival that took place in Meknes, the president of the jury, Sidi Mahdi El-Mandjra, a futurologist, one of our greatest Arab thinkers, fought with the jury and even left the jury who didn't want to give the grand prize to the movie. Instead, they gave the prize to the screenplay, but he disagreed and just upped and left!

Then, years later, he wrote in an Arab newspaper, *Al Quds*, that the best Arab director was Farida Benlyazid! As subjective as his opinion might be, it felt good, to be honest!

9. RECEPTION IN THE UNITED STATES
How was the movie received in the United States?

The screening in the United States reassured me. A university professor, Miriam Cook, was in Tangier for a university summer school. I met her, she saw the movie, and right away she invited me to come and show it in the United States. This was my first trip there, and I went to Duke—she was at Duke University, in North Carolina—but she also organized a whole tour to get the movie seen in other universities. Honestly, it did me a lot of good because the reception was good, very warm. Maybe they are used to different religions in the United States, they do not get offended, and they're curious about others. They also remain very polite even when they disagree. And it really helped me because I kept wondering: what have I done? Everybody is attacking me.

The movie was even seen at MIT. There were student papers written about it. What a truly wonderful tour! I have excellent memories of it.

10. **FILM RESURRECTION**
The movie has had a kind of renaissance after a few years. Could you tell us about it?
I was very lucky (and here let me take the opportunity to thank Florence Martin, a professor at Goucher College in Baltimore and William Higbee, a professor at the University of Exeter in the U.K.). Both professors have devoted part of their courses to Arabic cinema. They really liked the movie and they were able to obtain funds from the Arts & Humanities Research Council in the United Kingdom to clean up and digitize the movie.

I hadn't seen it in a long time, because since it was shot in 35 mm, the reels had become quite worn. I had the joy of rediscovering the beauty of its images and a of realizing that, in the end, I still believe in the same ideas today as I did then! We don't change that much…

In any case, it was invited once again with the same movie on a tour of American universities, which I found very touching, thirty years later. A screening was scheduled for April 1 [2020] at Harvard, but COVID happened, and we couldn't go. However, the movie has continued to be screened online, around the world. Its screening has been requested regularly. The latest one took place in July at Documenta in Kassel [Germany], and the film even stayed on its consulting platform for a month. I am delighted that the movie is going to the Block Museum [in Chicago].

11. AUTOBIOGRAPHICAL?

In your own spiritual journey, have you faced these two temptations—that of rejection and that of the most traditional orthodoxy? And did you have to find your own path a bit like your protagonist?

Yes, I think that every creation contains a part of autobiography, yet it is not my story. It is a story that I invented, but in which I put my own feelings, my own approach. It's true that we're raised in Islam. Then, we open up to the world and we see that it does not quite work that way... it's difficult to talk about faith, it turns out: you don't deal with ideas, you deal with a feeling. And from the moment you feel it, it becomes... something else. I have always said that each one of us holds a personal message if he listens to his inner voice. Hence, once you've discovered your inner voice, you can truly understand what Islam is.

Unfortunately, dogma wants us to be bound to the letter rather than to the mind, but what is important is the spirit!

The letter is, in a manner of speaking, an instruction manual on how to manage what you feel. Yet, sadly, the opposite takes precedence: you are forced to follow the dogma.

I always say that God is here. He is here. He will be here forever, and He wants us as we are. In the Qurʾān, it is said that if you want for everyone to be the same and pray day and night... Well, He created angels for that. But He wanted difference for humans. That's what His design is about: difference; each individual has his own approach. As I was working on the film, I knew I might be criticized and I felt like I was working on a thin line, that one could not say things that were unacceptable either. I must not invent anything. I am nothing or no one to invent. I just express my voice.

What's more, at the end of the movie, my friend Abdelhaï Diouri, an anthropologist, laughed and said to me: 'Farida, you've done something amazing!' He explained: 'You put yourself in a corner where no one can claim you.' And it's true that I was very careful so no one could tell me: 'Well, no, that's not in Islam, no.' Everything I say is substantiated and of course, my approach is absolutely not political but spiritual. Besides, for me, the last scene of the movie shows all religions coming together at the end of every individual's journey: they are on the mountain—for me, it is the Olive Mount; when they really embrace at the end of the movie, it is the yin and yang and that's it. If we agree that there is only one God, then He is the same for everyone and everyone follows his or her own path.

Farida is not done making films, as is clear from what she shares with her audience of film students: *Cervantès, near the end of his life, used to say: "I am old, I am sick, but I still write poetry. This is what I desire." You must stay alive till the very end!*[16] At the time of writing, she has started a new collection of short documentaries with Dounia Benjelloun on ancient architectures in the rural areas of Morocco: she is filming the old seats of power, of faith as well as the old granaries of the hinterland. Her passion for film-making aligns with her enduring clear-sighted love for her country and its multiple cultures. She has also secured a young woman producer for her documentary on Fatema Mernissi and a couple of producers for a feature film that might take her to India. These projects require her patience. As a case in point, the shoot of her first short on Amazigh architecture had to be postponed after the 2023 earthquake devastated a region close to where she was about to film. Yet, on the phone, she also declares joyfully, her laughter bubbling up in between her words: *Can you imagine? This devastating earthquake, while it killed so many people and destroyed granaries that were over two thousand years old, shook the earth so deeply that a myriad springs shot out! After a three-year drought, the people in the villages now have water!*

It is this aural image of her joy at the renewal of possibilities for the stricken survivors of the earthquake on which I wish to close this book. It encapsulates a moment in the latest spiral of her cinematographic and spiritual itinerary: out of a disaster comes the unpredictable possibility of salvation; out of material constraints comes filmic creativity. The overnight obliteration of the ancient granary she was going to film allows the livelihood of people in the Atlas to become suddenly less precarious. The vanishing of an ancient granary opens up hope. *I have always been attracted to the world of wonders*, the director says, as she mulls over the next subjects of her films.

NOTES

1. "An approach of listening, broad national consultation, and coconstruction, rooted in the firm belief that technical solutions to objective problems are not enough to weave social bonding and cannot alone guarantee the engagement of all, and that solutions emanating from the grassroots are unparalleled in their creativity and relevance when they find the space to express themselves." *CSMD General Report*, April 2021: 17. https://www.csmd.ma/documents/Rapport_General.pdf.

2. I can't help but notice that out of 35 members of the Commission, only 10 are women...

3. Farida Benlyazid'a masterclass, Mahir Center, Université Mohamed VI, Benguerir: June 2, 2021.

4. Telephone conversation with the author, July 28, 2021.

5. "Targets by 2035:

   – Increase in the female participation rate (from 18 to 45% in 2035);
   – Increase in the number of women in senior positions (from 11.4 to 35% in 2035);
   – Establish wage parity in the private sector (Reduce the wage gap from 15 to 5% by 2035);
   – All women must have the same opportunities as men to access education, protecting their fundamental right to compulsory education and childhood (Zero underage girls working and not going to school, Zero underage marriage);
   – Fight against illiteracy among women of all ages (mainly in rural area" *Appendix 2*: 136).

6. Promoting spaces for social-theological debate to advance thinking on issues closely related to women's rights, based on Ijtihad, as prescribed by the Qur'ān and the Sunna, and other foundations such as the general framework of the primary purposes (maqasid) of Islam and the concept of the general interest (maslaha) as advocated by the Malekite school, in the perspective of changing the debate on certain societal issues, such as the Ta'ssib in inheritance, the voluntary interruption of pregnancy (IVG), the social status of single mothers, the marriage of minors, and the legal guardianship of children. These forums for debate, which will be attended by representatives of religious bodies, concerned actors from civil society and experts (sociologists, doctors, psychologists, lawyers, etc.), should encourage the emergence of informed proposals on these issues, taking into account current societal transformations and respect for the international covenants ratified by Morocco (Annex 2, 138).

7. See "Réception des cinémas du Maghreb au Maghreb," Patricia Caillé, Florence Martin and Kamel Benouanès, dir. *Africultures*, No. 89/90, 2012: 40–43; "Le cinéma au féminin." *Quaderns de la Méditerrania/ Cuardenos del Mediterraneo*, No. 7, 2006: 221–224.

8. Mernissi, Fatema. *Les Sindbads marocains: Voyages dans le Maroc civique*. Rabat, Éditions Marsam, 2004.

9. "It is precisely the miraculous success of young people, when their elders trust them, that I describe in this book, which is the result of five years of research on civic initiative in southern Morocco." Ibid. Backcover.

10. Mernissi, Fatema. "Let's dream of galleries and rural museums to celebrate our Atlas carpet weavers," *Quaderns de la Mediterrània*, No. 7, 2006: 68.

11. https://www.blockmuseum.northwestern.edu/cinema/2022/a-door-to-the-sky-1988-farida-benlyazid.html.

12. Farid al-Atrash (1916–1974) was a prolific composer, singer, oud player and star actor in Egyptian musical films.

13. Both the sufi thinker Ibn 'Arabi (1165–1240) and the great Jewish philosopher Maimonides (1138–1204) were born in Andalusian Spain and traveled to Fez. Maimonides in 1160 and Ibn 'Arabi in 1196.

14. Moroccan theologian Asma Lamrabet has published feminist reformist readings of the Qur'ān (e.g., *Femmes Islam Occident: Chemins vers l'universel*, 2011; *Islam et femmes: les questions qui fâchent*, 2017).

15. Al-Qarawiyyn was created circa 859 and Salamanca University, the oldest university in Spain, was founded by royal decree in 1218.

16. Farida Benlyazid's master class, Mahir Center, Université Poltytechnique Mohamed VI, Bengerir: June 2, 2021.

BIBLIOGRAPHY

Aïdouni, Hamid et al. *L'œuvre cinématographique de Farida Benlyazid*. Ministère de la Communication, Rabat, 2010.

Amarger, Michel. "Le Maroc regarde ses identités plurielles." Interview with Farida Benlyazid, *Africiné*, Juillet 2006. http://www.africine.org/?menu=art&no=6969.

Amine, Khalid. "Theatre in Morocco and the Postcolonial Turn." *Textures*, September 21, 2009. http://www.textures-platform.com/?p=556.

Antrobus, Peggy, & Bizot, Judithe. "Women's Perspectives: Towards an Ethical, Equitable, Just and Sustainable Livelyhood in the 21st Century." *Isis International Women in Action*, Vols. 4.92 and 1.93: 28–35.

Armes, Roy. *African Filmmaking: North and South of the Sahara*. Edinburgh: Edinburgh University Press, 2006.

Ashcroft, Bill. "Towards a Postcolonial Aesthetics." *Journal of Postcolonial Writing*, Vol. 51, No. 4, 2015: 410–421.

Association Marocaine des Critiques de Cinéma. *L'œuvre cinématographique de Farida Benlyazid*. Rabat: Ministère de la Communication, 2010.

———. *Le Cinéma marocain: enjeu de l'industrie, enjeu de la création*. Revue Marocaine des Recherches Cinématographiques, No. 1, 2013.

Ba, Saër Maty, & Higbee, Will, eds. *De-Westernizing Film Studies*. London and New York: Routledge, 2012.

Bahmad, Jamal. "Rebels with a Cause: Youth, Globalization and Postcolonial Agency in Moroccan Cinema." *The Journal of North African Studies*, Vol. 19, No. 3, 2014: 376–389.

Benlyazid, Farida. *Lettre ouverte à mes amies d'enfance*. Tanger: Editions Khbar Bladna, 2019.

F. Martin, *Farida Benlyazid and Moroccan Cinema*,
Palgrave Studies in Arab Cinema,
https://doi.org/10.1007/978-3-031-40616-4

———. "Une Journée particulière." *Nos Années lycée. 100 ans Lycée Regnault.* Tanger: Litograph, 2013: 31–34.

———. "Réception des cinémas du Maghreb au Maghreb." Caillé, Patricia, Florence Martin et Kamel Benouanès, eds. *Africultures*, Vol. 89–90, No. 3–4 (2012): 40–43. http://africultures.com/reception-des-cinemas-du-maghreb-aumaghre-11159/.

———. "JUBILATION. Ce n'est qu'un début." Wassyla Tamzali, ed. *Histoires minuscules des révolutions arabes.* Montpellier, Chèvre Feuille étoilée, 2012: 185–189.

———. "Des hommes et des dieux." *Parfaire l'homme*, No. 2, mars avril 2011: 140–141.

———. "Le grand voyage." *Parfaire l'homme*, No. 1, décembre 2010: 81–85.

———. "La Modernité." In *Fatimita*. Tanger: Editions Khbar Bladna, 2010.

———. "¡Lahbiba Tanja!" *Aljamia*, No. 18, *Revista de la Consejería de Educación en Marruecos.* Ministerio de Educación y Ciencia, 2007: 81–86.

———. "Le cinéma au féminin." *Quaderns de la Méditerrania/Cuardenos del Mediterraneo*, No. 7, 2006: 221–224.

———. "¿Por qué el pañuelo?" *El Pais* (tribune), 14 septembre 2003.

———. "Image and Experience. Why Cinema?" In Sherifa Zuhur, ed. *Images of Enchantment: Visual and Performing Arts of the Middle East.* Cairo: American University in Cairo Press, 1998: 205–209.

———. *Aide-toi, le ciel t'aidera.* Pièce de théâtre. Baltimore: Johns Hopkins University, 1997.

———. "Une enfance tangéroise." In Mohammed Habib Samrakandi & Boubkeur El Kouche, dir. *Horizons Maghrébins – Le Droit à la mémoire: Tanger au miroir d'elle-même*, No. 31–32, 1996: 211–214.

———. "La terrasse: le lieu du possible." *Qantara: magazine des cultures arabe et méditerranéenne* 18, 1996: 66–67.

———. "La patience est belle." Chalier, Catherine, dir. *La Patience: Passion de la durée consentie.* Paris: Autrement, 1992: 195–205.

———. "Une journée dans la vie de L'Hajja Leitmeth." Jean-François Clément, dir. *Signes de l'invisible: Le Maroc.* Paris: Autrement, 1990: 80–91.

———. "Paul Bowles sans émotion." Jean-François Clément, dir. *Signes de l'invisible: Le Maroc.* Paris: Autrement, 1990: 117–123.

———. "The Gate of Heaven Is Open (1987)." In Miriam Cooke, Trans., Margot Badran & Miriam Cooke, dir. *Opening the Gates: A Century of Arab Feminist Writing.* Bloomington: Indiana University Press, 1990: 296–303.

Bettelheim, Bruno. *Psychanalyse des contes de fées.* Paris: Robert Laffont, 1976.

BineBine, Aziz. *Tazmamort: Dix-huit ans dans le bagne de Hassan II.* Paris: Denoël, 2009.

Bhabham Homi, *The Location of Culture.* London & New York: Routledge, 1994.

Bonnet, Véronique. "La Vida perra de Juanita Narboni de Farida Benlyazid: une réécriture filmique postcoloniale?" *Itinéraires: Lire les villes marocaines*, 2013: 81–94.

Bourget, Carine. "'Kaidakunna 'adhimoun' Revisited: Farida Benlyazid's 'Ruses de femmes' and Assia Djebar's 'La Beauté de Joseph'." *The French Review*, Vol. 86, No. 1 (October 2012): 147–159.

———. "Traditions orales et littéraires dans 'Une Porte sur le ciel' de Farida Benlyazid." *The French Review*, Vol. 81, No. 4, March 2008: 752–763.

Bowles, Paul. *Days. Tangiers Journal: 1987–1989*. Hopewell: The Ecco Press, 1991.

Box, Laura. "Women Playwrights and Performers Respond to the Project of Development." In Salhi Kamal, ed. *African Theatre for Development: Art for Self-Determination*. Bristol: Intellect, 1998: 141–152.

Boym, Svetlana. *The Future of Nostalgia*. New York: Basic Books, 2002.

Caillé, Patricia, Martin, Florence, & Benouanès, Kamel, eds. *Les Cinémas du Maghreb*. Paris: Africultures, 2012.

Caillé, Patricia, & Forest, Claude, eds. *Regarder des films en Afrique(s)*. Villeneuve d'Ascq: Presses Universitaires du Septentrion, 2017.

Carrée, Roland. "Farida Benlyazid: Se tourner vers le ciel." *Répliques*, No. 12, 2019: 120–145.

———. "Mohammed Abderrahman Tazi: Rester Debout." *Répliques*, No. 7, 2016: 62–89.

Carter, Sandra Gayle. *What Moroccan Cinema? A Historical and Critical Study 1956–2006*. Lanham: Lexington Books, 2009.

———. "Farida Benlyazid's Moroccan Women." *Quarterly Review of Film & Video*, Vol. 17, No. 4, 2000: 343–369.

Catusse, Myriam. *Le Temps des entrepreneurs? Politique et transformations du capitalisme au Maroc*. Tunis: Institut de Recherche sur le Maghreb Contemporain, 2008.

Caubet, Dominique. « La 'nayda' marocaine et ses espaces: de la scène musicale underground à la scène publique ». in Hanru, Raspail & Damani, eds. *Le Spectacle et le quotidien, Veduta / Biennale de Lyon 2009*. Lyon, Presses du Réel: 210–220.

Chalier, Catherine. *Le Désir de conversion*. Paris: Seuil, 2011.

Chérief, Sélim. *L'Homme qui avait été amoureux de Bette Davis*. Lyon: Rouge Inside, 2011.

Chion, Michel. *La Voix au cinéma*. Paris: Editions de l'Etoile, Cahiers du Cinéma, 1993 [1ère édition 1982].

Chraïbi, Zineb Abderrazik. *Mohamed Ben Ali R'bati, Naissance de la peinture marocaine, 1861–1936*. Rabat: Éditions Marsam, 2007: 16.

Cooke, Miriam. *Women Claim Islam*. London and New York: Routledge, 2000.

Corbin, Henry. Ralph Manheim, tr. *Creative Imagination in the Sufism of Ibn 'Arabi'*. Princeton: Princeton University Press, 1969.

Diouri, Moumen. *À qui appartient le Maroc?* Paris: Éditions L'Harmattan, 1992.

Driss-Jaïdi, Moulay. « Figures de la féminité dans trois films de Jillali Ferhati: Aïcha, Mina, Saïda et les autres. » Groupe de Recherche, *Jillali Ferhati: Une expérience unique*. Tanger: Association Marocaine des Critiques de Cinéma, 2011: 41–50.

Dwyer, Kevin. "Moroccan Cinema and the Promotion of Culture." *Journal of North African Studies*, Vol. 13, No. 3, 2007: 277–286.

———, & Tazi, M.A. *Beyond Casablanca: MA Tazi and the Adventure of Moroccan Cinema*. Bloomington and Indianapolis: Indiana University Press, 2004.

Edwards, Brian T. "Francophone Voices of the 'New" Morocco in Film and Print: (Re)presenting a Society in Transition." *The Journal of North African Studies*, Vol. 16, No. 3, 2011: 493–496.

De Franceschi, Leonardo. "Entre la maison et la ville, la lutte pour l'espace social." *Cinémaction*, No. 111, 2004: 62–66.

Gauch, Suzanne. *Maghrebs in Motion: North African Cinema in Nine Movements*. Oxford: Oxford University Press, 2016.

———. "Visions transnationales et les films de Farida Benlyazid." In Aïdouni, Hamid et al. *L'œuvre cinématographique de Farida Benlyazid*. Rabat: Ministère de la Communication, 2010: 44–48.

———. "Now You See It, Now You Don't: Transnational Feminist Spectatorship and Farida Benlyazid's *A Door to the Sky*." *Camera Obscura* 71, Vol. 24, No. 2, 2009: 106–137.

Gonzales-del-Valle, Luis T., & Federico Garcià Lorca, "La Niña que riega la albahaca y el principe pregunton," *Anales de la literature española contemporánea*, Vol. 9, No. 1/3, 1984: 295–306.

Gugler, Josef, ed. *Films in the Middle East and North Africa*. Austin: University of Texas Press, 2011.

Hamil, Mustapha. "Itineraries of Revival and Ambivalence in Postcolonial North African Cinema: From Benlyazid's *Door to the Sky* to Moknèche's *Viva Laldgérie*." *African Studies Review*, Vol. 52, No. 3 (December 2009): 73–87.

Higbee, Will, & Lim, Hwee Song. "Concepts of Transnational Cinema: Towards a Critical Transnationalism in Film Studies." *Transnational Cinemas*, Vol. 1, No. 1, 2010: 7–21.

Higbee, Will, Martin Florence & Bahmad, Jamal. *Moroccan Cinema Uncut: Decentred Voices, Transnational Perspectives*. Edinburgh: Edinburgh University Press, 2020.

Hjort, Mette. "On the Plurality of Cinematic Transnationalism." In Nataša D'urovic'ová & Kathleen Newman, eds. *World Cinemas, Transnational Perspectives*. New York: Routledge, 2010: 12–33.

Hocquart, Emmanuel. *Les Coquelicots. Une Grammaire de Tanger III*. Marseille: CIPM, 2011.

Johns Hopkins University Center for Communication Programs (JHU/CCP). *Communicating Safe Motherhood in Morocco—The Family Planning/Maternal and Child Health Phase V, Project, Final Report*. Baltimore: JHU/CCP, March 2000.

Kadiri, Abdeslam. "Lotfi Akalay: Tanger à la vie, à la mort." *Tel Quel*, No. 829, 19–25 octobre 2018: 50–53.

Khannous, Touria. "Realms of Memory: Strategies of Representation and Post-colonial Identities in North African Women's Cinema." *Journal X: A Journal of Culture and Criticism*, Vol. I, No. 6, 2001: 49–61.

Lahnait, Fatima, ed. *The Role of Binational Entrepreneurs as Social and Economic Bridge Builders Between Europe and North Africa*. Amsterdam, Berlin, Tokyo, and Washington, DC: IOS Press, 2009.

Lamrabet, Asma. *Islam et femmes: les questions qui fâchent*. Casablanca: En Toutes Lettres, 2017.

———. *Femmes, Islam, Occident: Chemins vers l'universel*. Casablanca: La Croisée des Chemins, 2011.

Lamrini, Rida. *Les Puissants de Casablanca*. Rabat: Editions Marsam, 1999.

Landau, Jacob M. Trad. Francine Le Cleac'h. *Etudes sur le théâtre et le cinéma arabes*. Paris: Maisonneuve & Larose, 1965.

Lebbady, Hasna. "Women in Northern Morocco: Between Documentary and the Imaginary." *Alif: Journal of Comparative Poetics*, No. 32, The Imaginary and the Documentary: Cultural Studies in Literature, History, and the Arts, 2012: 127–150.

Mahmood, Sabah. "Feminist theory, embodiment, and the docile agent: some reflections on the Egyptian Islamic revival." *Cultural Anthropology*. Vol. 16, No. 2, 2001: 202–236.

Martin, Florence. *Screens and Veils: Maghrebi Women's Cinema*. Bloomington & Indianapolis: Indiana University Press, 2011.

Martin, Florence, & Caillé, Patricia. "Reel Bad Maghrebi Women." In Nadia Yaqub, Rula Quawas, & Elizabeth Bishop, eds., *Bad Girls of the Arab World*. Austin: University of Texas Press, 2017: 167–184.

Martin, Florence. *"Bab al-samah Maftouh/A Door to the Sky*, Farida Benlyazid, 1988." In Gönül Dönmez-Colin, ed., *The Cinema of North Africa and the Middle-East*. London: Wallflower Press, 2007: 123–132.

———. *"Cinéma-monde*: De-orbiting Maghrebi cinema." *Contemporary French Civilization*, Vol. 41, No. 3–4, 2016: 461–476.

———. "Farida Benlyazid and Juanita Narboni: Two Women from Tangier." *Black Camera*, Vol. 6, No. 1, 2014: 124–138.

Martin, Lucile. "Le dossier du Sahara occidental." *Les Cahiers de l'Orient*, Vol. 102, No. 2, 2011: 43–57.

Mernissi, Fatima. *Le Harem politique: le Prophète et les femmes.* Paris: Albin Michel, 2010.

———. *Islam et démocratie.* Paris: Albin Michel, 2010.

———. "Rêvons de galeries et de musées ruraux pour fêter nos tisseuses de tapis de l'Atlas." *Quaderns de la Mediterrània,* No. 7, 2006: 67–70.

———. *Les Sindbads marocains: Voyages dans le Maroc civique.* Rabat: Éditions Marsam, 2004.

———. Trad, Claudine Richetin, *Rêves de femmes: Contes d'enfance au harem (Dreams of Trespass—Tales of a Harem Girlhood,* 1994). Paris: Albin Michel, 1996.

———. *Sultanes oubliées: Femmes chefs d'état en Islam.* Paris: Albin Michel, 1990.

Miller, Susan Gilson. *A History of Modern Morocco.* Cambridge: Cambridge University Press, 2013.

Mrabet, Mohamed, & Eric Valentin. *Mémoires Fantastiques.* Lyon: Rouge Inside Éditions, 2011.

Novak, Marcos. "Speciation, Transvergence, Allogenesis: Notes on the Production of the Alien." *Architectural Design,* Vol. 72, No. 3, 2002: 65–71.

Orlando, Valérie. *Screening Morocco: Contemporary Film in a Changing Society.* Athens: Ohio University Press, 2011.

———. *Francophone Voices of the "New" Morocco in Film and Print: (Re)presenting a Society in Transition.* New York: Palgrave Macmillan, 2009.

Propp, Vladimir. Trad. E. Mélétinski, M. Derrida, T. Todorov, & C. Kahn. *Morphologie du conte* [1928]. Paris: Seuil, 1970.

Roussel, Nelly. *Paroles de combat et d'espoir. Discours choisis.* Préface de Madeleine Vernet. Epône: Editions de l'Avenir Social, 1919.

Sabri, Tarik, & Ftouni, Laylal, eds. *Arab Subcultures: Transformations in Theory and Practice.* London and New York: I.B. Tauris, 2017.

Shafik, Viola. *Arab Cinema: History and Cultural Identity.* New York and Cairo: American University in Cairo Press, 1998 [2nd ed., 2007].

Shohat, Ella, & Stam, Robert. *Unthinking Eurocentrism: Multiculturalism and the Media.* 2nd ed. London and New York: Routledge, 2014.

Shohat, Ella. "Post-Third-Worldist Culture: Gender, Nation, and the Cinema." In Jacqui Alexander & Chandra Talpade Mohanty, eds. *Feminist Genealogies, Colonial Legacies, Democratic Futures.* New York: Routledge, 1997: 183–209.

Simour, Lhoussain. "(Re)Locating space in Hakim Belabbas's *khayṭ al-rūḥ* and Farida Benlyazid's *bāb sma maftūḥ.*" International Journal of Francophone Studies, Vol. 20, Nos. 1–2, 2017: 9–23.

Skalli, Loubna H. "Communicating Gender in the Public Sphere: Women and Information Technologies in the MENA." *Journal of Middle East Women's Studies,* Vol. 2, No. 2 (Spring 2006): 35–54.

Solanas, Fernando & Getino, Octavio. "Towards a Third Cinema: note and experiences for the development of a cinema of liberation in the Third World," *Cinéaste*, Vol. 4, No. 3, 1970: 1–10.

Tamzali, Wassyla, ed. *Histoires minuscules des révolutions arabes*. Montpellier: Chèvre Feuille Étoilée, 2012.

Teo Simarski, Lynn. "Through North African Eyes." *Saudi Amraco World*, January–February 1992: 30–35. https://archive.aramcoworld.com/issue/199201/through.north.african.eyes.htm [link active on September 20, 2023.].

Tozy, Mohamed. "L'évolution du champ religieux marocain au défi de la mondialisation." *Revue internationale de politique comparée*, Vol. 16, No. 1, 2009: 63–81.

Traoré, Aminata. *L'Étau: L'Afrique dans un monde sans frontières*. Arles: Actes Sud, 1999.

Vazquez, Angel. *La Chienne de vie de Juanita Narboni*, Selim Chérief, trans. Lyon: Rouge Inside Éditions, 2009.

Vermeren, Pierre. *Le Maroc de Mohammed VI: La transition inachevée*. Paris: La Découverte, 2011.

Zirani, Hayat. "Droits des femmes au Maroc: bilan et perspectives." In *IEM Annuaire 2010*. Barcelone: Institut Européen de la Méditerranée: 285–291.

Farida Benlyazid—Filmography

• Producer

Jillali Ferhati, *Jarha Fi-l Hâ'it / Une Brèche dans le mur* (fiction), France & Morocco, 1978.

• Scriptwriter

Jillali Ferhati, *Arais min kassab / Poupées de roseau* (fiction), France, Germany & Morocco, 1981.

Mohammed Abderrahmane Tazi, *Badis* (fiction), Morocco, Spain, 1989.

Mohammed Abderrahmane Tazi, *Al baht 3an jaouj imrati / A la Recherche du mari de ma femme* (fiction), Morocco, France, 1993.

Majid Rechich, *Kissat warda / L'Histoire d'une rose* (fiction), Morocco, 2000.

Mohammed Abderrahmane Tazi, *Fatema, la sultane inoubliable* (docufiction), Morocco, 2022

• Director and scriptwriter:

Identités de femmes Mosaïque, FR 3, France (documentary), 1979.

Bâb es-sama' maftûh / Une Porte sur le ciel (fiction), Tunisia, Morocco, France, 1988.

Aminata Traoré, une femme du Sahel (doc.), France, 1993.

Contrabando (reportage, 2M), Morocco, 1994.

Sur la terrasse (fiction, 15'), in *5 Films pour cent ans*, Morocco, 1995.

La Sardine de l'an 2000 (doc., ONP), Morocco, 1998.

La Pêche au Maroc, entre tradition et modernité (doc., ONP), Morocco, 1998.

Keid Ensa / Ruses de Femmes (fiction), Morocco, 1999.

Nia taghleb (film for TV, 2M), Morocco, 2000.

El boukma (film for TV, 2M), Morocco, 2001.

Dar elbeïda, yâ dar elbeïda / Casablanca, Casablanca (fiction), Morocco, 2002.

La Vida Perra de Juanita de Tanger / Juanita Bint Tanger / Juanita de Tanger (fiction), Spain, Morocco, 2006.

Avec Fayçal A. Bentahar, *Une Guerre à la télé*, Morocco, 2006.

Avec Abderrahim Mettour, *Casanayda* (doc.), Morocco, 2007.

Ster ma strer Allah / Secret de famille (film for TV, 2M), Morocco, 2009.

Le Sac (campaign against corruption short), Morocco, 2012.

Houdoud wa houdoud / Frontieras (docufiction, Cinétéléma), Morocco, 2013.

Tamy Tazi, créations au fil du temps (doc.), Morocco, 2013.

Tamy Tazi, défilé de mode 2013 (doc.), Morocco, 2013.

Musiques et Danses Amazighes (series of 10 docs), Morocco, 2015.

[*Les Femmes dans la musique amazighe; Les petits maestros; À travers les vallées en fleurs; Musique amazighe d'hier et d'aujourd'hui; Initiation aux musiques et danses amazighes; Moyen Atlas; Haut Atlas; Anti-Atlas; Aux confins du Sahara; Oriental et Rif*].

Noces Amazighes dans la vallée d'Anergui (series of documentaries), Maroc, 2017.

INDEX